货物放行时间测算指南

（第3版）

GUIDE TO MEASURE THE TIME REQUIRED FOR THE RELEASE OF GOODS

(VERSION 3)

世界海关组织
World Customs Organization
编著

贸易便利化分专业技术委员会
中 国 电 子 口 岸 数 据 中 心
编译

中国海关出版社有限公司
·北京·

图书在版编目（CIP）数据

货物放行时间测算指南：第3版：汉、英/贸易便利化分专业技术委员会，中国电子口岸数据中心编译. —北京：中国海关出版社有限公司，2021.9
ISBN 978-7-5175-0514-3

Ⅰ.①货… Ⅱ.①贸… ②中… Ⅲ.①海关管理-世界-指南-汉、英 Ⅳ.①F745.2-62

中国版本图书馆CIP数据核字（2021）第168914号

货物放行时间测算指南（第3版）
HUOWU FANGXING SHIJIAN CESUAN ZHINAN (DI-SAN BAN)

作　　者：世界海关组织　World Customs Organization
译　　者：贸易便利化分专业技术委员会　中国电子口岸数据中心
责任编辑：刘白雪
出版发行：中国海关出版社有限公司
社　　址：北京市朝阳区东四环南路甲1号　　邮政编码：100023
网　　址：www.hgcbs.com.cn
编 辑 部：01065194242-7521（电话）
发 行 部：01065194238/46/54/5127（电话）
社办书店：01065195616（电话）　　http://weidian.com/?userid=319526934
印　　刷：北京圣艺佳彩色印刷有限责任公司　　经　　销：新华书店
开　　本：787mm×1092mm　1/16
印　　张：15.25　　字　　数：280千字
版　　次：2021年9月第1版
印　　次：2021年12月第2次印刷
书　　号：ISBN 978-7-5175-0514-3
定　　价：65.00元

编译委员会

编译组

主　编：蔡　毅

副主编：包先雨　龙自立

译　者（按照姓氏笔画顺序）：

朱斯琦　郑文丽　柯培超　殷冷媛　程立勋

彭　礴　蔡伊娜

译者序

党中央、国务院高度重视优化口岸营商环境工作。习近平总书记在中央全面深化改革委员会第十八次会议上强调，要围绕实行高水平对外开放深化改革，深化商品、服务、资金、人才等要素流动型开放，加快营造市场化、法治化、国际化的营商环境。李克强总理指出，要坚持扩大开放，进一步推动通关便利化，更好融入国际市场，开展自由公平贸易，更有效利用两个市场、两种资源。为贯彻党中央、国务院的决策部署，海关总署作为优化口岸营商环境、促进跨境贸易便利化工作的牵头部门，会同相关部门和各地方政府，认真落实《优化营商环境条例》，持续深化“放管服”改革，对标国际先进水平，聚焦市场主体关切，采取一系列有效措施，推动我国口岸营商环境持续优化，跨境贸易便利化水平逐年提升。在世界银行营商环境评估中，我国“跨境贸易”指标全球排名已由2017年第97位大幅提高到2019年第56位，其中在进口、出口均为海运方式的经济体中排名已位居全球第7位。

货物通关时间是衡量贸易便利化的重要指标之一。近年来，在各地、各有关部门共同努力下，全国进口、出口货物整体通关时间大幅压缩。据统计，2020年12月，全国进口、出口整体通关时间分别为34.91小时和1.78小时，较2017年分别压缩64.16%和85.50%。自2020年全球爆发新冠肺炎疫情以来，全国上下统筹推进疫情防控和经济社会发展各项工作，主动作为，多措并举，采取针对性措施，尽可能减少疫情对通关时间的影响，巩固压缩整体通关时间成效，取得明显成效。

不断压缩进出口货物通关时间，体现了我国积极履行国际义务的决心，符合发展多边贸易体系的内涵。2017年2月，世界贸易组织（WTO）《贸易便利化协定》（TFA）正式生效。TFA提出，鼓励各成员单位“确定和公布平均放行时间”，定期测算和公布货物平均放行时间，并鼓励各成员分享实施经验。作为发展中国家，中国坚定支持多边贸易发展、全面实施TFA。世界海关组织（WCO）制定海关程序简化和协调的全球标准，提供操作工具，旨在通过优化边境通关程序，不断促进各国（地区）间贸易往来。WCO发布的“放行时间研究”（the Time Release Study，TRS）已成为国际公认的跨境贸易便利化评估工具之一，亦成为落实TFA、《区域全面经济伙伴关系协定》（RCEP）等协定的“规定动作”之一。

近年来，海关总署加强进出口货物通关时间研究、监测和通报等工作，结合我国实际，在 WCO 的 TRS 项目框架下开展“货物放行时间”研究。自 2018 年以来，国家口岸管理办公室定期向各省（区、市）口岸管理部门、各直属海关通报全国及各地进口、出口整体通关时间，及时协调指导各地采取措施巩固压缩整体通关时间工作成效。

为加快营造市场化、法治化、国际化的口岸营商环境，积极借鉴国际经验，定期开展放行时间研究确有必要、尤为重要。20 多年前，WCO 首次制定了 TRS 指南，为各国（地区）测量货物通关时间提供了可供参考的方法，2018 年 WCO 发布了最新的《货物放行时间测算指南》（第 3 版）。鉴于工作所需，组织翻译、早日出版和积极借鉴《货物放行时间测算指南》，引导跨境贸易各相关方共同开展放行时间研究，协同推进优化进出口通关流程，在确保监管有效前提下进一步提升跨境贸易便利化水平，对于持续优化口岸营商环境、促进贸易便利化、更好地服务国内国际双循环具有重要意义。

是为序。

编译委员会

2021 年 9 月

FOREWORD

前 言

The World Customs Organization (WCO) believes that seamless international trade plays a pivotal role in countries' economic prosperity. One of its continued top priorities in the 21st Century is therefore to improve trade flows between countries in a bilateral, regional and multilateral context through enhanced border clearance processes. To this end, the WCO not only sets out global standards on Customs simplification and harmonization, but also provides operational tools to ensure secure and more rapid trade flows across borders.

世界海关组织（WCO）认为，无缝连接的国际贸易对各国的经济繁荣起着举足轻重的作用。因此，21 世纪的首要任务之一便是通过改进边境通关程序，在双边、区域和多边背景下促进各国之间的贸易往来。为此，世界海关组织不仅制定了简化和协调海关程序的全球标准，而且提供了操作工具，以确保跨境贸易的安全和快速流动。

In today's highly globalized trade world, traders are increasingly exploring avenues to move their goods expeditiously across borders at reduced cost. There is a renewed impetus for trade facilitation at the global, regional and national level, which is in part due to the growing emphasis on speedy and harmonized implementation of the World Trade Organization (WTO) Trade Facilitation Agreement (TFA). It is in this context that the WCO, as part of its strategic commitment to improve global trade, has updated one of the most internationally recognized tools to measure the efficiency and effectiveness of international trade flows: the Time Release Study (TRS).

在当今高度全球化的世界贸易中，贸易商正在越来越多地探索各种以较低成本实现货物快速跨境运输的途径。贸易便利化在全球、区域和国家层面上得以重新推动，其部分原因在于各方越来越重视世界贸易组织（WTO）《贸易便利化协定》（TFA）迅速、和谐的实施。正是在此背景下，作为改善全球贸易的战略承诺的一部分，WCO 更新了最为国际公认的测量国际贸易流动高效性和有效性的工具之一：放行时间研究（the Time Release Study，TRS）。

The WCO first developed a TRS Guide over 20 years ago. The new version, the "Guide to Measure the Time Required for the Release of Goods (Version 3)", provides a globally accepted methodology to measure the actual time required for the release and/or clearance of goods, from the time of arrival until the physical release of cargo. The aim is to find bottlenecks in the trade flow process and take the corresponding policy and operational measures needed to improve the effectiveness and efficiency of border procedures, without compromising efficient trade control.

20 多年前，WCO 首次制定了 TRS 指南。新版的《货物放行时间测算指南（第 3 版）》（以下简称《指南》）提供了全球公认的方法，用于测算货物放行和/或清关所需的实际时间，即货物从运抵至实货放行所需的实际时间。其目的是在不影响贸易高效监管的情况下，找出贸易流动过程中的瓶颈，并采取相应的政策和操作措施，来提高边境管理措施的效能和效率。

The updated Guide reflects the new dynamics in the international trade arena to better respond to emerging realities, and encourages an inclusive approach whereby Customs and other trade stakeholders carry out a TRS in partnership, and jointly identify and address gaps. The new version takes on board the evolution of technology in processing, managing and ensuring not only trade facilitation, but also global trade security, and advocates the use of clearance and release data from relevant IT systems for more efficient and accurate analysis.

新版《指南》反映了国际贸易领域中的新动态，以便更好地应对新出现的实际情况，同时鼓励海关和其他贸易利益相关方以伙伴关系采用包容性方法开展放行时间研究，共同发现和弥补其中的差距。新版《指南》吸纳了处理、管理和确保贸易便利化和全球贸易安全方面的技术发展，倡导使用相关信息系统的清关和放行数据，以便进行更高效、更准确的分析。

It widely recognizes the importance of using periodic Time Release Studies for National Committees on Trade Facilitation (NCTFs) and other bodies to ensure sustainable monitoring and evaluation of the implementation of trade facilitation measures, so that this takes place in an effective and harmonious manner.

众所周知，对于国家贸易便利化委员会和其他机构来说，定期开展放行时间研究至关重要，这项工作可确保对贸易便利化措施的实施情况进行可持续的监测和评估，从而以有效与和谐的方式实施贸易便利化措施。

I encourage all WCO Members, as well as other stakeholders involved in trade facilitation, to make full use of the new TRS Guide in an innovative and collaborative way, and to continue sharing their experiences with the WCO for future development of the Guide and related tools.

我鼓励 WCO 所有成员，以及参与贸易便利化的其他利益相关方，以创新和协作的方式充分利用新版《指南》，继续与 WCO 分享经验，以便优化该《指南》及相关工具。

Kunio Mikuriya

御厨邦雄

SECRETARY GENERAL OF THE

WORLD CUSTOMS ORGANIZATION

世界海关组织秘书长

October 2018

2018 年 10 月

CONTENTS 目录

行动纲要

PLATFORM FOR ACTION

1. The Time Release Study (TRS) is increasingly being conducted by Customs administrations, in close cooperation with other stakeholders. Over the years, such Studies have targeted different border points, trade corridors and modes of transport (land, air and maritime), both to measure performance, and to improve it by developing appropriate policy/operational measures which follow the World Customs Organization (WCO) TRS methodology.

1. 各国海关与其他利益相关方正越来越多地开展放行时间研究。多年以来，该研究针对不同的边境口岸、贸易走廊和运输方式（陆运、空运和海运），依照世界海关组织（以下简称 WCO）公布的放行时间研究方法，制定适当的政策/操作措施，对其实施绩效进行测评并提升其绩效。

2. The rapid evolution of the international trade environment, the emergence of new procedures and technologies, and the ever-increasing pressure to reduce costs and times in the cross-border flow of goods, have made it imperative to keep the WCO TRS Guide up-to-date. It needs to reflect new developments and opportunities, with a view to constantly improving cross-border procedures. With this in mind, the WCO has updated the TRS Guide, based on the experience gained during TRS technical assistance missions, and the feedback received from Members and stakeholders.

2. 随着国际贸易环境的迅速演变、新的程序和技术的出现，以及压缩跨境货物流动的成本和时间压力的不断增加，WCO 的指南必须保持持续更新。它需要反映新的发展和机遇，以期不断改进跨境通关程序。为此，WCO 根据 TRS 技术援助任务获得的经验以及其成员和利益相关方的反馈，更新了该指南的内容。

3. The key elements of the updated TRS Guide (Version 3) include the following:

3. 《货物放行时间测算指南（第 3 版）》的关键要素包括以下几方面：

a. Detailed information on the use of TRS in the implementation, monitoring and evaluation of the TFA. The Guide sets out a concrete approach, including in the context of strategic planning to foster the implementation of TFA measures by National Committees on Trade Facilitation (NCTFs).

a. 在实施、监测和评估《贸易便利化协定》（TFA）的过程中应用TRS的详细信息。该《指南》设定的具体评估方法，包括在战略规划的背景下，推动国家贸易便利化委员会实施《贸易便利化协定》的措施。

b. An explanation of the possibility of conducting, as a first step, a simplified TRS. The latter maps out only that part of the clearance process that directly relates to Customs, and suggests appropriate measures to quickly address shortcomings.

b. 对开展简化TRS（作为第一步）可能性的解释。简化TRS仅给出与海关直接相关的部分通关程序，并提出可以迅速解决问题的适当措施。

c. Illustrations of different approaches to conducting TRS (for example, a consecutive or simultaneous TRS at all identified border points).

c. 运用不同方法开展TRS的实例（例如，连续或同时在所确定的边境口岸开展TRS）。

d. Detailed information on the use of modern technologies in data collection, collation and analysis for improving the TRS process (e. g. electronic processing systems, Single Window, smartphones, RFID seals, and GPS-enabled track and trace). This approach endeavours to exploit the growing use of ICT by Customs, other government agencies and private sector stakeholders.

d. 利用现代技术收集、整理和分析数据，以改进TRS过程（例如，电子处理系统、单一窗口、智能手机、射频识别标签及GPS跟踪技术）的详细信息。这种方法致力于挖掘海关和其他政府机构以及私营部门的利益相关方对信息和通信技术日益增长的使用。

e. Guidance on business process planning, and on performance measurement of entry/exit points and related trade lanes, including the development of model business processes with associated flows.

e. 业务流程规划、进出边境点及相关贸易通道绩效评估的指南，包括与各类流向相关的业务流程模型开发的指南。

f. A future-oriented approach to conducting a Joint TRS in a bilateral and multilateral context, and practical guidance on carrying out a TRS for performance management of regional trade corridors.

f. 在双边和多边背景下开展面向未来的联合实施 TRS 的方法，评估区域贸易走廊绩效的 TRS 实践指南。

g. An additional phase in the TRS methodology which encompasses "monitoring and evaluation" (Phase IV): countries conclude and evaluate one TRS cycle before preparing for the next, when adopting TRS as a strategic and periodic tool to enhance trade facilitation at national, regional and multilateral level.

g. 在 TRS 方法中增加了一个阶段，即"监测和评估"（第四阶段）：当各国将 TRS 作为提升国家、区域和多边贸易便利化的战略性和周期性的工具时，在准备开展下一个 TRS 之前，须结束并评估上一个周期的 TRS 工作。

h. Key principles and processes on conducting TRS in the context of international transit (especially its use in specific trade corridors for the movement/transit of consignments). There are also suggestions and examples for carrying out a Joint TRS at common border points involving neighbouring countries.

h. 国际过境运输背景下开展 TRS（尤其是其在特定贸易走廊中货物运输/过境的应用）的关键原则和流程还有一些在涉及邻国的共同边境口岸开展联合 TRS 的建议和案例。

i. Members' experience and best practice, which have been added to the Guide in order to provide practical perspectives, lessons learned and innovative solutions employed in carrying out TRS.

i. 该《指南》中添加了 WCO 成员的经验和最佳实践案例，以期提供有实用价值的观点、经验教训和在开展 TRS 中所采用的创新方案。

4. The Guide maintains the core methodology and recognizes Customs administrations as the lead agencies at borders to coordinate TRS projects. In close collaboration with otherrelevant

government agencies and private sector stakeholders, Customs administrations can plan and design the Study, with a focus on identifying and addressing bottlenecks in the flow process of cargo. Such collaboration can be achieved through the establishment of working groups and regular coordination meetings.

4. 该《指南》保留了原有的核心方法，并认可海关是协调开展 TRS 项目的边境牵头机构。在与其他相关政府机构和私营机构的利益相关方的密切合作中，海关应负责规划和设计 TRS 实施方案，重点关注确定和解决货物流动过程中的瓶颈问题，这种合作可以通过设立工作组和定期召开协调会的方式来实现。

5. Once the scope of the Study has been agreed by all the stakeholders, and following a trial exercise, it is possible to begin collecting data on the start and completion times of the different clearance procedures. Data may be collected through the use of pre-designed questionnaires, or retrieved from information systems or smart devices. The Guide notes that IT systems involving time-stamped activities provide better data quality. The analysis of results to establish average physical release times is conducted when all the required data has been collected, verified and validated.

5. 当所有利益相关方商定研究范围后，便可试运行，随后就可以开始收集清关程序中不同节点的起始时间和结束时间的数据。这可以通过使用预先设计的调查问卷收集，也可以从信息系统或智能设备中提取。该《指南》指出，带有时间戳记录的信息化系统可提供更高质量的数据。当所有需要的数据都收集、确认和验证完毕后，就可以对设置实货平均放行时间的实施结果进行分析。

6. The Study findings will form the basis of recommendations to address all the issues identified. All the results, findings and recommendations will ultimately be presented in a TRS Report for publishing. Given the national (and even international) impact of the Study, care must be taken to ensure its proper dissemination through the appropriate media channels and circulation to all stakeholders concerned. In addition to setting out average physical release times, the Report will identify areas where actions/procedures need to be improved, or policies adjusted, to address the bottlenecks identified. Finally, there should be a dedicated team responsible for the monitoring and follow-up of implementation of the

Report's recommendations.

6. TRS 的研究将针对发现的问题提出相应的建议措施。所有的结果、发现和建议最终都将在 TRS 报告中公布。考虑该研究对国家（甚至国际）的影响，必须慎重，以确保通过合适的媒体渠道进行适当的公布并向所有利益相关方进行适当的传播。除了列出平均实货放行时间外，该报告还将确定行动/程序需要改进或政策需要调整的领域，以解决所发现的瓶颈问题。最后，应设立一个专门小组，负责监测和跟踪报告中所提建议的落实情况。

01

引言

INTRODUCTION

7. Trade facilitation has become a central theme of economic growth and prosperity in the 21st century, supporting, among other things, the UN Sustainable Development Goals (SDGs). Several initiatives, measures and innovative solutions are increasingly being implemented by Customs administrations, partner government agencies and private sector stakeholders to ensure the rapid movement of cargo across borders.

7. 贸易便利化已成为21世纪经济增长和繁荣的中心主题，也是支持联合国可持续发展的目标之一。海关及其政府机构伙伴和私营机构利益相关方正不断实施若干倡议、措施和创新解决方案，以确保货物能快速跨境流动。

8. Customs administrations, as lead border agencies, play a vital role in expediting the international movement of goods. The World Customs Organization (WCO) believes that it is important for the Customs administrations, in collaboration with relevant government agencies and stakeholders, to assess the efficiency and effectiveness of border clearance processes, in order to optimize trade facilitation and thus ultimately improve overall performance.

8. 海关作为主要的边境部门，在加快货物的国际流动方面发挥着至关重要的作用。WCO认为，海关必须与有关政府机构和利益相关方合作，评估边境清关程序的效率和效能，以提升贸易便利化，从而提高整体绩效。

9. With this in mind, the WCO has developed a unique strategic tool, known as the Time Release Study (TRS), with which Customs and other government agencies, along with private sector stakeholders, can measure in a periodic manner the efficiency and effectiveness of the entire cross-border flow process related to imports, exports and transit movements of goods.

9. 为此，WCO开发了独特的策略工具，即TRS，海关、其他政府机构以及私营机构利益相关方可以定期评估与货物进出口和过境运输有关的整个跨境流动过程的效率和效能。

10. The tool seeks to accurately measure border process performance relating to trade flows, in particular the clearance and release of goods, and helps identify associated bottlenecks so that appropriate policy decisions to improve performance can be well designed and

effectively implemented. It allows the formulation of tailor-made solutions to address inefficiencies stemming from any actor in the overall clearance and release process in the international movement of cargo, thereby leading to a steady reduction in clearance times and trade transaction costs.

10. 该工具力求准确测算与贸易流动有关边境流程（特别是货物的清关和放行）的绩效，并有助于确定相关的瓶颈问题，以便能够妥善设计和有效执行提高绩效的适当决策。为稳步缩短清关时间和降低贸易交易成本，该工具允许使用定制化的解决方案，以解决在国际货物流动的清关和放行过程中由任何参与方造成的低效率问题。

11. Additionally, the tool has been attracting significant attention globally, given its increasing regular useby WCO Members, particularly in recent years. In parallel, it has also been supporting Members as an effective means of efficiently meeting obligations under the World Trade Organization (WTO) Trade Facilitation Agreement (TFA). Article 7.6.1 of the TFA encourages WTO Members to measure and publish their average release time of goods periodically and in a consistent manner, using tools such as the WCO Time Release Study.

11. 此外，随着 WCO 成员近年来越来越频繁地定期使用，TRS 在世界上已引起了极大的关注。同时，它一直是评估各成员高效履行 WTO 所规定义务的有效工具。《贸易便利化协定》第 7 条第 6 款第 1 项规定，鼓励 WTO 成员利用 WCO 的 TRS 等工具定期并以一致方式测算和发布其货物的平均放行时间。

12. Growing digitalization of international supply chains, and increasing uptake of information and communication technology (ICT) solutions in the business processes of Customs and other government agencies, have provided new opportunities for collecting more reliable and time-stamped data for TRS, thus improving the effectiveness of the tool.

12. 随着国际供应链的日益数字化，海关和其他政府机构在业务流程中越来越广泛地采用信息和通信技术（ICT）解决方案，这为 TRS 收集更可靠和有时间标记的数据提供了新机遇，有助于提高该工具的效能。

1.1 What is the Time Release Study (TRS)?

1.1 什么是放行时间研究（TRS）?

13. The Time Release Study is a strategic, internationally recognized tool to measure the actual time required for the release and/or clearance of goods, from the time of arrival until the physical release of cargo, with a view to finding bottlenecks in the trade flow process and taking the corresponding necessary measures to improve the effectiveness and efficiency of border procedures.

13. TRS 是一种国际公认的战略性工具，用于测算货物从运抵到实货放行所需的实际时间，以期发现贸易流程中的瓶颈并采取相应的必要措施，以提高边境清关程序的有效性和高效性。

14. Generally speaking, the TRS is a unique tool that countries are recommended to utilize in order to: measure the actual time required from the arrival of goods to their physical release; assess the efficiency and effectiveness of each actor in the flow process of cargo; identify bottlenecks affecting the release of goods; obtain empirical evidence for re-engineering existing procedures; identify opportunities for border management improvement; establish a baseline for border management performance measurement; and to improve border process efficiency in a periodic manner.

14. 一般来说，TRS 是建议各国使用的独特工具，它可以达到以下目的：

- 测算货物从运抵到实货放行所需的实际时间；
- 评估每个参与者在货物流动过程中的效率和效能；
- 确定影响货物放行的瓶颈；
- 获取重新设计现有程序的经验性证据；
- 确定边境管理改进的机会；
- 建立测量边境管理绩效的基准；
- 周期性地提高边境流程的效率。

15. The TRS measures the total time needed to complete all formalities. In other words, it can determine with precision the time for each separate procedure, such as the average time needed to prepare documents and to complete the formalities for each stakeholder responsible, and other average times in the movement of cargo between two or more countries along the international supply chain.

15. TRS 测量的是完成所有手续所需的总时间。换言之，它可以精确地确定每个单独程序所需的时间，例如制作单证和为每个利益相关方完成手续所需的平均时间，以及国际供应链上两个或多个国家之间货物流动的其他平均时间。

16. For example, in the context of the TRS, the time taken to finalize a Customs procedure can be divided into separate segments, such as the average time for documentary control and for physical examination of the goods. It is even possible to establish the average time needed by the competent authorities to issue licences, by measuring the average time from submission of an application for an import/transit/export/tariff quota licence, until effective issue of the requested licence by the competent authorities (the term "licence" is used generically for each administrative act and includes the licence, permit, authorization, approval or decision).

16. 例如，在 TRS 的背景下，完成海关监管程序所需的时间可以分为单独的几个部分，例如单证审核和实货检查的平均时间，甚至可以通过测算从提交进口/过境/出口/关税配额许可申请到主管部门有效签发所需许可证的平均时间，来确定主管部门签发许可证所需的平均时间（“许可”通常是指每一个行政行为，包括许可、准许、授权、批准或决定）。

17. It is important to note that, in some situations (e. g. low value, non-dutiable goods, and expedited shipments), release will be concurrent with clearance. The TRS methodology can be applied to measure the time needed for Customs to grant clearance after the completion of related formalities, including payment of duties and taxes. In the case of deferred payments, this may occur after the release of the goods.

17. 需要注意的是，在有些情况下（例如低货值、非应税货物和快速货运），放行与清关是同时进行的。TRS 方法可用于测算海关在完成相关手续（包括缴纳关税和其他税款）后清关所需的时间。在延期纳税的情况下，清关可在货物放行之后进行。

18. As defined in the Revised Kyoto Convention（RKC）, the term “release” means the action by Customs to permit goods undergoing clearance to be placed at the disposal of the person concerned, and “clearance” means the accomplishment of all formalities necessary to allow goods to enter home use, to be exported or to be placed under another Customs procedure. However, for the purpose of the TRS, release should normally be understood as the physical release of the goods. The figure below shows the main focus of the TRS.

18. 根据《经修订的京都公约》（RKC）的定义，“放行”是指海关允许将正在办理清关的货物交由当事人处理的行为；“清关”是指货物完成所有允许其在国内销售或使用、出口或转入下一个海关监管程序的必要手续。然而，为开展 TRS，放行通常被理解为货物的实货放行。下图显示了 TRS 的主要关注点。

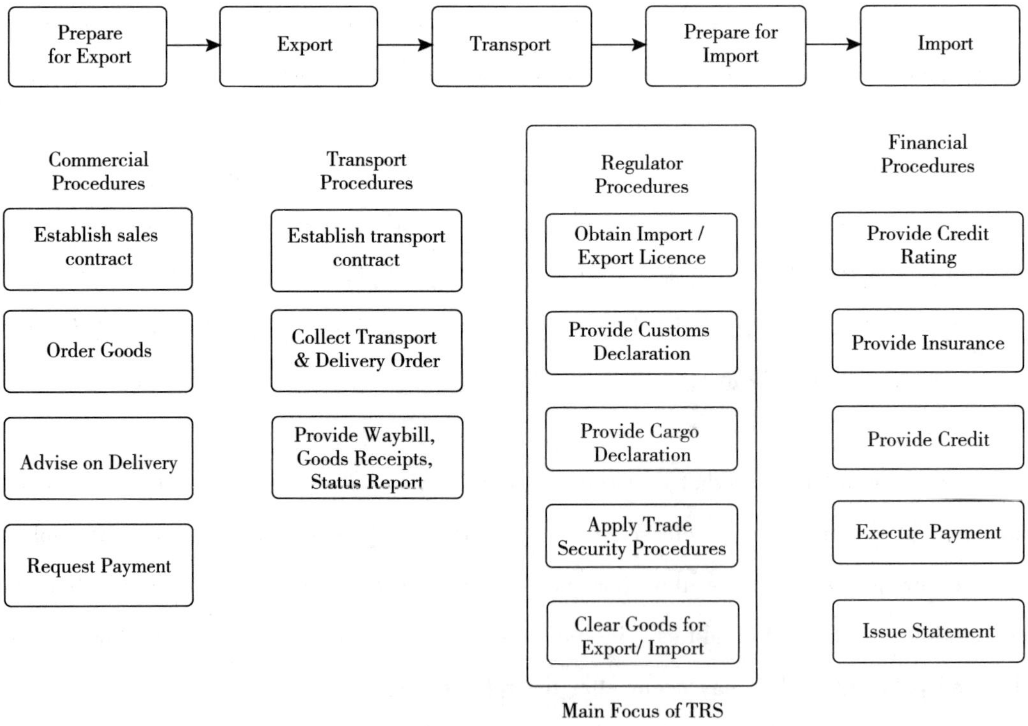

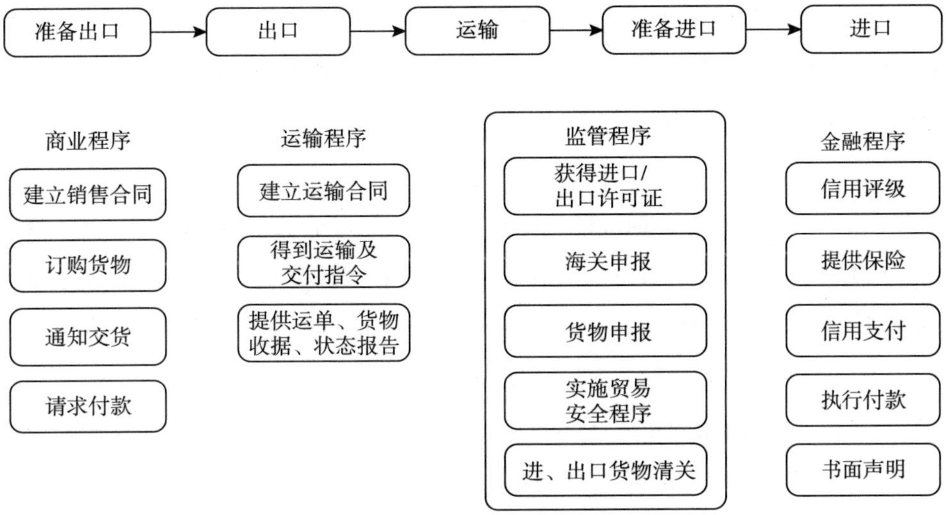

TRS的主要关注点

19. In terms of Customs procedures, this Guide focuses primarily on "Clearance for Home Use" and "Transit", because these are the procedures most often used. However, the principles of this Guide can also apply to any other Customs procedure, including "Exportation", "Warehousing", "Temporary Admission", "Inward Processing" and "Outward Processing".

19. 关于海关监管程序，该《指南》主要侧重“内销清关”（一般贸易进口清关）和“过境”，因为这是最常用的程序。然而，该《指南》的原则也可以适用于任何其他海关监管程序，包括“出口”“仓储”“暂准进口”“进口加工”和“出口加工”。

1.2 Objectives and important features of the TRS

1.2 TRS 的目标和重要特点

20. Although countries conducting a TRS may have several objectives, the overriding or principal objective is to identify and address bottlenecks in procedures related to the international movement of cargo. This objective remains crucial, both for the current international trade environment, and for how that environment might change in future.

20. 尽管开展 TRS 的国家可能有多个目标，但首要或主要的目标是确定和解决与国际货物流动有关的程序中的瓶颈问题。这一目标对于当前的国际贸易环境以及未来国际贸易环境如何变化至关重要。

21. However, Customs administrations are also motivated by additional objectives to conduct a TRS, based on national policy considerations and priorities. The Customs administrations of WCO Members have been carrying out Time Release Studies with primarily the following objective（s）in mind:

21. 然而，基于国家政策考虑和优先事项安排，海关也会因受到其他目标的激励而开展 TRS。WCO 成员的海关开展 TRS 的主要目标如下：

Measuring the overall performance of Customs and other stakeholders' business processes;

测算海关及其他利益相关方业务流程的总体绩效；

Identifying bottlenecks in the international supply chain and/or constraints affecting the release of goods, including with regard to the flow of information, documents and finance;

找出国际供应链中的瓶颈和/或影响货物放行的限制因素，包括信息流、单证流和资金流；

Assessing newly introduced and modified policies, procedures, techniques, technologies and infrastructure, or administrative changes;

评估新引进和修改的政策、程序、技术、科技和基础设施，或评估行政管理改革措施；

Establishing a baseline for trade facilitation performance measurement;

建立贸易便利化绩效测量基准；

Identifying opportunities for trade facilitation improvements;

发现改进贸易便利化的机会；

Measuring the arithmetic mean and/or median time between the arrival of the goods and their release into the economy;

测算货物从运抵到实货放行所需的平均时间和/或中位数时间;

Estimating with precision, based on a standardized system, the time required for each intervening event between arrival and release of the goods, i. e. unloading, storage, submission of the declaration, inspection, interventions by other government agencies and release of goods;

以标准化系统为基础,精确估计货物从运抵到放行之间每一次干预事件所需的时间,即卸货、储存、提交申报、查验、其他政府机构的干预和货物放行所需的时间;

Comparing the results obtained from previous Studies, especially following the introduction of policies or changes relating to Customs or border procedures (such as modernization, reform or trade facilitation programmes), to observe their progressive impact;

比较以往研究的结果,特别是在引进与海关或边境清关程序有关的政策或变化(例如现代化、改革或贸易便利化方案)之后,观察其逐渐产生的影响;

Collaborating on the TRS with neighbouring countries sharing borders, as well as others within a Customs/Economic Union or otherwise, in order to identify bottlenecks at common border crossings or in a supply chain from export to import (including transit), and to take necessary coordinated corrective measures and implement solutions;

与共享边界的邻国以及关税/经济联盟内的国家或其他国家合作开展 TRS,以确定共同边境口岸或供应链从出口到进口(包括过境)的瓶颈,并采取必要的协调纠正措施和实施解决方案;

Promoting the image of Customs administrations and other trade stakeholders with regard to commitment to trade facilitation;

提升海关和其他贸易利益相关方在贸易便利化承诺方面的形象;

Exploring opportunities to introduce WCO modern standards and instruments related to

Customs and other border regulatory processes;

探索引入与海关和其他边境监管流程有关的 WCO 现代标准和工具的机会；

Monitoring and evaluating the implementation of the WTO TFA;

监测和评估 WTO《贸易便利化协定》的执行情况；

Promoting coordinated border management;

促进协调边境管理；

Implementing the Single Window environment; and

实施单一窗口；

Introducing realistic policies related to service standard levels or client charters in Customs and other government agencies.

在海关和其他政府机构中引入与服务标准水平或客户章程相关的实用政策。

A. Different choices or approaches when conducting a TRS

A. 开展 TRS 的不同选择或方法

22. In previous years, when the TRS methodology was being developed, it was recommended that the tool be used at one border crossing point only. Today, whilst countries may conduct a TRS at an individual border crossing point if they wish, it is becoming more common (given the huge increase in trade volumes) to conduct a TRS at a number of border crossing points, or at all border crossing points, where clearance takes place.

22. 前些年，在制定 TRS 方法时，一般建议仅在一个边境使用该方法。如今，各国可根据需要在单个边境开展 TRS，随着贸易量的大幅增长，在多个或所有存在清关业务的边境口岸开展 TRS 变得越来越普遍。

23. Nevertheless, when Customs administrations do not have sufficient experience in carrying out a TRS, or when they are conducting a TRS for the first time and/or resources

are limited, it is recommended that the first Study cover one crucial border crossing point only. This would be a simple TRS approach often used to measure the single busiest port/border crossing point, and it would constitute a simplified approach to conducting a Study, and pave the way for a more comprehensive TRS to be done in future.

23. 然而，当海关在开展 TRS 方面没有足够的经验，或者首次开展 TRS 以及/或者资源有限时，建议首次开展 TRS 的范围仅限于一个主要边境口岸。这是一种简易的 TRS 方法，通常用于对单个最繁忙的港口/边境口岸进行评测，并可为将来开展更全面的 TRS 积累经验。

24. In more difficult situations, when a Customs administration is not able to conduct its first TRS at the identified strategic office (s) in a comprehensive manner which involves all stakeholders, it is also possible for the Study to cover only that part of the national clearance process which is directly related to Customs. When such an approach is adopted initially, the Customs administration should endeavour to carry out a more comprehensive TRS, involving other government agencies and stakeholders, at the earliest possible opportunity, and preferably within one year. This allows sufficient time for the Customs administration to enhance its understanding and to address internal issues, such as organizational and human resource capacity or integrity issues, whilst working to achieve buy-in both within the organization, and from other stakeholders, before conducting a fully-fledged TRS.

24. 在更困难的情况下，当海关无法在确定的战略性海关办事处全面开展涉及所有利益相关方的首次 TRS 时，也可以只涵盖与海关直接相关的那部分清关流程。当开始使用此方法时，海关应努力争取尽早，最好在一年内，开展涉及其他政府机构和利益相关方的更全面的 TRS。这将使海关在开展全面的 TRS 前，能尽力在组织内部和其他利益相关方之间达成共识，而且可以留出充足时间来深入理解 TRS 并解决内部问题，例如组织、人力资源或廉政问题等。

25. However, as stated earlier, it has become more common to carry out Time Release Studies at some or all border crossing points where clearance takes place (as well as for different modes of transport). Studies conducted in respect of more than one border

crossing point are either " simultaneous " or " consecutive " . The TRS methodology described in this Guide clearly supports these types of Studies.

25. 然而，如前所述，在一些或所有边境口岸以及对不同的运输方式开展 TRS 已经变得越来越普遍。对一个以上边境实施的研究，要么是“同时实施”，要么是“连续实施”。该《指南》中描述的 TRS 方法明确支持这些类型的研究。

26. As it is often challenging to conduct a TRS at all national locations, it would also be justifiable to target a few strategic Customs offices or border crossing points because national laws, regulations, procedures and policies related to cargo flow processes at borders are generally applicable to the whole Customs territory. In order words, operational procedures are usually standardized and harmonized throughout a country, unless there are operational issues which are very specific to a Customs office/border point.

26. 由于在一个国家的所有边境开展 TRS 经常具有挑战性，所以也可将一些战略性的海关办事处或者边境口岸作为开展 TRS 的对象，因为与货物跨境流动流程相关的国家法律、法规、程序和政策通常适用于该国的整个关境。换言之，除非某个海关办事处/边境口岸存在非常特殊的业务问题，否则，操作程序通常在全国范围内都是标准化和统一的。

27. Bearing in mind all the options for conducting a TRS, it should be noted that when only one or a few border points are measured, the results of the Study can be used to modify/adjust legislation or procedures, or to introduce measures that can be replicated across other border crossing points, thereby ensuring harmonization throughout the country.

27. 牢记开展 TRS 的所有选项，应当注意的是，当仅测算一个或几个边境口岸时，研究结果可用于修改/调整立法或程序，或者引进一些在其他边境口岸可复制的措施，从而确保全国的程序协调统一。

B. The TRS as a continuous improvement cycle

B. TRS 是一个持续改进的循环过程

28. The rationale behind conducting TRS is based on the premise that it should be adopted

as a continuous improvement cycle. It is essential to undertake Time Release Studies periodically to find opportunities for further improvement. Thus, undertaking a TRS will provide Customs administrations with a baseline of current performance regarding border procedures by identifying bottlenecks, making it possible to subsequently explore solutions to address the problem.

28. 开展 TRS 必须基于以下前提，即它应该是一个可持续改进的循环过程。必须定期开展 TRS，以寻找进一步改进的机会。因此，通过开展 TRS 找出瓶颈，能为海关提供当前边境清关流程绩效的基准，从而有可能找到解决问题的办法。

29. Administrations that periodically undertake Time Release Studies have reported that the time taken for release or clearance of cargo has decreased steadily due to the implementation of improvements and corrective measures designed as a result of the bottlenecks/problems identified. The implementation of corrective measures takes time for most countries, and so each TRS cycle should allow the country sufficient time for this before it embarks on the next TRS cycle. Anecdotal experience of Customs administrations indicates that a TRS should not be carried out before allowing "reasonably sufficient" time to implement identified corrective measures, and allowing these measures to stabilize in order to observe their impact.

29. 根据海关定期开展的 TRS 的报告，通过 TRS 发现瓶颈/问题，进而采取整改措施，有助于稳步减少货物放行或清关所需的时间。对于大多数国家而言，实施整改措施是需要时间的，因此，应允许该国在开始下一个 TRS 周期之前有足够的时间来实施整改措施。海关的实践经验表明，应允许有“合理充足”的时间来实施确定的整改措施，并确保这些措施稳定实施，以观察其效果。

30. The figure below outlines the full cycle of a standard TRS, covering the steps or activities involved in a cycle, as well as how one TRS cycle, upon conclusion, leads to the next TRS cycle.

30. 下图展示了标准的 TRS 周期，包括周期中涉及的步骤或活动，以及 TRS 周期结束后如何进入下一个周期。

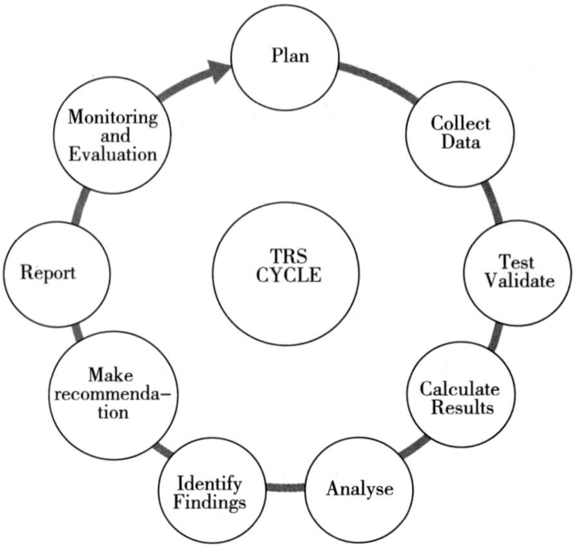

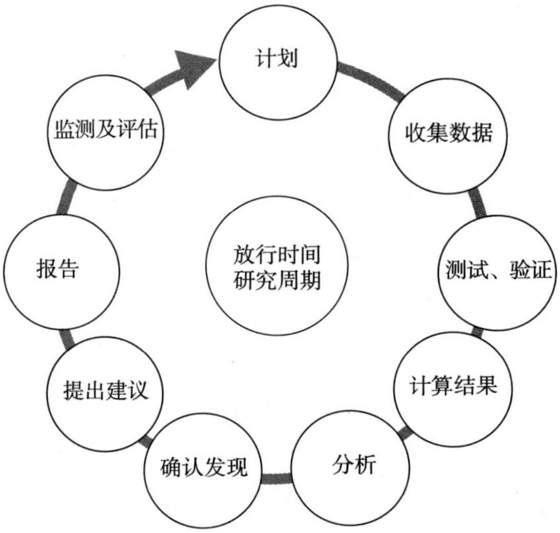

31. Many administrations have established pre-set work or clearance standards, such as client charters and performance pledges, which indicate the average time that should be taken to complete any particular process. In such cases, the results of the Study could be used to evaluate the extent to which these standards or estimated times are being met. The Study will also give useful insights into bottlenecks within the clearance system, including the reasons for not being able to meet pre-set work standards. It will help identify improvement measures that could be undertaken to achieve the stated goals, providing

greater transparency and predictability.

31. 许多海关已经制定了预设的工作标准或清关标准，例如客户章程和绩效承诺，这些标准设定了完成某项特定流程所需的平均时间。在这种情况下，研究结果可用于评估满足这些标准或预估时间的程度。TRS，还将对清关系统内部的瓶颈问题提供有用的建议和意见，包括不能满足预设的工作标准的原因。它将有助于确认实现既定目标的整改措施，同时提供更高的透明度和可预见性。

32. If no Study has been undertaken previously, then the first Study can be used as a reference basis for future comparisons when improvements are made in the flow process of cargo.

32. 如果之前没有开展过 TRS，那么在改进货物流动程序时，首次研究可作为未来比较的参照依据。

C. Applicability of the TRS for export procedures and beyond national borders

C. TRS 在出口程序和境外的适用性

33. This Guide mainly focuses on the time taken from the arrival of the goods at the port/airport/land border, until their release to the importer or to a third party acting on the importer's behalf. However, the methodology in this Guide can equally be applied to a cargo flow process involving export, or to a situation involving more than one country.

33. 该《指南》主要关注从货物运抵港口/机场/陆路边境到将其放行交付给进口商或者代表进口商的第三方所花费的时间。然而，该《指南》中的方法同样适用于出口货物的流动过程，或涉及多个国家的情形。

34. Time Release Studies for export procedures may be useful for those countries that have not yet introduced modern Customs export procedures, although many Customs administrations provide a release status within a few minutes of registration of the goods declaration for export through an automated Customs clearance system. The "Export TRS", from registration of the goods declaration to release, may be meaningful for some countries that impose export Customs duties, since the assessment of duties and risk management could take time.

34. 许多国家的海关采用了自动清关系统，出口货物在申报登记后的几分钟内就可实现放行。但对于尚未采用现代化海关出口程序的国家，在出口程序的环节开展TRS将大有裨益。同时对于那些征收出口关税的国家，开展出口TRS，测算从货物申报登记至放行所需的时间，也具有重要意义，因为关税评估和风险管理需要时间。

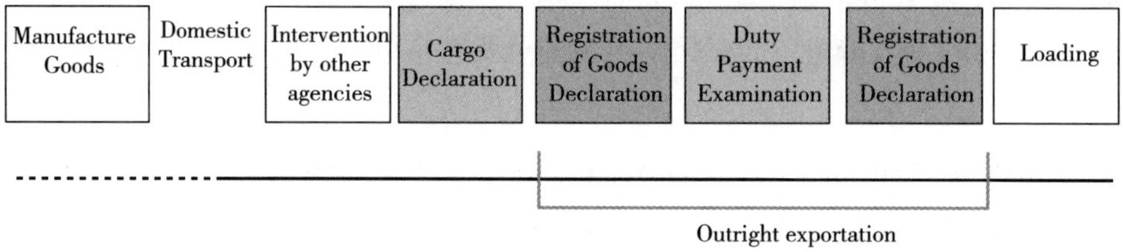

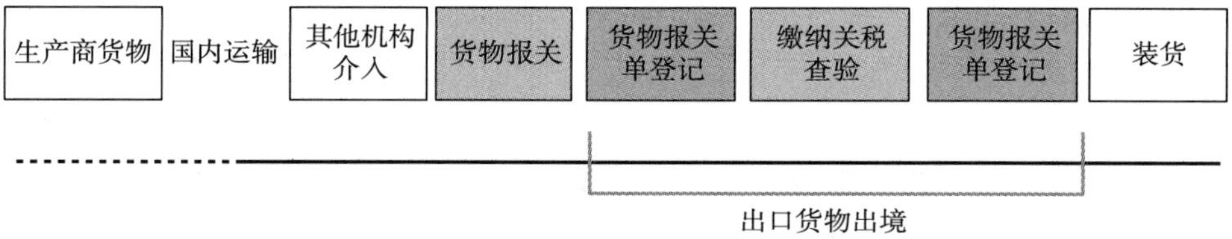

35. There are some challenging issues for a TRS involving export. In many cases, manufacturers determine the schedule for domestic transportation of export goods to the port, based on a ship's schedule, the cut-off date/time for delivery of goods to the container yard, or even the timing of an order from foreign customers. In addition, the starting point for export could be ex-factory, the consignment's arrival at the container vanning site, or the registration of the goods declaration. Nevertheless, undertaking a TRS involving export merits consideration in order to respond to the interests of business stakeholders. It is also worth noting that export performance in a certain region (with a neighbouring country) could also be measured by a TRS involving export, in combination with a TRS for transit procedures.

35. 对于涉及出口的TRS来说，存在一些挑战性的问题。在多数情况下，制造商会根据船期、集装箱堆场收货的截止日期/时间甚至国外客户的订单时间，来制定在国内将出口货物运输至港口的时间表。此外，出口的起点可以是货物出厂、货物运抵集装箱装运地点或货物申报登记。然而，为了满足商业利益及相关方的利益，应该开展出口TRS。值得注意的是，也可以采用出口TRS与过境程序TRS相结合的方法，来测算某个地区（与邻国）的出口绩效。

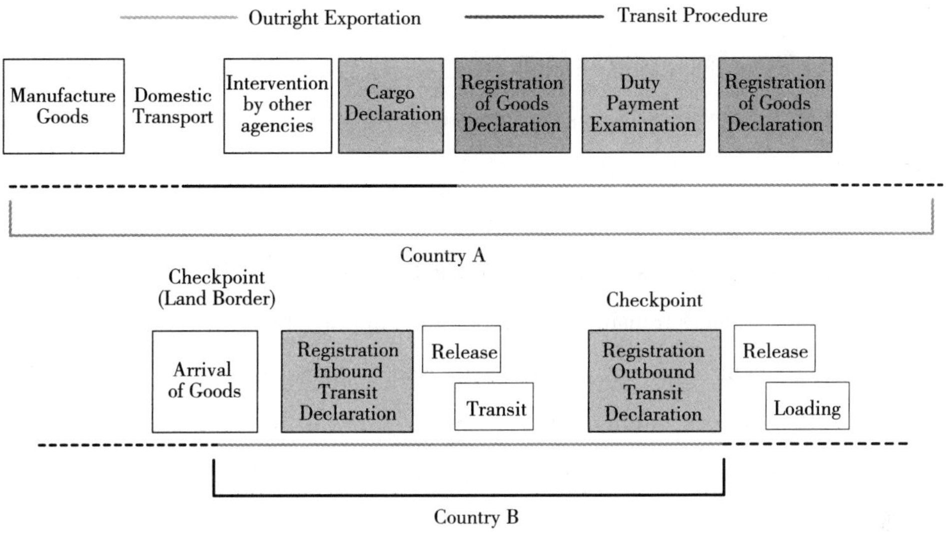

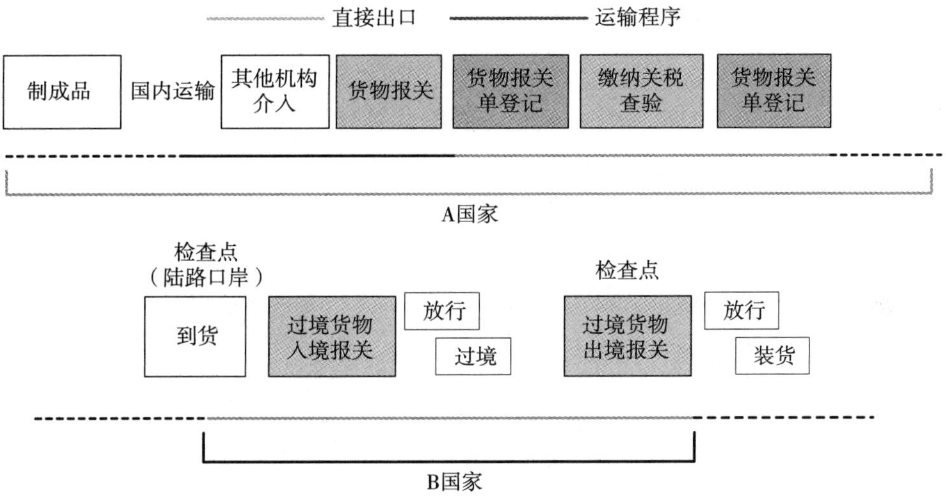

36. The TRS methodology is also applicable to measuring the efficiency and effectiveness of trade relations between two or more countries. Guidance on how to conduct a "Joint TRS" at a bilateral or multilateral level is in Appendix 3.

36. TRS 方法还适用于测算两个或多个国家之间贸易关系的效率与效能。关于如何在双边或多边层面上实施“联合 TRS”的指南，见附录 3。

37. Bilaterally, two countries may agree to carry out a Joint TRS at common or different border points by replicating the methodology with a few adjustments to achieve the desired goal. A high degree of commitment from both countries, as well as from trade stakeholders,

will be needed.

37. 在双边层面，两个国家在做适当调整后基于相同方法，可以在共同的或不同的边境口岸开展联合 TRS，以实现预期目标。两国以及贸易利益相关方都需高度重视该项工作。

38. In the same way, the methodology can be used to carry out a TRS at multilateral level, covering even international transit. This particularly applies to specific trade corridors in respect of the movement/transit of consignments from seaports to hinterlands in landlocked countries, including transit through other countries. As with the TRS at bilateral level, a high degree of commitment from all countries will be needed, as well as from trade stakeholders.

38. 同样地，该方法可用于在多边层面上开展 TRS，甚至可以将国际过境运输纳入其中。尤其适用于将货物从海港转运到内陆腹地的特定贸易走廊，包括途经其他国家的情形。与双边 TRS 一样，此项工作的开展需要所有相关国家以及贸易利益相关方的高度重视。

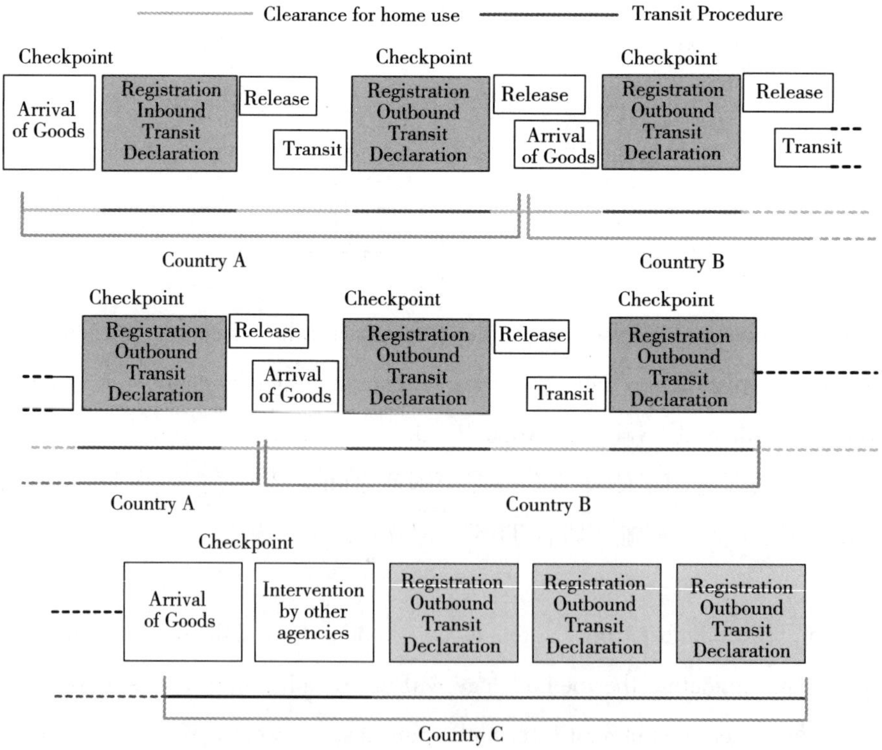

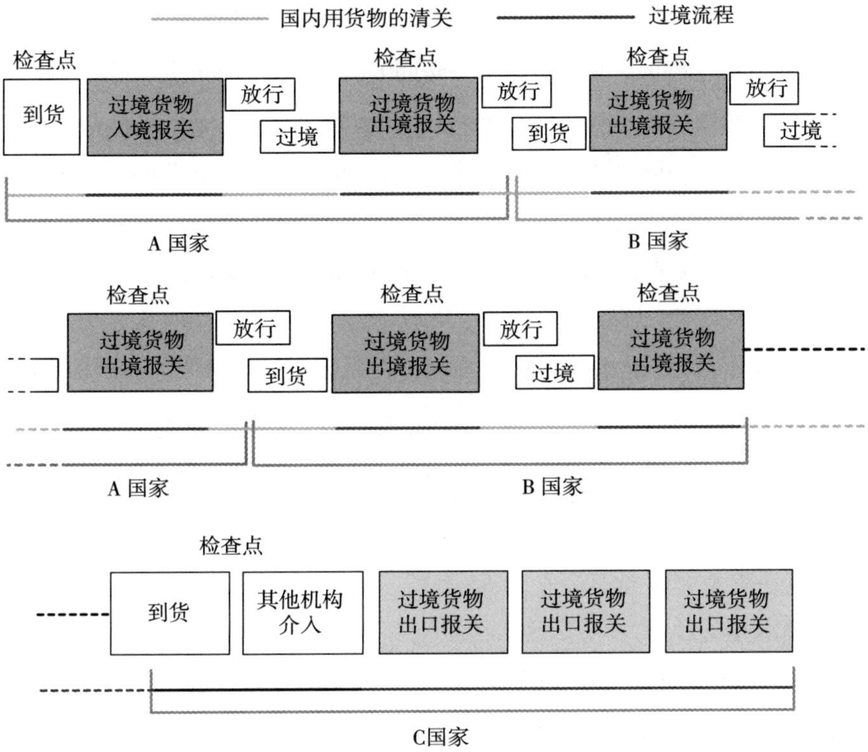

D. The TRS as a national benchmarking tool

D. TRS 被视作国家之间比较的基准工具

39. The TRS was not initially designed as a benchmarking tool. The traditional ideology, which remains valid, is that it is not meaningful to compare TRS results among different countries since trade conditions such as infrastructure, border procedures, IT development, resource availability, and border agency capacity are rarely, if ever, identical in reality.

39. TRS 设计的初衷并非将其作为一个基准工具。现实中，各国的基础设施、边境程序、信息技术发展、资源可用性和边境机构能力等贸易条件很少相同，因此，传统观念认为比较不同国家之间的 TRS 结果没有意义。该观念仍有道理。

40. Statistical standards concerning both the sampling and the calculation methods must be

adhered to if useful and reliable results are to be obtained. Additionally, laws, procedures and resources vary from one Customs administration to another. For this reason, comparisons of results from different Customs administrations are neither useful nor reliable, since Studies can seldom be undertaken in identical conditions and operating environments. In essence, a TRS should not be considered to be a competition between Members or attempt to place a value judgement or ranking on the operations of an administration.

40. 若要获得有效和可靠的结果，必须遵循抽样和计算方法的统计标准。此外，由于成员方海关的法律、程序和资源各不相同，所以比较不同成员方海关的TRS结果既不可靠也没有实际意义，因为几乎无法在相同的条件和操作环境中实施TRS。TRS本质上不应作为WCO成员之间的竞争手段，也不应依此对某成员方海关进行价值评判或管理水平的排名。

41. Nevertheless, TRS could be used in a country as a national benchmarking tool for certain purposes, particularly from the macro perspective. In this case, inherited conditions or situations in each country have to be properly taken into account, since the effectiveness/ineffectiveness of border agencies might not necessarily be the main cause of any delay.

41. 然而，从宏观的角度来看，TRS可以作为国家基准工具用于一定目的的评估。在这种情况下，必须适当考虑每个国家独特的条件或情况，因为边境机构高效或无效的监管程序并不一定是造成所有延误的主要原因。

42. Given similar situations, involving, for example, the same mode of transport or the same legislation, the TRS can be used as a benchmarking tool to support realistic service standard levels for Customs administrations and other trade stakeholders, as the results of Studies undertaken at different Customs offices could be compared to raise the performance of trade stakeholders.

42. 在相同的条件下，例如涉及相同的运输方式或相同的法规时，TRS可作为基准工具来评估海关和其他贸易利益相关方的真实服务水平。通过比较不同海关之间的TRS结果，可以帮助贸易利益相关方提高服务绩效。

E. Stakeholder engagement

E. 利益相关方的参与

43. The effective involvement of relevant stakeholders serves to ensure that TRS outcomes are based on the best and most comprehensive information available to identify bottlenecks and trade facilitation opportunities in the border process.

43. 利益相关方的有效参与能够确保 TRS 的结果是基于可获取的最佳和最全面的信息，能找出边境流程中的瓶颈和贸易便利化的机会。

I. Border and other agencies

I. 边境和其他机构

44. The policy document "Customs in the 21st Century" ("C21") identifies Coordinated Border Management (CBM) as one of the ten building blocks for the role and mission of Customs in the 21st century. CBM represents an approach to managing borders which involves public service agencies working across portfolio boundaries in a coordinated manner to achieve a shared goal, thus providing a cohesive government response to the challenges of border management.

44. WCO 的政策文件《21 世纪海关》（"C21"）将边境协调管理（CBM）确定为 21 世纪海关履行职能和使命的十大基石之一。边境协调管理提供了边境管理的方法：为实现共同的目标，公共服务机构以协调运作的方式对边境实施联合管理，从而共同应对边境管理面临的挑战。

45. The spirit of CBM has also been reflected in Article 8 ("Border Agency Cooperation") of the WTO TFA, which requires each Member to coordinate their activities with respect to the agencies and authorities responsible for border controls and procedures involving the import, export and transit of goods.

45. 边境协调管理的精神也体现在 WTO《贸易便利化协定》第 8 条（"边境监管机构合作"）中，该条款要求每个成员应协调负责对货物进出口、过境实施边境监管和办理清关程序的各部门、机构的活动。

46. What constitutes appropriate involvement and communication among border agencies will differ from country to country. The fact is that each Member has its own governmental and administrative structure, and adopts international obligations through domestic legislation in its own way for trade procedures.

46. 各国边境机构实现适当参与和沟通的措施各不相同。事实上，每个成员方都有各自的政府和行政组织架构，并以各自方式通过国内立法来履行贸易程序上的国际义务。

47. The following list provides examples of agencies and organizations that are typically involved ina TRS: Customs, Quarantine, Standards Board, Immigration, Border Police Authority, Port Authority, Airport Authority, Land Border Authority, Ministry of Finance/Economy, Ministry of Transportation, Ministry of Trade/Commerce, Ministry of Agriculture and Animals, Ministry of Health, Food and Pharmaceuticals, and Ministry of Environment.

47. 通常参与 TRS 的机构和组织有：海关、检疫机构、标准委员会、移民局、边防警察局、港务局、机场管理局、陆路边境管理局、财政/经济部、交通部、贸易/商务部、农业和动物部、卫生部、食品药品局和环境部。

48. With a view to the Study's relevance and efficiency, only those agencies which actually impact on the cargo clearance process should be included. These can act as the national voice of others which intervene to a lesser extent in the flow process of cargo. The involvement of border agencies is indispensable to the TRS, as they may be able to provide Customs with the necessary data which it does not have, and to formulate solutions to address non-Customs bottlenecks. For example, if bottlenecks relating to border agencies have been identified, such agencies are likely to know which measures could be recommended, and the measures would then be included in the National TRS Report.

48. 从研究的相关性和效率出发，参与 TRS 的机构应该仅包括那些实际影响货物清关过程的机构。在国家层面，这些机构可代表对货物流动干预程度较低的其他方面的意见。边境机构的参与，对 TRS 而言是必不可少的。他们能够向海关提供海关所没有的必要数据，并且能为解决非海关导致的瓶颈问题提供方案。例如，如果与边境机构有关的瓶颈问题已经确定，这些机构知道可以建议采取哪些措施，而后这些措施很可能将被纳入国家的 TRS 报告。

49. It is important to bearin mind that the TRS can be very technical. The officials involved should not only be in a position to take decisions, but also have good overall technical knowledge. Therefore, it is crucial that officials from other border agencies involved in the TRS have relevant knowledge of trade issues, particularly issues which are the competence of their respective institutions.

49. 需要指出的是，TRS 的技术性很强。参与决策的官员不仅要具有决策权，而且要具有良好的综合技术知识。因此，参与 TRS 的其他边境机构的官员需要熟悉与贸易相关的问题，尤其是隶属各自机构职权范围内的问题，这一点至关重要。

Ⅱ. Private sector

Ⅱ. 私营机构

50. Customs-to-Business Partnership is identified as one of the ten building blocks for the role and mission of Customs in the WCO Customs in the 21st Century policy document. This policy document argues that Customs needs to understand the concerns of business, while business needs to know the requirements of Customs. It also highlights that there is a need to translate this relationship into a partnership that results in mutually beneficial outcomes.

50. WCO 的政策文件《21 世纪海关》中将“关企伙伴关系”确定为 21 世纪海关履行职能与使命的十大基石之一。该政策文件认为，“海关需要了解企业的关注点，同时企业需要了解海关的监管要求”。该文件还强调，海关与企业之间的关系应成为一种互利互惠的伙伴关系。

51. To achieve a successful outcome to the TRS, it is imperative to actively engage the private sector and to take its views into consideration. Consequently, it is important to have a good understanding of the interests of the private sector and to communicate regularly with

the private sector organizations and members that may be affected by particular aspects of TRS implementation.

51. 让私营机构积极参与TRS并且听取他们的意见，对研究取得成功十分重要。因此，海关应充分了解私营机构的利益关注点，并定期与可能受到开展TRS特定方面影响的私营机构组织和成员保持沟通。

52. The following list provides examples of business participants that could be involved in the TRS: chambers of commerce, freight forwarders, Customs brokers (agents), seaport authorities, airport authorities, warehouses, railway industry, transport industry, shipping companies, airlines, international couriers, and express couriers.

52. 参与TRS的商业利益相关方一般有：商会、货代公司、报关行、港务局、机场管理局、仓库运营商、铁路运营商、运输公司、船运公司、航空公司、国际快件公司和快递公司。

53. For instance, in cases where the port authority and airport authority are wholly operated by the private sector, the TRS may need to be undertaken in cooperation with them to measure the time of arrival of goods. The involvement of Customs brokers (associations) is indispensable to the TRS, as they may be able to provide Customs with the necessary data that it does not have. They are also likely to suggest possible measures which could be introduced in the country once bottlenecks are identified. These measures would then be included in the National TRS Report.

53. 例如，如果港务局和机场管理局完全由私营机构运营，为测算货物的到达时间，则需要与他们合作开展TRS。报关行（协会）对于TRS来说也是必不可少的，他们可以向海关提供海关没有的必要数据。一旦发现了瓶颈问题，他们可能会提出可在全国推广的措施。这些措施将被纳入国家的TRS报告。

54. A TRS typically provides an opportunity for Customs, other border agencies and business to work together for mutual benefit and can create the conditions to evaluate progress in implementing the WTO Trade Facilitation Agreement. The TRS could identify bottlenecks in Customs and border procedures, and even in non-government sector

transactions, providing opportunities to further improve current conditions.

54. 通常，TRS 可以为海关和其他边境机构以及企业提供互利合作的机会，并为评估 WTO《贸易便利化协定》的执行情况创造条件。TRS 有助于发现海关和边境流程，甚至非政府部门事务处理过程中的瓶颈问题，进而提供进一步改善现状的机会。

55. It is also critical that the individual circumstances of each Member be taken into consideration in creating the TRS Working Groupwith business.

55. 在与企业组建 TRS 工作组时，应充分考虑各成员的情况，这一点至关重要。

02

开展TRS的国家战略考虑或利益

STRATEGIC CONSIDERATIONS OR BENEFITS TO A COUNTRY IN CONDUCTING A TRS

56. The WCO has been encouraging its Members to conduct Time Release Studies periodically in order to leverage the opportunities that a TRS brings to Customs administrations, other partner government agencies and the business community in the clearance of goods.

56. WCO 一直鼓励其成员定期开展 TRS，以便利用其给海关和其他政府伙伴机构以及商业团体在货物清关上所带来的机会。

57. Recently, the use of TRS has also been recommended under Articles 7.6.1 and 7.6.2 of the World Trade Organization Trade Facilitation Agreement (WTO TFA). The TRS tool should be used as a key performance measurement tool to assess, evaluate and enhance the implementation of the WTO TFA measures.

57. 最近，世界贸易组织《贸易便利化协定》（WTO TFA）第 7 条第 6 项第 1 款和第 2 款都建议开展 TRS。TRS 工具是评估和加强 WTO《贸易便利化协定》措施实施的关键绩效测算工具。

58. Under the Agreement, WTO Members are encouraged to measure and publish their average release time of goods in a periodic and consistent manner. The TRS methodology is explicitly mentioned in the TFA (Article 7.6) as an aid to Members in carrying out such exercises.

58. 根据该协定，WTO 鼓励其成员定期以一致的方式测算并公布货物的平均放行时间。《贸易便利化协定》（第 7 条第 6 项）明确提出，TRS 是 WTO 成员开展此类活动的一种辅助工具。

59. International development partners within the trade arena have also been advocating that the TRS be used as a strategic enabler to support the implementation of trade facilitation measures, particularly those included in the WTO TFA.

59. 贸易领域的国际发展伙伴也一直提倡将 TRS 当作支持贸易便利化措施（尤其是 WTO《贸易便利化协定》所涵盖的那些措施）实施的战略性推动力。

60. The National Committee on Trade Facilitation (NCTF) within a country can use the

TRS in the strategic planning and proper sequencing of the TFA by accurately and comprehensively assessing trade facilitation needs and priorities, as well as byperiodically monitoring and measuring the outcomes of the implementation of specific facilitation measures and associated policies and programmes.

60. 各国的国家贸易便利化委员会可以应用TRS工具，对贸易便利化的需求和优先事项进行准确、全面的评估，并定期监测和衡量执行具体便利化措施以及相关政策和方案的结果，从而对《贸易便利化协定》进行战略规划和统筹安排。

61. A coordinated approach which engages all relevant stakeholders in conducting the TRS can help enhance coordinated border management at national, regional and international levels, thus strengthening inter-agency cooperation. The latter is a key building block in trade facilitation, and is laid down in various WCO instruments, such as the WCO Revised Kyoto Convention and the WCO SAFE Framework of Standards, as well as in the WTO TFA. Such an approach can also help enhance regional integration, including by helping Members join and integrate into regional economic communities, based on their strategic and policy considerations.

61. 促使所有利益相关方协作参与TRS，有助于加强国家、区域和国际各层面的边境协调管理，从而加强机构间的合作。后者是贸易便利化的关键组成部分，被纳入世界海关组织的各类文件（例如WCO《经修订的京都公约》和WCO《全球贸易安全与便利标准框架》以及WTO《贸易便利化协定》）中。这种基于战略和政策考虑的方式，可以帮助成员加入并融入区域经济共同体，有助于加快区域一体化进程。

62. Increasingly, the regional trade community is finding that the TRS is a strategic tool for improving intra-regional trade, and Joint Time Release Studies involving neighbouring countries are being carried out at common border points. These Studies can equally be used in measuring the performance of a transit corridor involving a few countries, from one end to another, especially in respect of the movement of consignments from seaports to hinterlands in landlocked countries, including transit through other countries.

62. 区域贸易共同体日益发现，TRS是改善区域内贸易的战略工具，相邻国家在共同边境开展口岸联合TRS。这些研究同样可以用于测算涉及几个国家的过境走廊的绩效，特别是用于测算货物从海港到内陆腹地的运输（包括途经其他国家的过境运输）的绩效。

63. With the above in mind, and considering the significance of the TRS, the latter has become a well-established tool that helps enhance trade facilitation in any country, regardless of the size, complexity or level of the economy. Its benefits go far beyond trade facilitation and beyond those actors which are directly involved in the flow process of cargo: the benefits extend to other areas directly and indirectly related to Customs, other government agencies and the business community, thus improving a country's overall economic competitiveness.

63. 考虑上述情况和 TRS 的重要性，TRS 已成为可帮助提升所有国家（不论其经济规模、复杂程度或水平如何）贸易便利化水平的一种常用工具。它的益处远远超出了贸易便利化的范围，也超出了直接参与国际贸易货物流动过程的各方，而且与海关、其他政府机构和商界直接或间接相关的其他领域也跟着受益，进而能提升国家整体的经济竞争力。

64. The TRS can also assist Members with " perception management " through a comprehensive and evidence-based performance measurement and improvement strategy.

64. TRS 还可以通过全面的、基于证据的绩效评估和改进策略，协助成员进行"感知管理"。

2.1 Benefits to national governments

2.1 对政府部门的好处

65. The TRS provides the following benefits to national governments:

65. TRS 可为各国政府带来以下好处：

Improves the efficiency of Customs administrations and other government agencies involved in the flow process of cargo related to importation, exportation or transit of goods, or any other Customs regime related to release or clearance of cargo;

提高与货物进口、出口、过境以及其他货物放行或清关有关的任何海关制度相关的货物流动程序所涉及的海关和其他政府机构的效率;

Allows Customs and other stakeholders to explore synergies, and to work together in addressing national concerns or obstacles which represent a source of delay or problems in the movement of cargo;

促使海关和其他利益相关方齐心协力，共同解决国家关切的问题或者导致货物运输出现延误或问题的障碍;

Creates better conditions for accelerating the international movement of cargo subject to import, export, transit or any other Customs regime related to the release or clearance of cargo, thereby reducing transaction costs for traders and encouraging domestic and international investment;

创造更好的贸易条件，加快办理国际货物的进口、出口、过境，以及其他任何有关货物放行或清关的海关手续，从而降低贸易商的交易成本，促进国内和国际投资;

Enhances opportunities for expansion of national productivity, leading to the improvement of the country's international competitiveness in the global market; and

提高国家生产力，提升国家在全球市场上的国际竞争力;

Supports the government's macroeconomic initiatives through growth and development by strengthening efficiency and effectiveness of cross-border agencies.

加强跨境机构管理的效率和效能，促进经济发展和增长，以支持政府的宏观经济计划。

2.2 Benefits to the business community and consumers

2.2 对工商界和消费者的好处

66. The TRS provides the following benefits to the business community and consumers:

66. TRS 可为工商界和消费者带来以下好处：

Enables the business community to partner with Customs and other government agencies to improve the trade flow process of cargo in relation to a country's import, export or transit release/clearance process, providing them with a better trading environment;

推动工商界与海关和其他政府机构合作，以改进国家的进口、出口或过境放行/清关的货物贸易流程，进而为他们提供更好的贸易环境；

Reduces the financial burden that the business community is likely to face as a result of any possible inefficiency from one or more government agencies in the trade flow;

减轻工商界可能面临的，在贸易流动中由一个或多个政府机构的低效率所导致的财务负担；

Improves transparency and predictability for the business community with regard to the release or clearance process, thus leading to better inventory management and just-in-time deliveries;

为工商界提高放行或清关过程的透明度和可预测性，从而改善库存管理和适时交货；

Creates favourable conditions for legitimate business to benefit from the implementation of trade facilitation measures or initiatives, such as pre-arrival processing, Single Window and Authorized Economic Operator;

为守法企业创造有利条件，使其从实施贸易便利化措施或计划（例如运抵前手续办理、单一窗口和经认证的经营者）中获益；

Enables private terminals and warehouse operators, freight forwarders and others to operate and improve their businesses in a dynamically efficient environment;

使私营码头和仓库运营商、货运代理和其他经营者能够在动态、高效的环境中运营和改善他们的业务；

Provides competitive and fair prices to consumers, who will not have to pay additional costs as a result of inefficient procedures or unjustified practices which may add cost to goods during release or clearance before the goods reach consumers; and

为消费者提供有竞争力和公平的价格，使消费者无须支付由低效程序或不合理做法而产生的额外费用——这些程序或做法可能会使货物在到达消费者手中之前，在放行或清关过程中增加成本；

Improves consumer choice and accessibility to foreign or domestic products.

给消费者带来对国内外产品的更多选择和购买渠道。

03

TRS方法概述

OVERVIEW OF TRS METHODOLOGY

67. The Time Release Study should be divided into four core phases, to be followed in a sequentialmanner until the Study is concluded (leading to a new Study cycle in due course). The phases are an integral part of the Study and set out the methodology in full. They are described below.

67. TRS 分为四个核心阶段，要依次进行，直到研究结束（在适当的时候启动一个新的研究周期）。这些阶段是 TRS 不可分割的组成部分，它们完整地阐述了研究的方法，如下图所示。

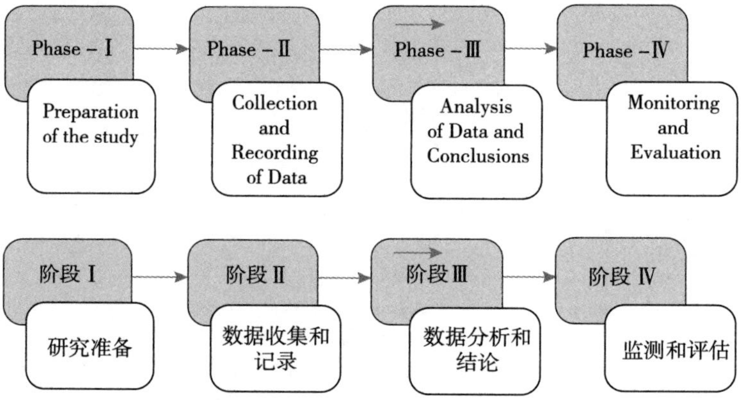

3.1 Phase I – Preparation of the Study

3.1 阶段 I ——研究准备

68. This is the most important phase since it determines the design and scope of the Study. Detailed preparation is therefore essential to ensure the success of the Study and the credibility of its results.

68. 确定研究的计划和范围是最重要的阶段。因此，细致的准备工作对于确保研究的成功及其结果的可信度至关重要。

A. Establishment of a Working Group

A. 组建工作组

69. The first step is to establish a Working Group responsible for the overall project. This is

necessary in order to bring together all the relevant officials, including those from other government agencies, who will be involved in the project from the outset. In cases where Customs administrations are conducting the Study with little prior experience, it is also important to provide the Working Group with Terms of Reference which clearly define what is expected of it. Guidance on this process, including a list of the functions and responsibilities of the Working Group, is in Appendix 2 to this document. However, since TRS in a country is supposed to be carried out periodically, the Terms of Reference may require less input in the context of subsequent Studies.

69. 第一步是组建一个负责整个项目的工作组，它由所有相关官员包括其他政府部门官员组成，这些人员从一开始就参与项目研究。在进行该研究时，如果海关的经验不足，则必须向工作组提供能明确界定对其预期内容的职权范围。此过程的内容包括工作组的职能和责任清单，详见附录2。一个国家应定期开展TRS，因此在随后开展的研究中，职权范围无须增添那么多的内容。

70. Theparticipation of as many players as possible in the supply chain (e. g. Customs brokers and other trade operators) is highly recommended in order to ascertain the time taken for the entire clearance chain, i. e. from the time of arrival of the goods at the port/airport/land border, to the time they are physically removed from the Customs area or physically released. These players should also form part of the Working Group from its inception.

70. 强烈建议让尽可能多的供应链上的各方（例如报关行和其他贸易经营者）参与进来，以确定整个清关过程所需要的时间，即从货物运抵边境（港口/机场/陆路边境）时起，到货物实际离开海关监管区域或货物实货放行时止。这些参与者应该从一开始就成为工作组的一员。

71. The Working Group should be responsible not only for the preparation, planning and implementation of the project, but also for ensuring good coordination between all the parties and agencies involved. In order to achieve this, and to address any misunderstandings, it will be necessary to explain the objectives, the approach envisaged, and the advantages to be gained by Customs, other government agencies, Customs brokers

and other trade operators.

71. 工作组不仅应负责项目的准备、规划和实施，还应协调好各参与方和机构。为了实现这一目的并消除所有误解，工作组有必要向海关、其他政府机构、报关行和其他贸易经营者解释 TRS 的目标、拟采取的方法以及能从中获得的好处。

72. In addition, all parties involved in implementing the Study should be made aware that its results will contribute to improving cargo clearance processes, and bring other benefits to the nation as a whole, in terms of improved economic competitiveness and supply chain efficiency. It will also complement the interests of all staff and trade stakeholders.

72. 此外，所有参与研究的各方应达成共识：研究结果将有助于改进货物清关流程，能为国家带来其他的整体利益，包括提升整个国家的经济竞争力和供应链效率。它还将符合所有职员和贸易利益相关方的利益。

B. Determination of the scope and design of the Study

B. 确定研究范围和研究设计方案

73. It is recommended that the Study be relevant and targeted to a specific situation or to the national trading environment. Since situations may differ from country to country, it is suggested that, as far as resources permit, the Study should include a comprehensive description of all the events in the clearance chain. This approach will require the participation of Customs brokers, trade operators, banks, and other border agencies involved in border clearance (e. g. Health and Agriculture). Every player will thus be able to consider each of its own processes across the entire clearance chain, with a view to improving and enhancing the existing system.

73. 该研究应针对特定情况或各个国家的贸易环境。由于各国的情况可能各不相同，在资源允许的情况下，建议研究应包括对清关链条中所有情况的全面描述。这需要报关行、贸易经营者、银行和其他参与边境清关的机构（例如卫生部、农业部）的合作。因此，每个参与者都能够考虑自身在清关全链条中每个流程的角色，以改进并提升现有制度。

74. In determining the scope and design of the Study, the Working Group must first decide the following:

74. 在确定研究范围和制订研究计划时，工作组必须首先确定以下事项：

Will the Study consider Customs performance only, or will it take into account the performance of relevant agencies involved in border clearance (CBM perspective)?

该研究是仅限于评估海关绩效，还是从边境协调管理的视角，将评估范围扩大到涉及边境清关的相关机构？

Will the Study measure the time from arrival of the goods at the port, airport or land border station until they are released and physically removed from the Customs control area or physically released? If so, it should also involve other parties, such as trade operators, Customs brokers, other relevant agencies (e. g. Health and Agriculture), banks and other economic operators.

该研究是否测算货物从运抵边境（港口、机场或陆路边境）到货物被放行并从海关监管区实际运走或实货放行的时间？如果是这样，还应涉及其他各方，如贸易经营者、报关行、其他相关机构（如卫生部、农业部）、银行和其他经营者。

Will theStudy be internal to the Customs administration, and measure the time from when the Customs declarations are presented to Customs until the time when goods are released by Customs-and/or will it include a scenario covering the completion of all border clearance formalities?

该研究是否限于海关内部，测算从向海关申报到海关放行货物的时间？是否包括完成所有边境清关手续的情况？

Will the Study be based on automated or manual Customs procedures, or both?

该研究是基于自动还是人工的海关监管程序，抑或两者兼而有之？

Will the Study consider export clearance and transit procedures, or be a Joint Study with neighbouring countries sharing a land border, or with other countries within a Customs/

Economic Union?

该研究是否会考虑出口清关和过境程序，或者与共享陆路边境的邻国或与关税/经济联盟内的其他国家实施联合研究？

Will the Study be conducted to evaluate the impact of implementation of a particular WCO instrument/ tool, or of one or more related WTO TFA measures?

该研究的开展是否用以评估实施某一特定的 WCO 文件/工具产生的影响，或者实施一个或多个 WTO《贸易便利化协定》相关措施产生的影响？

75. If an administration wishes to undertake the Study using both automated and manual systems, it must take this into account when choosing the method of data capture and the Customs offices to be included.

75. 如果想要同时使用自动和人工系统进行研究，则必须考虑数据采集方法和所涵盖的海关办事处。

C. Planning

C. 规划

76. Planning constitutes another important aspect of the Study. The plan can easily be modified before the Study has significantly progressed. However, once the Study is well under way, the plan should not be changed.

76. 规划是研究的另一重要组成部分。在研究取得显著进展之前，可以很容易地修改计划。然而，一旦研究已经开展，就不应再改变计划。

77. The TRS Working Group should be aware that it is possible to conduct a TRS in one or more locations. Accordingly, Customs administrations may decide to conduct the Study at more than one location simultaneously, or at various locations consecutively, subject to resource availability and other considerations.

77. 工作组应意识到，可以在一个或多个地点开展 TRS。因此，考虑到资源的可用性和其他因素，海关可以决定是否在多个地点同时或连续开展研究。

78. Aside from deciding whether the Study will take place at one or more locations and whether it will be "simultaneous" or "consecutive", the Working Group should decide a number of other issues or steps during the planning stage. These are outlined below.

78. 除了决定该研究将在一个还是多个地点开展，以及"同时"还是"连续"开展外，工作组还应在规划阶段决定以下这些问题或步骤。

79. When planning a TRS, it is important for the Working Group to realize that the Study may be conducted over a longer period than that recommended in this Guide, particularly if the Study is to take place at several locations consecutively. It should be noted that, for a "simultaneous" or "consecutive" Study, each Customs office/border point selected for the Study will normally be involved in its preparation and execution.

79. 在规划 TRS 时，工作组必须意识到，该研究实际花费的时间可能比该《指南》建议的时间更长，特别是在多个地点连续进行研究的时候。应注意的是，对于"同时"或"连续"研究，用于研究的每个海关办事处/边境口岸通常都要参与研究的准备和实施工作。

80. As mentioned earlier, a "simultaneous" TRS means that a Customs administration will carry it out at more than one location at the same time. In contrast, a "consecutive" TRS involves carrying out the TRS at one location at a time followed by additional Studies conducted at other border posts.

80. 如前所述，"同时" TRS 意味着海关将在多个地点同时开展 TRS。相比之下，"连续" TRS 则先在某个时间、某个地点开展 TRS，随后在其他边境开展额外研究。

81. Fundamentally, Customs administrations may decide whether to conduct the TRS at one station, or at a number of stations, depending on whether they consider it justifiable and relevant.

81. 从根本上而言，海关决定在一个还是多个地点开展 TRS，取决于他们认为该研究是否合理和具有相关性。

82. Irrespective of whether the Study is conducted in a simultaneous or consecutive manner, it is recommended that its work and outcomes be consolidated into a single National TRS Report. This should outline the reality on the ground at each location and provide other crucial information upon the conclusion of the whole process.

82. 无论研究是同时还是连续进行，建议将 TRS 工作和成果合并成一份国家 TRS 报告。该报告中应包括每个地点的实际情况，并且在整个流程结束时提供其他关键信息。

83. Usually, the TRS Action Plan, which is drafted at the very early inception stage of the TRS, gives some indication of when the crucial steps are going to be fully concluded. The seven core steps which the Group has to carefully consider in planning a TRS are indicated below and should be followed in chronological order. However, once the TRS process becomes embedded in a country, some of these steps may potentially be omitted or require less time, particularly in terms of preparation. The steps are the following:

83. 通常工作组应在 TRS 最初阶段起草 TRS 行动计划，说明何时全面完成关键步骤。工作组在规划 TRS 时，必须按时间顺序仔细考虑以下七个核心步骤。然而，一旦 TRS 程序与某个国家的实际情况相结合，其中的某些步骤可能会被省略或花费更少的时间，尤其是在准备阶段。

Determination of the duration, period and timing of the TRS;

确定 TRS 的持续时间、周期性采样和开展时间；

Determination of the geographic scope;

确定地理范围；

Types of goods and traffic;

货物类型和运输方式；

Sampling;

抽样流程；

Business process;

业务流程;

Determination on whether it is necessary to use a questionnaire;

确定是否需要使用调查问卷;

Test run.

试点研究。

Ⅰ. Determination of the duration, period and timing of the TRS

Ⅰ. 确定 TRS 的持续时间、周期性采样和开展时间

84. "Duration of the Study" refers to the time taken to complete various TRS activities, including the TRS Report. The duration has to be sufficient to allow the Working Group time to draft and finalize the TRS Report. In view of all the activities to be carried out by the Working Group (including regular meetings, visiting places where flow process operations are handled, collecting the data from arrival to release of the goods), it is recommended that the duration of the Study as project be a minimum of six months. However, it will sometimes be possible to carry out subsequent Time Release Studies in less time, once the Customs administration has gained sufficient knowledge and experience.

84. "研究的持续时间"是指完成包括 TRS 报告在内的各种 TRS 工作所要花费的时间。"持续时间"必须足以让工作组有时间起草和完成 TRS 报告。考虑工作组将开展的所有活动(包括召开例会、实地调研流程操作办理场所、收集货物从运抵到放行的数据),建议研究项目的持续时间至少为 6 个月。然而,如果海关在 TRS 方面具有足够多的知识和经验,那么以后的 TRS 将可能在较短的时间内完成。

85. The "TRS period" is normally shorter; it often serves as a reference or base point for collecting live clearance data of sample declarations. Ideally, the period should last at least five or seven consecutive working days (five days when Customs declarations are not processed at weekends, and seven days when the declarations are processed at weekends). This should not

unduly disrupt normal Customs operations, and will ensure that a sufficiently large number of declarations are captured to have a good representative sample. If the Study is conducted in a fully automated clearance environment, the period could be significantly longer than five or seven days.

85. “TRS 的样本周期”通常较短。它通常用作收集报关样本实时清关数据的参考点或基点。理想情况下，该周期应至少持续五天或七天（周末不办理海关申报的为五天，周末办理海关申报的为七天）。此项工作不应过度干扰海关的正常业务，并要确保能获得足够多的报关单，以取得具有代表性的样本。如果研究是在一个完全自动化的清关环境中进行的，那么这个周期可以大大超过五天或七天。

86. The period chosen for the Study should be one of normal traffic. Seasonally fluctuating periods, such as before or after holidays (where the volume of traffic tends to be particularly low or high) should be avoided, because these often do not reflect the normal traffic flow. The TRS period should be distinguished from the overall duration of the Study, which also involves other activities, including collecting all the data for the TRS (explained further in Phase II of the TRS methodology).

86. 研究的样本周期应选择在正常的货运时段内。应避开季节性波动的时段，如节假日前后（货运量往往过高或过低），因为这些时段的数据不能反映正常的货运量。TRS 样本周期应与研究的持续时间区别开来，因为后者还涉及其他工作，包括收集 TRS 的所有数据（在 TRS 方法概述的第二阶段中进一步阐述）。

Ⅱ. Determination of the geographic scope

Ⅱ. 确定地理范围

87. The Customs administration, in consultation with relevant stakeholders, should determine whether the Study is to be conducted nationwide (i. e. at all the Customs offices), or only in certain regions or certain individual offices. The Working Group can usually make a proposal after examining the relevant factors, and put this to the administration for decision. For the initial Study, it is suggested that the busiest Customs office in terms of traffic be chosen. For example, in many countries, a significant percentage of traffic goes through only one or two locations. These ports, airports or land border crossings could be used as a starting point for the Study.

87. 海关应与利益相关方进行协商，确定是开展全国性的（全国所有海关）TRS，还是仅限于某些地区或个别海关办事处。工作组通常可以在综合考虑相关因素后提出建议，并提交管理部门做决定。对于首次研究，建议选择货运量最大的海关办事处。例如，在一些国家，大部分货物只在一两个地点进出，可以从这些港口、机场或陆路边境开始进行研究。

88. The following criteria could influence the choice of Customs offices:

88. 以下标准会影响海关办事处的选择：

Volumes of traffic – it is suggested that the Study be conducted at points of entry with a large volume of traffic; and

货运量——建议在货运量较大的进境边境开展研究；

Types of consignments – it is recommended that the Study be conducted at points of entry which process a large variety of consignments and are not limited to only certain commodities, such as bulk goods or chemicals. Normally, such Customs offices/border points should deal with the flow of goods which are crucial for the domestic economy (for example, the most import, transit and export goods). However, under certain circumstances, they may deal with inputs for manufacturing, or with finished goods required to establish, run and maintain critical infrastructural projects, etc.

货物类型——建议在货物类型丰富的进境边境开展研究，而不要选择货物类型较单一，如局限于散装货物或化学品的边境。一般情况下，货物类型丰富的海关办事处/边境口岸处理对国内经济至关重要的货物流动（如绝大多数的进口、过境和出口货物）。然而，在某些情况下，他们可能会处理生产原料，或者建立、运行和维护关键基础设施项目所需的成品货物。

Ⅲ. Types of goods and traffic

Ⅲ. 货物类型和运输方式

89. The choice of goods to be covered by the Study will depend on the type of goods entering or

exiting the country. It is recommended that, at least for the initial Study, the administration include all goods entering through the selected points of entry, in order to develop a holistic assessment of efficiency. However, the administration may decide to select only a particular category or categories of goods entering or exiting the country. Some of the options are:

89. 研究所选取的货物由该国进出境货物类型决定。建议至少应在首次研究中，将选定边境口岸的所有进口货物都纳入研究范围，以便对边境效率进行整体评估。也可以只选择该国的一种或几种特定类型的进出境货物开展研究，可选的货物类型包括以下几种：

Goods falling within certain regimes, such as dutiable goods, non-dutiable goods, exempted goods, or goods imported under preferential and free trade arrangements;

特定制度规定下的货物，如应税货物、非应税货物、免税货物或根据优惠和自由贸易安排进口的货物；

Goods which fall under different procedures, such as goods intended for home use, goods intended for free zones, goods intended for inward processing, goods intended for warehousing, transit, export, etc.;

适用不同监管方式的货物，如用于境内使用的货物、自由区货物、进境加工货物、仓储货物、过境货物、出口货物等；

Containerized goods, pallets, break bulk, etc.;

采用不同包装方式的货物：集装箱货物、托盘货物、散装货物等；

Other criteria, such as type of goods (for example, perishable goods), tariff headings, value, goods from Authorized Economic Operators (AEOs), etc.

其他分类标准，例如货物种类（如易腐货物）、税目、价格、经认证的经营者（AEO）货物等。

90. These categories of goods are given by way of example, and further criteria could be developed. In determining the choice of traffic involved in the Study, the Working Group

should take into account the geography of the Customs territory and the level of traffic relative to the volume of all traffic nationally.

90. 以上货物分类仅供参考，可根据实际情况制定更多分类标准。在选择要研究的运输方式时，工作组应考虑关区的地理位置以及采用该运输方式的货运量在全国总运输量中的占比。

91. It may be possible to eliminate from the Study certain traffic of minor importance, or traffic that constitutes less than a certain percentage of total traffic.

91. 可以从研究中排除某些不重要的，或者货运量占总运输量不到一定百分比的运输方式。

92. Given the large volume and special nature of postal andexpress courier traffic, this should normally be analyzed separately. However, with growing e-commerce, the number of postal and express courier parcels is rapidly increasing and should accordingly be considered as part of the Study in order to speed up legitimate e-commerce flows.

92. 由于邮政和快递的业务量大、性质特殊，通常应单独分析。随着电子商务的发展，邮政和快递包裹的数量正在迅速增加，因此应将其作为研究的一部分，以加快跨境电子商务货物的合法流通速度。

93. Depending upon the resources available, the Study may be carried out for all types of traffic（e. g. air, sea, rail or road）during the same period, or carried out consecutively for different means of transport and for different locations.

93. 在资源充足的前提下，可以在同一时期内对所有类型的运输方式（如空运、海运、铁路或公路运输）都进行研究，也可依次对不同的运输工具和不同的地点进行研究。

94. Special attention may be paid to a particular type of consignment, such as consignments for which immediate release is required. In that case, the Study should either be devoted solely to this type of consignment, or be a more comprehensive Study, covering all consignments, with a separate sample of the particular type of consignment selected from the population for detailed study（see important information in the below box, including

pertaining "Sampling").

94. 需要特别注意特定类型货物，例如需要立即放行的货物。在这种情况下，要么仅对该类特殊货物进行单独研究，要么开展更全面的、包括所有货物的研究，并从总体中选择一个该特殊类型货物的独立通关样本进行详细研究。（重要信息请参阅下表，包括"抽样"）

ELEMENTS TO BE CONSIDERED ON DETAILED DRAWING PLAN (EXAMPLE)

Who? (Establishment of the Working Group)

Points	Example
Who (which division) in the Customs administration should be in charge of the TRS?	Director of Facilitation Director of Customs Clearance
Which government agencies should be involved in the TRS?	Department of Trade, Department of Quarantine
Which private entities should be involved in the TRS?	Customs brokers, forwarders, carriers

When? (Overall duration for data collection and period of the Study)

Points	Example
When is the target timing of the TRS?	The 1 week of April
How many days are necessary for the overall collection of TRS data?	Overall duration for data collection of the Study is maybe 4 consecutive weeks
How possible can you organize the overall schedule?	• 1 week for data collection on procedures in the trade-related agencies • 2 weeks for data collection on procedures in the trade-related agencies and Customs • 3rd & 4th week for data collection on Customs and release of goods

Where? (Choice of Customs offices)

Points	Example
How many Customs offices should be involved in the TRS?	All Customs offices, the biggest Customs office
Which Customs office should be involved in the TRS?	Airport Customs, seaport Customs, Customs for transit
Should the TRS cover the period from arrival of the goods to physical removal of the goods from the Customs control area, or Customs procedures only?	From arrival to removal from the Customs control area

What? (Type of goods)

Points	Example
Should it include automated (ICT) Customs procedures or manual (paper-based) procedures only?	Both manual and automated (ICT) Customs procedures
Which means of transport should be included?	Air, sea, rail, road, river
Which type of goods should be included?	All, FCL, LCL, conventional
What value criteria of goods should be set?	High, medium, low, non-dutiable
For which core events will times be captured?	Arrival, lodgement/registration of required documents, examination and drawing of sample, discharge, border release given, border clearance given, removal from border control, received at owners' premises

How? (Sampling, collecting and recording data)

Points	Example
How many samples should be taken into account?	20% of all Customs declarations
How should samples be selected?	Use last two digits of Customs declaration ID Number
How can you obtain the necessary data on "Arrival of goods"?	Carriers, Customs IT system
How can you obtain the necessary data on "Unloading of goods"?	Port operator, Customs IT system
How can you obtain the necessary data on "Intervention by trade-related agencies and other stakeholders"?	Border Agency
How can you obtain the necessary data on "Physical release of goods"?	Warehouse operator

详细抽样计划需考虑的因素（示例）

人员（工作组的组建）	
要点	举例
TRS 由海关的哪些部门、哪些人员负责？	贸易便利处处长、通关处处长
哪些政府部门应参与 TRS？	贸易部门、检疫部门
哪些私营主体应参与 TRS？	报关行、货运代理、承运人
时间（数据收集的总时长和研究的时段）	
要点	举例
TRS 的目标时段？	4 月中的 1 周
收集 TRS 总体数据需要多少天？	收集所有研究数据需要连续四周的时间
整体进度如何安排？	第一周收集贸易相关机构程序的数据； 第二周收集贸易相关机构和海关程序的数据； 第三和第四周收集贸易海关及货物放行的数据
地点（海关办事处的选择）	
要点	举例
应有多少海关办事处参与 TRS？	所有海关办事处、最大的海关办事处
哪些海关办事处应参与 TRS？	机场海关、港口海关、过境地海关
TRS 涵盖的是从货物运抵到实际离开海关监管区的全过程，还是仅到办结海关手续为止？	从货物运抵到实际离开海关监管区

（续表）

研究对象（货物类型）	
要点	举例
应涵盖海关自动化（ICT）清关程序，还是只包括人工（纸质）清关程序？	应同时包括人工和自动化清关程序
应包括哪些运输方式？	空运、海运、铁路运输、公路运输、河运
应包括哪些种类的货物？	所有货物、整箱、拼箱、传统货物
应如何设置货物的价值标准？	高、中、低、无税
需要采集哪些核心事项的发生时间？	到达、所需单证的提交/登记、样品抽取和检查、手续办结、准予放行、准予清关、解除边境管控、货主场所收货
操作方式（抽样、收集和记录数据）	
要点	举例
应抽取多少样本？	申报单总数的20%
如何选择样本？	按报关单编号最后2位数字抽取
如何获取必要的“货物运抵”数据？	承运商、海关信息化系统
如何获取必要的“货物卸载”数据？	港口运营商、海关信息化系统
如何获取“受贸易有关机构和其他利益相关方干预”的必要数据？	边境机构
如何获得“货物实货放行”的必要数据？	仓库运营商

Ⅳ. Sampling

Ⅳ. 抽样流程

95. When the volumes of consignments or time constraints make it impossible to capture all transactions in the period selected, sampling should be used. If a sampling method is used, a sampling strategy must be developed. The latter should consider the nature of the consignments to be measured, the primary purpose of the analysis, the types of statistical techniques that might be used, and the relative ease or difficulty in the mechanics of listing the transactions and drawing the sample.

95. 当受货物量或时间限制，从而无法在所选时段内获取所有交易信息时，应使用抽样方法。如果采用抽样方法，则必须制定抽样规则。抽样规则应综合考虑待测算货物的性质、分析的主要目的、可能使用的统计方法以及获取交易信息和抽取样本的难易度。

96. When the population cannot cover one hundred percent (100%) of all transactions to be captured for the Study, the Working Group shouldensure that the sample selected is statistically valid. The administration conducting the Study should justify the sample size in the TRS Report.

96. 当样本总体无法百分之百覆盖研究所需获得的所有交易时，工作组应确保所选样本的统计有效性。开展 TRS 的海关应在 TRS 报告中说明样本量的合理性。

97. Care should be taken to ensure that the samples are representative of the transactions covered by the Study (sample reliability), as this will reflect the degree of variability that exists in the population.

97. 研究时应注意确保样本能足以代表研究所涉及的所有交易（样本可靠性），因为这将反映样本总体的可变程度。

98. The sample size required for meaningful estimates of the population or sub-population parameters will also depend on the degree of precision in making the estimates (sampling error). Generally, the larger the sample used, the more representative it will be of the population for the Study.

98. 对总体数据或分组数据参数进行有意义估算所需的样本量，也依赖于估算的精确度（抽样误差）。一般来说，使用的样本量越大，研究样本总体的代表性就越强。

99. Reliable results can be obtained if a sound sampling method is used. The principles below should be observed.

99. 可靠的结果源于采用合理的抽样方法。抽样时应遵守以下原则：

All samples must be selected randomly or with a known selection probability. This can be done by using random number generators for automated procedures. For manual procedures, systematic means to ensure randomness in selecting transactions should be developed. Established sampling methodologies can be used to make this truly representative.

所有样本的抽取应是随机的或基于公认的选择概率。可以通过使用随机数生成器来实现自动化抽取。对于人工作业，应制定系统化的方法，以确保样本选择的随机性。建立合理的抽样方法，将有助于实现抽样的真正代表性。

If sub-populations, for example goods that undergo physical examination, are to be studied separately, a stratified random sampling method should be used, where separate samples are established for each sub-population. It should be noted that comparing samples from these sub-populations with those from the main population could lead to errors.

如果要单独研究分组数据，例如接受实货查验的货物，则应采用分组随机抽样方法，为数据分组建立单独的样本。应注意的是，这些分组数据样本与总体数据样本可能存在一定的偏差。

100. It is suggested that books on statistical research methodology be consulted if additional or more in-depth information is needed on sampling issues. If necessary, external experts could be used to advise on the sampling method and process.

100. 如果需要了解关于抽样问题的更多或更深入的信息，建议查阅统计研究方法类的书籍。如有必要，可以聘请外部专家对抽样方法和抽样过程进行指导。

Ⅴ. Business process

Ⅴ. 业务流程

101. The Working Group should design national business processes for all cargo clearance processes, per mode of transport or border crossing point to be covered by the TRS. Each business process should include Customs, the other main government agencies, and the private sector involved in the flow process for the potential cargo or location (s) which will be the focus of the Study.

101. 工作组应对 TRS 所覆盖的所有货物清关过程、每一种交通方式、每一个跨境边境制定一套全国性的业务流程。对于作为研究焦点的潜在货物或地点，每个业务流程应包括海关、其他主要政府机构以及涉及货物流动的私营部门。

102. The national business process can be understood as the sequence of activities and tasks which an international consignment undergoes in the form of the physical movement of cargo, document processing, examination, inspection, intervention by other stakeholders, payment of duties/taxes/fees, release of goods, etc. The national business process model should be a clear reflection of how the cargo clearance process is carried out in reality. In addition, it should distinguish between the intervals of the process that fall within the competence of the Customs authority, and those that depend on the other cross-border regulatory agencies. As far as possible, this should be reflected in the questionnaire or in the way data is analysed. A business process model for different modes of transport is in Appendix 2 to this document.

102. 该全国性的业务流程可以理解为处理国际货物的一系列工作和任务，包括货物实体移动、单证处理、审核、查验、其他利益相关方的干预、关税/其他税费缴纳、货物放行等。该全国性业务流程模型应该清楚地反映实际的货物清关流程。此外，还应区别属于海关职权范围的程序办理时段以及其他跨境监管机构负责程序的办理时段。这些内容应尽可能反映在调查问卷或数据分析中。不同运输方式的业务流程模型见附录2。

Ⅵ. Determination on whether it is necessary to use a questionnaire

Ⅵ. 确定是否需要使用调查问卷

103. A questionnaire can be used to capture key elements of the clearance process. The questionnaire form will ensure that the information is captured in a structured format, particularly when the clearance process is not fully automated.

103. 调查问卷可用来收集清关过程中的关键信息。特别是在非完全自动化的清关过程环境下，调查问卷表能确保所需信息以结构化的形式获得。

104. In a non-fully automated environment, when Customs administrations have very little experience of conducting a TRS, it is recommended that a simple questionnaire be used

that records the " time-stamps " of the main procedures or processes. A complex questionnaire that requires the recording of numerous time-stamps and other complex features leads to inaccurate data collection when Customs administrations have little experience.

104. 在非完全自动化的清关流程下，建议缺乏开展TRS经验的海关使用简单的调查问卷，来记录反映主要程序或流程的“时间戳”。因为复杂的调查问卷内容包含了众多的“时间戳”和其他复杂要素，将会影响所收集数据的准确性，特别是在海关部门开展该研究的经验不足的时候。

105. However, as the Customs administration gains experience in conducting a TRS, the Working Group may, in time, consider designing a complex questionnaire for the start of a new TRS cycle. The questionnaire form should be designed to capture significant relevant data required for the Study (which the Working Group will be able to do if they are well acquainted with the business process). The form should contain a series of questions to be answered by all the parties involved in the Study. It could be a single form, containing information to be entered by all the relevant agencies participating in the Study, or it could be a number of forms, containing information on the processes relevant to the respective participants. Multiple questionnaires or forms are not normally recommended for capturing time-stamps.

105. 当海关在TRS方面积累了足够经验之后，工作组可以考虑在下一个TRS周期中使用复杂的调查问卷。调查问卷表是为采集研究所需要的重要相关数据而设计的（如果工作组对业务流程非常熟悉，则可以这样做）。该表格应包含需要参与研究的各方都回答的一系列问题。它可以是一张单一的表格，包含所有参与机构都要录入的信息；也可以是一系列表格，由参与研究的各机构分别填写。一般不建议使用系列调查问卷或表格来采集“时间戳”。

106. If a number of forms are used, it is desirable to evaluate the items of data together (once all the data has been captured) in order to ascertain the time taken for the overall clearance chain. However, it is preferable to use a single form that is agreed by all the agencies involved in the clearance process. This will be more convenient, since all the data

will be captured in a chronological sequence.

106. 如果使用系列表格，在所有数据收集完毕后，最好对所有数据项进行统一评估，以便确定整个清关流程所需要的时间。但是，建议优先使用清关流程参与各方都认可的统一表格来收集数据，这样做更简便，因为所有数据是按时间顺序进行采集的。

107. Although the questionnaire depends on the country, mode of transport or even the location, there are important elements that should be included, and some of these elements are also shown template questionnaires set in Appendix 2.

107. 虽然调查问卷的内容根据国家、运输方式以及边境地点的不同而有所差异，但都应该包括附录 2 中的调查问卷模板所列明的重要要素。

108. Given that over 60% of WCO Members are Contracting Parties to the Revised Kyoto Convention, and in view of the ongoing efforts to improve and harmonize the flow process of cargo in these Members, a simpler, standard national form may capture all the required information. However, the form should be adjusted to reflect possible small differences regarding different locations or modes of transport.

108. 鉴于 60% 以上的 WCO 成员是《经修订的京都公约》的缔约方，同时各方都在致力于改善和协调成员国间的货物流通，所以可以使用一种更简单且统一的表格来收集所有必要的信息。但是，表格内容仍应根据具体情况进行调整，以反映不同地点或运输方式之间可能存在的细微差异。

109. In those countries where most or all clearance processes are fully automated, it is possible that a questionnaire will not be needed to collect the necessary data. This is because the time-stamps which are normally collected using the questionnaire form can be inserted directly into a smartphone, tablet or other electronic device.

109. 对于基本上或完全实现清关过程自动化的国家，可能不需要采用调查问卷来收集必要的数据。因为通过调查问卷收集到的“时间戳”，可以直接从智能手机、平板电脑或其他电子设备中获取。

110. Nevertheless, the Working Group should always be aware of the structure which a questionnaire form could take. This is helpful in terms of knowing how the information will be obtained, and what the logical sequence will be for the entire clearance process. It will also become important when the WCO TRS software is used to analyse the data obtained.

110. 然而，工作组还是应熟悉调查问卷表的结构设计。这将有助于了解信息的获取途径以及整个清关流程的逻辑顺序，同时对使用 WCO 发布的 TRS 软件分析样本数据也大有裨益。

111. It is also possible that, in a fully automated environment, the form will be designed to include a barcode and that the time-stamps will be able to be captured much more quickly and accurately by using a barcode reader.

111. 在完全自动化的环境下，还可以将条形码嵌入相关表格中，使用条形码阅读器更快速、更准确地获取“时间戳”。

Ⅶ. Test run

Ⅶ. 试点研究

112. It is advisable that a test run be conducted once the questionnaire has been designed and the personnel collecting and recording the data have been briefed. However, a test run should also be conducted when questionnaire formsare not used (i. e. when the clearance process is fully automated). This is important in order to ascertain that data collection takes place exactly as prescribed. It will also provide the opportunity to remedy any problems that might be encountered due to a lack of understanding by the personnel collecting and recording the data.

112. 建议在调查问卷设计完毕后开展试点研究，在开始前要向收集和记录数据的人员简要介绍调查问卷的情况。即便不使用调查问卷表（当清关过程完全自动化时），也应进行试点研究，因为这将确保数据采集过程完全按照预设规定进行，还将有助于及时发现并解决在研究过程中由于数据收集和记录人员缺乏了解所带来的问题。

113. The test run can be carried out over two days so that all the parties involved in the Study knowhow to resolve any problems that might be encountered during the test. It is recommended that the questionnaire be circulated in advance to all the parties. In addition, those who will be using electronic devices to collect the data need to have them in advance.

113. 试点研究可在两天内完成，以便参与各方都能了解该如何解决测试过程中可能遇到的问题。建议将调查问卷提前分发给参与各方。此外，那些用于收集数据的电子设备也应提前发放给相关人员。

114. All the observations from the test run should be recorded and, if possible, any issues identified should be resolved before conducting the Study. After the test run, butbefore the actual Study, it is possible that quick adjustments might be needed. However, it is worth to note that in situation where questionnaire form is not used test-run might not carried out.

114. 应完整记录试点研究过程中出现的所有结果，如果可能的话，应在开展正式研究之前解决试点研究过程中发现的所有问题。试点研究结束之后，实际研究开始之前，应根据实际运行情况对研究过程进行及时调整。值得注意的是，在没有使用调查问卷的情况下，可以不开展试运行。

3.2 Phase Ⅱ – Collection and recording of data

3.2 阶段Ⅱ——数据收集和记录

115. Data collection is influenced to a great extent by whether the clearance process is mostly manual or automated. The collection of data involves certain essential elements.

115. 数据收集在很大程度上受清关过程主要是人工化还是自动化的影响。数据收集包含了某些特定的基本要素。

116. When collecting data for the purpose of conducting a TRS, there are two options which can be used:

116. 开展 TRS 时，有两种方式可以收集数据：

A. Collection of data manually

A. 人工收集数据

117. Data is collected manually by using one or more questionnaire forms where the data cannot be collected electronically. The collection and recording of data should take place using the pre-designed form（s）. As many WCO Members have a partially automated clearance process, the form will not be used to collect all the data from arrival of the cargo until release. The entire set of data collected from arrival to release, including the data collected manually, will subsequently need to be inserted into the WCO TRS software for further analysis.

117. 当无法以电子方式收集数据时，可以通过一份或多份调查问卷表来人工收集数据。数据的收集和记录应使用预先设计好的表格。由于 WCO 的许多成员方都有部分自动化的清关过程，因此不用收集从货物运抵到放行的所有数据。从运抵到放行的整个数据集，包括人工收集的数据，随后都需要导入 WCO 发布的 TRS 软件中，以进行下一步的分析。

B. Collection of data automatically

B. 自动收集数据

118. Data can be collected from computer systems and additional electronic devices, such as smartphones, RFID seals, GPS-enabled track and trace, other used during the flow process. This option allows Customs administrations, other government agencies and relevant stakeholders to extract their respective time-stamped activity records of the cargo clearance process. The time records related to the accomplishment of various events identified are measured, extracted from IT systems and uploaded into the WCO TRS software platform. A hybrid approach combining both of these options can be used for the collection of data when the interval from arrival to physical release of cargo contains elements where actions are carried out manually and with the aid of electronic devices.

118. 数据可以从计算机系统和在货物流通过程中使用的其他电子设备（例如智

能手机、射频识别标签、GPS 跟踪和追踪设备）中获取。这种方式可以让海关和其他政府机构以及利益相关方提取各自在货物清关过程中带有时间戳的活动记录。随后，对与完成各个确定事项相关的时间记录进行测算，并将其从电子系统中提取出来后上传到 TRS 软件中。当货物从运抵到实货放行的时间段中包含人工监管和借助电子设备监管时，可以组合使用人工和自动两种方法来收集数据。

119. When data is collected for the purpose of TRS analysis using only option two above, the TRS Working Group is advised to capture the data and immediately structure it in a manner compatible with the TRS software. This is important because, while the manual option involves circulation of one or more questionnaires at various points in a sequential manner, the data obtained electronically by using option two comes from different points within Customs and other stakeholders' domains (unless the whole process is fully electronic), and may not necessarily follow a sequential flow process for the clearance of goods.

119. 当仅使用自动收集数据的方式来收集 TRS 所需的数据时，建议 TRS 工作组在获取数据后，立即用与 TRS 软件兼容的方式对数据进行结构化处理。这是因为，使用选项 2 以自动化方式获得的数据（除非整个过程完全自动化）来自海关和其他利益相关方领域内的不同地点，数据的顺序与货物清关流程可能不一致。而人工收集数据时是按顺序在不同地点分发一份或多份调查问卷表。

120. For the data collection process, the Working Group needs to consider the key areas below.

120. 对于数据收集过程，工作组需要考虑以下关键问题。

Ascertain which processes are accomplished with the aid of computers and electronic devices, and which processes are manual. This will help the Working Group to better define the method (s) for collecting the necessary data.

确定借助计算机和电子设备自动完成的流程，以及人工完成的流程。这将有助于工作组更好地确定收集数据的方法。

Ascertain the processes and the parties responsible for collecting and recording the data.

确定收集和记录数据的流程和责任方。

Some data is known in advance. For example, Customs brokers, freight forwarders and shipping agents will usually have most of the general information relating to the goods and their arrival prior to submission of the declaration to Customs (particularly when goods are not subject to a pre-arrival declaration). In a manual setting, this information could be entered into the questionnaire form as soon as it is received. It is therefore preferable for the questionnaire forms to be given to Customs brokers, freight forwarders and shipping agents in advance to fill in the relevant available information prior to submission of the goods declaration.

部分通关信息是可以提前知晓的。例如，报关行、货运代理和船运代理在向海关提交报关单之前（特别是当货物无须提前申报时），通常已经掌握了与货物及其运抵有关的大部分基本信息。在人工收集数据的过程中，可以在收到这些信息的第一时间将其填入调查问卷表中。因此，最好在货物报关前，提前向报关行、货运代理和船运代理发放调查问卷表，以便他们提前填写相关已有信息。

When data is entered into the form at the Customs office during the clearance process, it is desirable that the officers tasked with entering the data be other than those processing the transactions. This will avoid delays in the routine processing operations.

如果数据是在清关过程中于海关办事处录入表格的，负责录入数据的人员最好不要是办理业务的一线人员，以避免常规流程操作导致的延迟。

Certain administrations allow the lodgement of goods declarations and initiate a number of processes (such as risk management) prior to the arrival of thegoods, or even prior to their loading/departure. Customs may either assess the information or request it in relation to cargo interventions before the actual arrival. Where the decision is made not to examine the goods, the latter may be released by Customs even before their arrival, or at the moment of arrival, depending upon national legislation.

某些海关允许在货物运抵之前甚至在货物装载/发运之前提交货物申报，并启动一系列作业流程（例如风险管理）。海关可在货物实际运抵前，对与货物干预措施有关的信息进行评估或要求提交此类信息。如果决定不查验该货物，海关可以根据所在国法律，在货物运抵前或运抵时放行货物。

Administrations may also choose to measure the steps in the pre-arrival process itself, i. e. the difference between the time of the lodgement of the goods declaration and the time that Customs grants the actual release of the goods. These time-stamps would have to be included in the automated system or the questionnaire form in such a manner as not to distort the results of the processing and release of goods after arrival.

海关也可选择测算提前申报流程各个步骤的时间，即从货物提交申报至海关同意放行的时间。这些时间戳在嵌入自动化系统或调查问卷表时，不得影响货物运抵后的处理和放行结果。

As indicated earlier, a recommended way to collect the data is to use both of the two available options, i. e. a hybrid approach, but only when there is not a fully automated environment. It is important to bear in mind that Customs and the other stakeholders involved in the clearance process might all have different automated processes involving computer systems or other electronic means, and that a more precise approach to collecting data will be to extract it from the different computer systems or electronic devices, and to integrate it with the data collected manually.

如前所述，只有在不是完全自动化的环境下，才建议采用组合方式收集数据，即自动和人工两种方式同时使用的组合方法。值得注意的是，海关和参与清关过程的其他利益相关方，可能有不同的由计算机系统或其他电子设备组成的自动化流程。因此，收集数据更精确的方法便是把数据从不同的计算机系统或电子设备中提取出来，再与人工手动收集的数据进行整合。

In countries where the clearance process takes place using the Single Window system, significant data is concentrated in that system. In the Single Window environment, it is important that the data is collected in a structured manner for the purpose of TRS analysis. In essence, less manual data will be required to be collected in a Single Window environment, depending on the level and number of other government agencies and stakeholders involved or interfaced with the Single Window. Data relating to peripheral processes (i. e. outside the Single Window environment) should therefore be collected using the TRS-designed form. Alternatively, additional electronic devices may be accessed or used to obtain relevant data.

在使用单一窗口处理清关流程的国家，数据大量集中在该系统中。在单一窗口环境中，为了开展 TRS 分析，以结构化的方式收集数据是很重要的。一般而言，参与单一窗口或与单一窗口对接的其他政府机构和利益相关方的级别越高、数量越多，在单一窗口环境中需要人工收集的数据就越少。因此，单一窗口环境以外的流程数据应采用 TRS 预设的调查问卷的方式收集。此外，也可以通过访问或使用其他电子设备的方式来获取相关数据。

In capturing and recording the time, a 24-hour clock should be used in order to facilitate subsequent calculations. For example, if the time is given in a day/week/month format as part of a certain process, it should be converted into a 24-hour format by using the relevant statistical approach. Similarly, it is essential to ensure that a standard date format is used, especially when data is collected from various systems.

在截取和记录时间时，应使用 24 小时制，以方便后续的计算。例如，如果某个流程以日/周/月的格式标示时间，则应使用相关的统计方法将其转换为 24 小时的格式。同样，必须确保使用标准日期格式，特别是当数据采集自各种不同系统时。

121. In instances when arrival, release or other times in a manual or automated system are already recorded as part of normal document processing, the sample data could be collected retrospectively. This would eliminate the need to collect data on a pre-designed form during the release process itself, and also avoid any identification of the samples to those involved in releasing them. This historical measurement has certain advantages over live transactions, in that monitoring actual movements may delay or accelerate release times because staff are aware that their activities are being recorded.

121. 当人工或自动系统中的货物运抵、放行或其他时间已被作为正常单证办理流程记录的一部分时，可以在事后收集样本数据。在这种情况下，就不需要在放行过程中使用预设的表格来收集数据，也无须让参与货物放行的各方对样本进行识别。相较于对实时操作的测算，基于历史数据的测算更具优势，因为在实时状态下，操作的工作人员知道其作业过程正在被记录，所以对货物运输实时监测可能会导致放行时间出现延迟或者提前。

122. However, it is also important to recognize that long historical measurement might has disadvantage when comparing with more recent or actual data. The reason for this is that the time taken can be much easier explained in the context of latter.

122. 然而要意识到，与较新或实际的数据相比，比较久远的历史数据测算的劣势更明显。原因是，较新或实际的数据，所测算的时间更清晰明了。

123. Administrations with automated clearance systems should use those existing systems to capture the time-stamps at each step in the clearance process. Where an administration does not have an automated clearance system but intends to develop one, it should incorporate the time-stamps for each step of the clearance process in the automated system once the latter has been developed.

123. 已经拥有自动清关系统的海关，应使用现有系统来获取清关流程中每个步骤的时间戳。目前未有但计划开发自动清关系统的海关，应在系统开发时，将清关流程中每个步骤的时间戳嵌入该自动化系统中。

3.3 Phase Ⅲ – Analysis of data and conclusions
3.3 阶段Ⅲ——数据分析和结论

A. Verification of data
A. 数据验证

124. It is important to note that any analysis using raw data can only be accurate if all the required data is captured and is of a high quality. Accurate data not only means that it is factual, but also that it is sufficient to cover relevant processes, intervention points, actions

and interventions related to the flow process, so that it can be analysed within the context of the TRS. It might be necessary and useful to look at recorded data captured from previous TRS cycles to understand and follow a common approach for a comparative analysis.

124. 值得注意的是，只有所有需要的数据都已高质量采集完毕之后，基于原始数据的分析才更精确。精确的数据不仅仅意味着其具有真实性，更应该足以涵盖与货物流通相关的过程、干预节点、活动和干预项，这样该数据才可以在 TRS 背景下进行分析。参考 TRS 历史周期中所采取的数据记录是必要且有用的，这将有助于理解和开展比较性分析。

125. Data that has been entered with errors, or using a different method than in the agreed parameters, will distort the results of the analysis. It is therefore essential to verify the quality of the data by ensuring that it is captured accurately. This can be done by verifying the sequence and structure of the data (if possible, for all the transactions, or randomly) before analysing it. It is also important to take into consideration the business process model related to the flow process of cargo.

125. 如果输入的数据有错误，或者使用的方法与设定的参数不同，将使分析结果失真。因此，必须对数据质量进行验证，以确保收集数据的准确性。在分析数据之前，可以用顺序验证和结构验证的方式对数据进行验证（条件允许的情况下，可以采用全样本或随机样本验证）。数据验证时，应考虑与货物流程相关的业务流程模式。

126. Data collected using the questionnaire may be less accurate than that collected using computer systems or other electronic devices. In this regard, the Working Group may like to ascertain the level of accuracy of manually captured data by carrying out the manual collection of data using questionnaire forms for a few intervention points, and then automating these and comparing the results. This should normally be done during the test run step.

126. 使用调查问卷收集的数据与使用计算机系统或其他电子设备收集的数据相比，准确性较低。因此，工作组可对一些干预节点采用问卷形式人工收集数据，再对其进行自动化处理和结果比较，从而验证人工采集数据的准确性。这通常应在试点研究阶段完成。

B. Analysis of data

B. 数据分析

127. When the situation requires, and it is possible to collect both manual and automated data, it is advisable to do a preliminary check of the data by separating automated procedures from manual ones. However, the time taken for each process, action and intervention – either manual or automated – should be merged in a structured manner and analysed using a holistic method.

127. 如果情况允许，可以同时用人工和自动化方式来收集数据，并且建议把自动化程序收集的数据和人工收集的数据分开，进行初步校验。但是，每个流程、活动和干预项所花费的时间（无论是人工的还是自动的），都应进行结构化合并和整体分析。

128. Past experience indicates that it is possible to explore alternatives for data analysis, such as the use of Excel or other analytical software. The use of WCO TRS software is recommended for data analysis and for producing statistical reports. "A Basic Guide to the Use of the WCO TRS Online Software" can be found in Appendix 4.

128. 以往经验表明，可尝试使用其他方式对数据进行分析，例如使用 Excel 或其他分析软件。在进行数据分析和生成统计报告时，建议优先使用 WCO 发布的 TRS 软件。《WCO TRS 在线软件基本使用指南》见附录 4。

129. The TRS software facilitates the compilation and analysis of the data captured, which is crucial for a TRS. It gives concreate results based on the data which is insert.

129. TRS 软件有助于整理和分析所收集的数据，它对于 TRS 来说至关重要。它可根据导入的数据给出具体的分析结果。

130. The initial results from data analysis should, where necessary, be followed up with stakeholders and participants in the supply chain to validate findings and identify underlying

reasons for certain behaviours. For example, factors influencing the timing of lodgement of Customs declarations by importers or their service providers should be explored.

130. 必要时，应由利益相关方和供应链参与方跟进数据分析的初步结果，以便对结果进行验证并确定某些行为的潜在原因。例如，应分析由进口商或其服务提供商造成的，影响申报单提交时间的因素。

131. Depending on the Study objectives, the average time taken for all goods may be calculated, and subsequently for a combination or multiple combinations of independent variables. For example, the aim may be to find the difference in the time taken to release goods declared manually and those declared electronically. Further calculations could be made to find the difference between the times for these two types of declaration in the context of specific processes. These calculations could be repeated for a multiple number of combinations, for example, comparing release times of AEO and non-AEO consignments.

131. 根据研究目标，可以计算出所有货物花费的平均时间，然后计算独立变量的单个组合或多个组合所需的时间。例如，想要测算人工申报和电子申报的货物放行时间差异。通过进一步计算，可以找出这两种申报类型在特定流程中的时间差异。这些计算可以对多个组合重复进行，例如，比较 AEO 和非 AEO 货物的放行时间。

132. The results obtained can then be studied to ascertain if they meet the requirements of the Customs administration and/or the expectations of stakeholders/clients, and to suggest possible improvement measures.

132. 然后，根据研究所得出的结果，确定是否符合海关的要求以及/或者利益相关方/客户的期望，并提出下一步要采取的整改措施。

C. Final Report

C. 最终报告

133. The TRS Working Group should finalize the Report of the Study within the established time frame (which is often included in the TRS Action Plan as part of the preparation for

the Study）. It is crucial that the TRS Report be factual, relevant and tothe point, particularly in terms of addressing the problems considered to be the source of delays in the cargo flow process.

133. TRS 工作组应在既定的时间框架（该框架通常作为研究准备的一部分并包含在 TRS 行动计划中）内完成研究报告。TRS 报告必须遵循实事求是、有针对性和有的放矢的原则，特别是在解决造成货物流通延误的根源问题方面。

134. Although the Working Group is free to draft a Report which it considers reflects the country's actual situation and context, a typical TRS Report should include the objectives of the Study, the methodology used, the number and names of stakeholders involved, the analysis of data, the findings, and the recommendations for improving the flow process of cargo, taking into account the scope of the Study. A model format of a TRS Report is in Appendix 5.

134. 虽然工作组可以自主起草一份反映本国实际情况和背景的报告，但标准的 TRS 报告应包括以下内容：研究目标、采用的方法、涉及的利益相关方的数量和名称、数据分析、研究结果和对货物流程的改进建议，以及研究的范围。TRS 报告模板见附录 5。

135. Furthermore, it should allow for a subsequent TRS cycle to take place once the main recommendations from the previous TRS have been implemented. This will ensure coherence and sustainability when conducting future Time Release Studies.

135. 此外，一旦前一轮 TRS 提出的主要改进措施已执行，就要开展新一轮的 TRS。这将确保未来 TRS 的一致性和可持续性。

136. As indicated earlier, a simply TRS approach is often used to measure the single busiest port/border crossing point; a "simultaneous" TRS is a Study conducted at the same time for different locations and modes of transport within a Customs territory; and a "consecutive" TRS is a Study conducted in different locations at different points in time.

136. 如前所述，简单的 TRS 方法通常用于测算单个最繁忙的港口/边境口岸；"同时" TRS 是对同一关境内不同的地点和运输方式同时进行的研究；"连续" TRS

是在不同地区、不同时间开展的研究。

137. A single TRS Report will enable policy and decision-makers to read just one Report instead of multiple Reports. It will also enable them to take a holistic view when discussing and finalizing corrective policies and operational measures included in the Report by the Working Group. It is recommended that – whether the TRS is conducted simultaneously or consecutively – one TRS Report be prepared that captures the complete Study.

137. 单一的 TRS 报告可让政策决策者只需阅读一份而不是多份报告，也便于他们在讨论和最终确定工作组在报告中所提出的整改政策和操作措施建议时，更具全局观。无论是同时还是连续开展的 TRS，都建议只编制一份涵盖完整 TRS 的报告。

138. Although the TRS Working Group will have to write its own Report, based on its specific requirements and specificities, the structure of a possible TRS Report is set out in Appendix 5 as a reference. This can be adapted to the circumstances in which the performance of a particular Study or Studies takes place.

138. TRS 工作组必须根据具体要求和具体情况编写报告，附录 5 为 TRS 报告结构模板。该模板内容可根据特定 TRS 所开展的实际情形进行调整。

139. When drafting the Final Report, the Working Group should include an Action Plan on the measures to be implemented. The Plan should be based on issues identified during the TRS and the categorization of various trade facilitation measures under the WTO TFA. Additional measures can be added, where needed. All suggested measures can then be prioritized, based on the national strategic planning and sequencing of trade facilitation measures, and/or on their consolidation/enhancement. Appendix 5 outlines a possible TRS Report structure, whilst Appendix 6 contains a model National Action Plan.

139. 工作组在起草最终报告时，应将实施措施的行动计划包含其中。该行动计划应基于 TRS 发现的问题以及 WTO《贸易便利化协定》中各种贸易便利措施的分类。如果需要，还可以添加其他措施。所有措施和建议可以根据国家战略规划、贸易便利化措施的实施顺序以及/或者措施的巩固/强化需要来确定优先顺序。附录 5 为 TRS 报告结构模板，附录 6 为国家行动计划模板。

D. Press release and/or presenting the Report in forums

D. TRS 报告的对外发布

140. In the spirit of transparency and cooperation, the results of the Study should be made available to all participating and relevant parties, thereby encouraging direct/indirect intervention to address identified bottlenecks/problems.

140. 本着透明与合作的精神，TRS 的成果应提供给所有参与方和相关方，并鼓励他们通过直接或间接干预的手段解决已发现的瓶颈问题。

141. As part of the larger outreach effort and the dissemination of information concerning ongoing efforts to improve the cargo clearance process, the TRS Report should be made available to the public and – given that all actors in the cargo clearance process normally need to improve on an ongoing basis – it should not rank trade stakeholders or countries on their performance.

141. TRS 报告应作为提升外展项目和宣传有关改进货物清关流程不懈努力的一部分，向外界发布。同时，鉴于货物清关过程中的所有参与方通常需要持续改进，该报告不应对贸易利益相关方或合作伙伴的绩效进行排名。

142. It is recommended that the Working Group draft a press release on the key outcomes of the Study Report and make it available to all the Study stakeholders for information. If possible, it should also be made available to the generalpublic, as a way of increasing transparency with regard to Customs and related procedures, as well as highlighting the challenges in the cargo clearance process. Additionally, sharing the Report in the form of a press release demonstrates, among other things, Customs' commitment and ongoing efforts regarding trade facilitation.

142. 建议工作组就研究报告中的主要成果起草一份新闻稿，并提供给参与研究的所有相关方。如有可能，还应将研究结果向社会公众公布，因为这是提升海关及其相关程序透明度的途径，也可让使公众了解货物清关过程所面临的挑战。此外，以新闻稿的形式发布报告内容，可向公众展现海关在提升贸易便利化方面的决心和为此所付出的不懈努力。

143. In some instances, the press release could be issued in the context of an exit conference, where trade stakeholders and others are invited to discuss issues related to the Study, including challenges and opportunities which have arisen in conducting a TRS. However, the press release could be a simple paper, informing of the outline and key outcomes of the Study. A model of a simple press release is in Appendix 7.

143. 在某些情况下，新闻稿也可在结项报告会上发布，邀请贸易利益相关方和其他相关方就研究提出的各项问题进行讨论，内容包括在整个研究实施过程中所遇到的机遇和挑战。新闻稿可以是对研究大纲和主要成果的简单概述。简单的新闻稿模板详见附录7。

144. It is important to note that, for those countries which enjoy the benefit of special and differential treatment under the WTO TFA, their sharing of TRS Reports with relevant international bodies, such as the WCO, can provide opportunities for further technical assistance and support in implementing the Study recommendations. This may be required to avoid duplication of effort and resources, as well as to better define priorities for optimal utilization of resources.

144. 值得注意的是，对于那些在WTO《贸易便利化协定》框架下享受特殊和差别待遇的国家来说，与WCO等相关国际机构分享其TRS报告，将更有机会在研究所提建议的实施方面获得进一步的技术援助和支持。这或许是一种避免重复工作和资源浪费，以及更好地确定国际援助资源使用优先权的必要方式。

145. Customs administrations are encouraged to communicate to the WCO the results of the TRS, as reflected in the Final TRS Report, within a reasonable time period in order to enable the WCO to analyse and better understand the work done, and to better advise the administration on key issues emanating from the Study.

145. WCO鼓励各成员方海关在合理时间内，向其通报TRS的最终报告所涵盖的研究结果，以便WCO分析和更好地了解已完成的研究工作，并更及时地通知其成员方海关在TRS中发现的关键问题。

146. If the Customs administration desires, the WCO can provide opportunities for the Report to be shared with the international Customs community in meetings and forums, such as the WCO Permanent Technical Committee, the WCO Working Group on the Trade Facilitation Agreement, and at WCO-organized global events.

146. 根据成员方海关的意愿，WCO 可以为其提供在国际海关界的会议和论坛上分享该报告的机会，例如 WCO 常设技术委员会、WCO《贸易便利化协定》工作组，以及 WCO 举办的其他全球性活动。

3.4 Phase Ⅳ – Monitoring and evaluation

3.4 阶段Ⅳ——监测和评估

A. Level one: National and regional monitoring and evaluation

A. 第一层面：国家和区域监测与评估

147. It is recommended that Customs administrations create a mechanism that will ensure continuous monitoring and evaluation of the implementation of recommendations listed in the TRS Final Report. It is advisable that the entity responsible for monitoring and evaluation be recommended by the TRS Working Group, in consultation with higher-level decision-makers in the respective Customs administration.

147. 建议海关建立相关工作机制，以持续监测和评估 TRS 最终报告中所列建议的执行情况。负责监测和评估的单位，建议由 TRS 工作组推荐，并与其海关高层决策者协商确定。

148. As a number of Customs administrations have conducted a TRS before, and are performing Studies in cooperation with other stakeholders, there is anecdotal experience that can facilitate the process of monitoring and evaluation. In a national context, the Working Group can consider, among other things, the following suggestions:

148. 一些海关开展过 TRS，并且正在与其他利益相关方合作开展研究，因此已拥有一些有利于监测和评估程序的实际经验。在国家层面上，工作组可以考虑下列建议：

Recommending that the TRS monitoring and evaluation exercise be done via a National Committee on Trade Facilitation (NCTF), which could ensure that the recommendations are implemented by Customs and all other trade stakeholders in a coordinated and efficient manner; and

建议由国家贸易便利化委员会对 TRS 进行监测和评估，以确保海关和其他贸易利益相关方能高效协同地执行改进建议；

Proposing that Customs monitor and evaluate the implementation of all the recommendations on an ongoing basis at a more operational level.

建议由海关在更具操作性的层面上，持续地对所有改进建议的实施情况进行监测和评估。

149. Although two approaches are suggested above, it is equally possible for the TRS Working Group to explore other options for monitoring and evaluation. However, considering the national priority given to implementation of the WTO TFA as part of a "whole-of-government" approach, and the multi-stakeholder nature of the National Committee on Trade Facilitation, the first of the two suggestions seems to be the best option for monitoring and evaluating the TRS results and ensuring the implementation of its recommendations. In countries where a NCTF already exists or where progress is being made towards establishing this type of Committee, Customs should play an important role on the Committee, including in the monitoring and evaluation of a TRS. Legally, the Committees are often constituted with a firm mandate to work, and coordinate national efforts, towards further trade facilitation.

149. 除了上面建议的两种方法之外，TRS 工作组也可以探索其他监测和评估的方法。考虑到作为"整体性政府"策略的一部分执行 WTO《贸易便利化协定》被视为国家重点工作，以及国家贸易便利化委员会包含多个利益相关方的特点，上述第一项建议应该是监测和评估 TRS 结果并确保建议措施落实的最佳选择。在已成立国家贸易便利化委员会或正在组建该类委员会的国家中，海关应在该类委员会中发挥重要作用，包括对 TRS 提出的改进建议的实施情况进行监测和评估。从法律上讲，该委员会通常被赋予明确的职能，来开展工作并协调各相关方，以进一步促进贸易便利化工作。

150. The Committee could conduct monitoring and evaluation through regular feedback from all the relevant government agencies and private sector stakeholders. For example, the Committee could ask each stakeholder to describe its progress in implementing its respective recommendations resulting from the TRS.

150. 国家贸易便利化委员会可通过所有政府相关机构和私营部门利益相关方的定期反馈对改进建议的实施情况进行监测和评估。例如，委员会可以要求每个利益相关方汇报其在开展 TRS 提出的建议方面所取得的进展。

151. In countries where the establishment of a NCTF is not on the government's immediate agenda, the Working Group should recommend that Customs monitor and evaluate the recommendations listed in the TRS Report, in close coordination with all the relevant stakeholders. Customs, within its sphere of competence and power, should create the most convenient mechanism to engage in discussion with those stakeholders.

151. 对于那些尚未将设立国家贸易便利化委员会列入政府当前工作议程的国家，工作组应建议由海关来密切协调所有利益相关方，对 TRS 报告中列出的建议的实施情况进行监测和评估。海关应在自身的权力和职能范围内，建立最便利的、囊括各利益相关方的研讨机制。

152. In situations where the Study goes beyond national borders, the Working Group may consider recommending that a regional economic community or a joint grouping of countries involved, which fits within the context of the Study, monitor and evaluate the implementation of recommendations. If it is proving challenging to find a suitable regional framework, the Working Group may recommend that Customs administrations carry out monitoring and evaluation at the respective national level.

152. 在跨国开展研究的情况下，工作组可以建议由一个区域经济共同体或多国联合小组，在符合研究背景的前提下，监测和评估建议的执行情况。如果难以找到合适的区域框架，工作组也可以建议由各国海关在各自的国家层面开展监测和评估。

153. If the task of monitoring and evaluation is assigned to a regional economic community, trade stakeholders related to the specific region have to provide regular updates and feedback, using the appropriate national channels. The updates can be given at the national level and presented at regional meetings on Customs or trade issues.

153. 如果由区域经济共同体来担任监测和评估的工作，那么与该特定区域有关的贸易利益相关方必须通过适当的国家渠道定期提供反馈。最新情况可反馈给各国政府，并在与海关或贸易问题有关的区域会议上进行介绍。

154. When monitoring and evaluation are carried out by the respective Customs administrations of the territories where the Study was conducted, each Customs administration must consult trade stakeholders. It must then provide the other Customs administrations with feedback on the implementation of the recommendations pertaining to it as a result of the TRS. The updates can be given at ad hoc and/or regular meetings between all the Customs administrations involved.

154. 当由开展研究所在关境的各海关负责监测和评估时，各海关必须咨询贸易利益相关方，并必须向其他海关反馈 TRS 相关建议的实施情况。可以在所有参与研究的各海关之间召开的临时和/或例行会议上反馈最新情况。

B. Level two: WCO assessment of the TRS Report and recommendations

B. 第二层面：WCO 对 TRS 报告和建议的评估

155. This level is optional. Customs administrations may like to share their TRS Report, reflecting the national or regional context, with the WCO for its assessment. This will not only assist them in identifying any gaps in the Study conducted, but will also help in allocating resources for future Time Release Studies or trade facilitation activities, as needed. At the request of the Customs administration involved, the WCO will provide a thorough assessment of the TRS carried out within the national or regional context.

155. 该层面是可选项目。有的海关可能希望与 WCO 分享反映其国家或地区情况的 TRS 报告，并供其评估。这不仅有助于他们在所开展的研究中找到现存的差距，而且有助于他们根据需要为未来的 TRS 或贸易便利化活动调配资源。应参与研究的海关的请求，WCO 将对在国家或区域范围内开展的 TRS 进行全面评估。

156. In performing the assessment, the expert (s) will, if the Customs administration involved agrees, useprevious TRS Reports and evaluate the degree of improvement of Customs and other actors.

156. 在进行评估时，如果参与研究的海关同意，专家将对比先前的 TRS 报告，以评估该海关和其他参与方的改进程度。

157. If asked to assess the methodology and accuracy of any TRS conducted, the WCO may, at the request of the Customs administrations involved, and taking previous TRS Reports into consideration, provide the administrations with a letter indicating the extent of conformity of the TRS with the TRS Guide, and confirming their accurate use of WCO TRS methodology.

157. 如果应参与研究的海关的请求，对开展 TRS 的方法和准确性进行评估，WCO 可综合考虑以前的 TRS 报告，向该海关提供一份文书，说明其 TRS 与 WCO《TRS 指南》的一致程度，并确认其是否正确使用了 WCO TRS 方法。

Next cycle of the Time Release Study
下一个 TRS 周期

158. TRS is a continuous improvement cycle that should be conducted periodically. However, once a TRS is conducted, the subsequent TRS should take place only after a reasonable period of time, when key recommendations from the previous Study have been implemented. It is recommended that the knowledge and expertise gained from the previous TRS be captured and applied to enhance future Studies.

158. TRS 是一个需要定期进行的持续改进的循环。当一轮 TRS 完成后，其提出的主要改进建议已执行时，再进行下一轮研究。建议将以往 TRS 中获得的知识和经验收集起来，用以提升今后的研究。

附录

APPENDICES

APPENDICES[①]

APPENDIX 1 – CHALLENGES AND WAY FORWARD

APPENDIX 2 – THE TRS WITHIN A COUNTRY ENVIRONMENT

APPENDIX 3 – THE TRS WITHIN AN INTERNATIONAL/REGIONAL ENVIRONMENT

APPENDIX 4 – A BASIC GUIDE TO THE USE OF THE WCO TRS ONLINE SOFTWARE

APPENDIX 5 – MODEL FORMAT OF A FINAL REPORT

APPENDIX 6 – MODEL NATIONAL ACTION PLAN FOR IMPLEMENTATION OF THE TRS RECOMMENDATIONS

APPENDIX 7 – MODEL PRESS RELEASE

APPENDIX 8 – MEMBERS' EXPERIENCE

附录[①]

附录 1　挑战与应对方法

附录 2　国内环境下的 TRS

附录 3　国际/区域环境下的 TRS

附录 4　WCO TRS 在线软件使用指南

附录 5　最终报告的格式模板

附录 6　实施 TRS 中建议措施的国家行动计划模板

附录 7　新闻发布模板

附录 8　各成员方的经验

---

① Please note these are guidelines only and do not always need to be followed precisely. You may choose to use some and not others, and if you feel it is appropriate, the guidelines can be adapted to suit your particular border environment. If you need further assistance or clarification about how to apply the appendices, please contact the WCO Secretariat (see contact details on the last page).

① 请注意，这些附录内容仅是《指南》的参考内容，无须全部采用。可选择性使用《指南》的某部分内容。适当时，可以对《指南》进行调整，以适合特定的边境环境。对于如何使用附录，如果需要进一步的帮助或说明，请与世界海关组织秘书处联系（联系方式在最后一页）。

APPENDIX 1 – CHALLENGES AND WAY FORWARD

附录 1　挑战与应对方法

1. When conducting a TRS, either with or without the involvement of other international trade stakeholders, Customs are likely to be exposed to a number of challenges, problems and/or complications. These often arise because the TRS generally entails some level of complexity, regardless of whether the Study is carried out nationally, regionally or multilaterally.

1. 在开展 TRS 时，无论国际贸易流程中其他利益相关方是否参与，海关部门都可能面临许多挑战、问题和/或复杂情况。不论是在国内、区域还是多边开展 TRS，都具有一定的复杂性。

2. Although the number of challenges or difficulties encountered while conducting a TRS can vary widely, when challenges do arise they are likely to come from different sources, some of which are more common than others. Due to possible complications while conducting a TRS, it is recommended that Customs administrations familiarize themselves in advance with some of the potential challenges, problems and/or complications, and also with the various possible ways of addressing them.

2. 因为各国的实际情况不同，开展 TRS 时遇到的挑战或困难也会各有不同，而且挑战和困难可能来自不同方面，但是，一些挑战和困难是相似的。开展 TRS 时随时会出现复杂情况，因此建议海关部门提前熟悉那些潜在的挑战、问题和/或复杂情况，以及应对它们的方法。

3. A list of such potential challenges, problems and/or complications is below, with possible ways of either mitigating or resolving them. It draws on the past experience of some WCO Member Customs administrations in carrying out a TRS, and on possible problems that have been foreseen. The list is not at all exhaustive, but provides a basic options for Customs administrations to consider in advance when preparing for a TRS.

3. 下文将列举一些潜在的挑战、问题和/或复杂情况，以及应对它们的常用方法。这些方法源自一些 WCO 成员方以往在执行 TRS 方面的经验和已预见的问题。该清单并不详尽，但可为海关部门在准备 TRS 时提供基本参考。

A. Customs officials who are Members of the TRS Working Group are unable to devote time to the TRS project

A. TRS 工作组中的海关人员无法全职参与

4. In the experience of many countries, when the TRS project is fully implemented by a Customs administration, without support from consultants and private companies (which is the ideal scenario), it is imperative that Customs officials who are Members of the Working Group be given adequate time to focus on the project, even if they have other responsibilities or activities. However, there are cases where adequate time is not given for Customs officials to implement TRS projects. Inadequate time to prepare and implement the TRS frequently occurs due to issues such as employees being allocated several tasks at the same time, and to a lack of motivation and cooperation within Customs.

4. 根据多国的经验，在没有顾问和私营公司支持的情况下实施 TRS，海关部门必须给作为工作组成员的海关关员足够的时间来参与该项目，即使他们还有其他职责或任务。但是，在有些情况下，海关关员没有足够的时间来开展 TRS 项目。由于存在诸如工作人员被同时分配多项任务以及单位内部缺乏动力和协作意识等问题，致使经常出现准备和开展 TRS 的时间不足的情况。

5. To resolve the above problems, strong Customs leadership is very important, and should preferably go beyond simply addressing the issue of inadequate time resources. It is recommended that, at the very outset of the project, Customs administrations designate officers with the right skills and competences to be part of the TRS Working Group. The Head of the Customs administration should monitor the project on a regular basis, and he or she should nominate someone with the right profile to manage the team.

5. 要解决上述问题，拥有海关领导的强有力支持是非常重要的，而且最好不仅仅是解决时间和资源不足的问题。建议在项目开始之初，海关部门就指定具有适当技能和领导能力的官员加入 TRS 工作组。海关部门负责人应提名一名身份适当的官员来管理该团队，并定期监督该项目。

6. In situations where the designated officers are unable to dedicate enough time to the project, they should either be released fromsome of their existing duties, or be released entirely from their other work to focus on the TRS project. The leader or the coordinator of the project should be able to contact the Head of Customs easily and directly, and if possible, he or she should be the person reporting to the Head of Customs.

6. 如果指定官员无法为该项目投入足够的时间，应将他们从其现有职责中脱离出来，或者将其完全从其他工作中脱离出来，以专注于 TRS 项目。项目负责人或协调员应该能够方便、直接地与海关负责人联系，并且在可能的情况下，直接向海关负责人汇报相关工作。

7. During a TRS cycle, it would be preferable for reorganization of Customs staff not to affect staff members who are assigned to the TRS Working Group. If one or two Members of the Customs Working Group are reallocated elsewhere, there should be a mechanism to replace them as quickly as possible.

7. 在一个 TRS 周期中，海关的人员调整最好不要影响分配到 TRS 工作组的工作人员。如果工作组中的一两个海关成员被重新分配到其他岗位上，则应该有一种机制来保障有人尽快接替他们的工作。

B. Inadequate cooperation with the relevant stakeholders

B. 有关利益相关方不充分合作

8. Establishing a Working Group with the mandate to carry out a TRS is a determining factor in the success of any TRS cycle. As outlined in the TRS methodology, it is one of the first steps in preparing for any TRS when the Working Group from one cycle cannot be maintained for the next.

8. 组建一个负责开展 TRS 的工作组，这是 TRS 成功开展的决定性因素。正如 TRS 方法所述，当一个 TRS 周期结束时，实施 TRS 准备工作的第一步就是组建 TRS

工作组。

9. A complete TRS cycle is a comprehensive process which entails several activities, and the need to create a Working Group led by the Customs administration should be considered to be one of the top priorities in conducting a Study. However, creation of a Working Group is only effective if it comprises the relevant players with a key role in the cargo, information or finance flow process. For example, it might not be sensible to conduct a national TRS focusing on maritime transport without involving the national port authority if it holds relevant data.

9. 一个完整的TRS周期是一个牵涉许多活动的综合过程，建立由海关部门领导的工作组是实施该研究的首要任务。然而，只有在货物、信息、资金流动等方面能够发挥关键作用的相关方都参与的情况下，建立的工作组才有效。例如，以海运为主的国家开展TRS时，如果不邀请拥有相关数据的港务局参与，将是不明智的做法。

10. Bearing this in mind, it is recommended that Customs administrations liaise with the most relevant players with akey role in the cargo flow process. Discussions with key trade stakeholders, including the private sector, should be held at a very early stage to ensure that they feel involved, and have a role to play in the process. Involving stakeholders at the earliest possible stage will also give them "ownership" of the TRS project.

10. 因此，海关部门应与在货运流程中发挥关键作用的相关方保持联系。在早期阶段，应与主要贸易相关方包括私营机构进行讨论，引导他们积极参与TRS并发挥各自应有的作用。尽早让利益相关方参与进来，也将提升他们主动开展TRS项目的意识。

11. On the other hand, in some cases, Customs might face problems due to a lack of cooperation from stakeholders. In some of the TRS Reports received by the WCO, the Organization noted that Customs faced difficulties in securing cooperation from other trade stakeholders, including other government agencies (OGA). One of the things reported in such cases is that lack of cooperation slows down the process of conducting a

TRS. Inadequate cooperation may arise from different quarters, but on many occasions involves either the private sector or other government agencies – sometimes even both. Nevertheless, if it involves the private sector, this is much easier to address.

11. 当然，在某些情况下，海关可能会面临利益相关方缺乏合作的问题。WCO 在收到的一些 TRS 报告中出现，一些海关在获得其他贸易利益相关方（包括其他政府机构）的合作方面面临困难。在这种情况下，缺乏合作会延缓实施 TRS 的进程。不充分的合作可能来自不同方面，但多数是来自私营机构或其他政府机构，或者两者兼而有之。如果问题业自私营机构，则该问题较易解决。

12. If the issues arise from the private sector side, it is important to emphasize the benefits that the sector is likely to gain when Time Release Studies are conducted periodically. Such benefits range, for example, from reducing trade bottlenecks (thus leading ultimately to trade facilitation), to reducing trade transaction costs. In the worst-case scenario, Customs administrations may wish to consider ways of enforcing private sector cooperation under their respective national legislation.

12. 如果问题来自私营机构，则向该机构强调定期实施 TRS 给其带来的好处是非常重要的。例如，这些好处包括减少贸易瓶颈（最终实现贸易便利化），减少贸易交易成本等。在最坏的情况下，海关部门可以考虑通过国家立法来加强与私营机构的合作。

13. If the lack of cooperation emanates from another government agency, it is recommended that Customs strengthen their relationship with the non-cooperating institution, or obtain support from a government body with the power to instruct all other trade stakeholders to cooperate. Political will is the crucial way of ensuring positive cooperation on the part of OGA. Indeed, political will is sometimes needed at the highest government level, i. e. from the President's or Prime Minister's Office, given the insufficient authority of Customs as a border agency.

13. 如果缺乏合作是由另一个政府机构引起的，建议海关加强与该机构的关系，或向有权指示其他所有贸易利益相关方进行合作的政府部门寻求支持。政治意愿是确保其他政府机构积极合作的关键途径。实际上，海关作为边境机构的权力不足，有时需要最高政府层面的政治意愿。

C. Lack of data to carry out TRS at the national and regional level

C. 在开展 TRS 时缺乏国家和地区层面的数据

14. Data is a significant asset for government and business alike, and it can be defined and used for multiple purposes, including when countries conduct a TRS. Data is vital to the TRS – indeed, one cannot be carried out nationally, regionally, or multilaterally without it. As indicated previously, TRS data can be collected manually or electronically: in the former case, with the aid of paper survey forms which circulate along the clearance points or circuits, in the latter, through different electronic systems.

14. 数据对于政府和企业而言都是重要资产，可被定义并用于多种用途，包括用于国家开展 TRS。数据对于 TRS 至关重要，如果没有数据，就无法在国家、地区或多边层面开展 TRS。如前所述，TRS 数据可以通过人工或自动方式收集：若使用人工收集方式，需要借助纸质调查表在清关地点或货物流通沿线进行；若使用自动收集方式，则需要通过不同的电子系统来获取。

15. TRS implementation involves, amongst other things, the capture of data or time records inrespect of the intervention of one or more trade stakeholders. Such data therefore needs to be collected manually or electronically from different sources to calculate the average time between the arrival of cargo and its physical release. However, there have been situations in which the application of TRS methodology has gone beyond simply capturing data on the Customs administration's intervention, and trade stakeholders have been unwilling to share their own data with the TRS Working Group.

15. 开展 TRS 的重要工作之一是获取一个或多个贸易利益相关方干预的数据或时间记录。因此，这些数据需要从不同来源以人工或自动方式收集，以计算货物从运抵到实货放行所需的平均时间。然而，在某些情况下，TRS 方法的应用已经超出了简单地获取海关部门所干预的数据，并且贸易利益相关方不愿与 TRS 工作组分享自己的数据。

16. One reason for the reluctance of trade stakeholders to share information, especially with local government institutions or on an intergovernmental basis, is data protection (although other reasons are also likely). One of the quickest ways to address this issue is to provide a clear explanation of the purpose of the Study, the type of data, and how the Study can potentially provide value-added to all trade stakeholders, including those who are unwilling to share their data. When this solution is not enough to resolve the problem, other options can be explored, particularly the possibility of looking at existing national legislation or proposing national or intergovernmental Memoranda of Understanding between the parties involved, with clear guidelines on the implications of using the data for a purpose other than that agreed.

16. 贸易利益相关方，尤其是地方政府机构或政府之间不愿分享信息的原因之一是数据保护（尽管也可能有其他原因）。解决此问题最快的方法之一是明确解释该研究的目的、数据类型以及该研究可为所有贸易利益相关方（包括不愿分享自己数据的利益相关方）提供的潜在的价值。如果此方法不足以解决问题，还可探索其他方法，特别是研究现有国家立法或在有关缔约方之间提出国家或政府间谅解备忘录的可能性，应明确规定不得将相关数据用于商定的用途之外。

17. As the issue of data protection may take time to resolve, the Working Group should openly discuss it at the earliest stage of preparing for the TRS, and explore quick ways of dealing with the problem so that possible solutions can subsequently be found much more promptly.

17. 由于数据保护问题可能需要时间来解决，工作组应在准备 TRS 的早期阶段公开讨论这一问题，并探索快速处理这一问题的方法，以便能够更迅速地找到可能的解决办法。

18. It is also possible that TRS data is available, but is not collected appropriately or is not reliable. In this case, the Working Group should first analyse the data, then assess it. If the data has been collected manually, one of the first options could be to assess whether it would be prudent to repeat the data collection process. When electronic data is still available, it might perhaps be more realistic to obtain the data in electronic format. The

digital revolution is generating exponential opportunities for electronic data access, capture, aggregation and analysis, and so the expectation of more effective Time Release Studies can now be met.

18. 可能存在 TRS 数据可用但未正确收集或数据不可靠的问题。在这种情况下，工作组应首先对数据进行分析和评估。如果这些数据是通过人工收集的，那么可以评估重复数据收集过程的可行性。当相关电子数据也可用时，以自动方式重新获取相关数据更现实。数字革命为访问、获取、聚合和分析电子数据提供了快速、便捷的机会，因此，现在有望实现更有效的 TRS。

D. Agreeing on the TRS Report

D. 寻求 TRS 报告共同意见

19. After carrying out the different activities, including collecting, gathering and analysing TRS-related data and drafting the TRS Report, it can sometimes be a challenge to actually agree on the content of the Report. A TRS Report should clearly reflect the work which was carried out, and contain relevant information on, interalia, the reason for conducting the TRS, the activities performed by the Working Group in order to conclude the TRS cycle, statistical analyses and results, findings and recommendations.

19. 在完成了包括收集、汇总和分析与 TRS 有关的数据以及起草 TRS 报告在内的各种活动之后，可能面临的一项挑战是就报告的内容达成一致。TRS 报告应清晰地反映所开展的工作，并包含以下相关信息：开展 TRS 的原因、工作组为得出 TRS 周期、统计分析和结果、研究发现和建议而开展的活动。

20. The Report should be factual and identify all of the potential bottlenecks hindering trade. As the Report should contain factual information, and will often reveal unacceptable practices, the parties involved will not always agree on its content and structure. This is particularly the case when the problems which have been exposed during the Study clearly indicate that a particular non-private sector party bears some degree of blame for a specific or overall delay.

20. 报告应实事求是，并确定影响贸易货物流动的所有潜在瓶颈。由于报告包含的都是真实信息，并且通常会揭示一些相关方不能接受的做法或事实，因此，有关各方有时无法就报告的内容和结构达成一致。特别是当研究过程中发现的问题明确表明某些非私营机构当事方对某一具体或总体延误负有一定程度的责任时，更是难以就报告达成一致。

21. In the event that the final TRS Report cannot be agreed among all trade stakeholders, the worst-case scenario is that, ultimately, a decision is made not to agree on the Report, thereby invalidating all the work done. This situation cannot normally be resolved, and all the stakeholders will then agree not to release the Report.

21. 如果所有贸易利益相关方无法在最终的 TRS 报告上达成一致意见，最坏的情况是该报告最终不被通过，从而使所有已完成的工作变得无效。这种问题通常无法解决，该最终报告也将无法发布。

However, a less problematic situation might be that trade stakeholders disagree on the Report, but do not demonstrate an intention to abandon it. In such cases, or when there is misunderstanding, it is important that stakeholders with concerns present a valid, evidence-based argument to justify their view. Similarly, the TRS Working Group members who hold different positions should also be able to justify the facts in the Report or to present some other kind of evidence. In both situations, refusal to accept release of the TRS Report, or disagreement on the Report, should be handled with a great degree of sensitivity, and it is important to avoid conflicts.

然而，较易解决的问题是，各贸易利益相关方对报告内容存在分歧，但并不表示有意放弃该报告。在这种情况下或对报告存在误解时，有顾虑的利益相关方要提出一个有效的、基于证据的论据来证明他们的观点是正确的，这是非常重要的。同样，持不同立场的 TRS 工作组成员也应该能够证明报告中的事实或提出其他证据来证实。在这两种情况下，应以高度敏感的态度去处理拒绝接受 TRS 报告的发布或对报告有异议的情况，避免冲突是很重要的。

APPENDIX 2 – THE TRS WITHIN A COUNTRY ENVIRONMENT
附录2　国内环境下的TRS

A. General functions and responsibilities of the Working Group
A. 工作组的一般职能和职责

1. The Working Group should be given the authority by the Customs administration or NCTF to take all the decisions deemed necessary for implementation of the Study.

1. 海关部门或国家贸易便利化委员会应授权工作组进行所有关于实施该研究的必要决定。

2. A Customs official at senior management level should head and chair the Working Group, and should have an understanding of the national trade environment. The chair should provide regular updates to the Customs authority and/or NCTF regarding work on the TRS, to ensure that management are aware of how work is progressing and of possible challenges.

2. 海关部门高级官员应领导和主持工作组的工作，并应了解国家贸易环境。工作组组长应定期向海关部门和/或国家贸易便利化委员会汇报TRS工作的最新情况，以确保管理层了解相关工作的进展情况和可能面临的挑战。

3. The Working Group should consist of an optimal number of members to ensure the efficiency of the Study. The experience of Members to have conducted a TRS indicates that past Working Groups have consisted of around 12 members. An information session may be necessary to brief all the interested parties about the Study.

3. 工作组成员数量应达到最佳状态，以确保该研究的效率。WCO成员开展TRS的经验表明，工作组大约由12名成员组成。工作组有必要向各相关方发布关于该研究基本情况的信息。

4. Certain members of the Customs administration may be considered key to the Working

Group. The latter should include one or two specialists in each of the following fields:

4. 海关部门的某些成员是工作组的关键成员。工作组应在以下每个领域安排1~2名专家:

- Customs procedures;
- Organizational matters and administrative structures;
- Statistics; and
- Computers (a computer specialist may be useful even if manual procedures form the basis of the Study, since analysis of the results could be carried out by computer).

- 海关监管程序领域;
- 组织人事和管理机构设置领域;
- 数据统计领域;
- 计算机(即使研究基于人工程序,但结果分析是通过计算机进行的,所以计算机专家对此项工作也是有帮助的)领域。

5. In order to maintain the Working Group's efficiency, its members may have more than one role. For example, a statistician/computer specialist may be the same person, as may the chair/Customs procedure specialist.

5. 为了保证工作组的效率,其成员可能需要扮演多个角色。例如,统计学专家/计算机专家可能与工作组组长/海关监管程序专家是同一个人。

6. If the Study is concentrated solely in one or in a very small number of Customs offices, the heads of these offices should participate in the Working Group. The heads of other Customs offices which are not participating in the Study could also be invited to participate in the analysis of the results. However, if the Study is conducted in the area of jurisdiction of a particular Customs office, then it is imperative that the head of that office attend the analysis of the results, or appoint someone else to do so. This will aid impartiality, as well as help in the Study's actual execution.

6. 如果该研究仅涉及一个或很少的海关办事处,则这些海关办事处的负责人应加入工作组。也可邀请未参与研究的其他海关办事处负责人参与结果分析。但是,如果研究是在特定海关办事处的管辖范围内进行，则必须由该部门的负责人参与结果分析，或指定其他人参与。这将增加研究的公正性，并有助于研究的实际实施。

7. The Working Group should familiarize itself with its Terms of Reference, in particular the objectives and outcome ofthe Study, so as to ensure that there is no deviation from the specific output expected of the Group.

7. 工作组应熟悉自己的职权范围，特别是研究目标和研究结果，以确保不偏离工作组预期的输出结果。

8. The Working Group should also prepare detailed instructions and guidelines which cover the creation, review and validation of the TRS Work Plan, and which comprise the following:

8. 工作组还应编制详细的开展 TRS 的说明和指南，包括 TRS 计划的制订、审查和确认。其主要内容如下：

- Aim of the Study;
- Scope and methodology;
- Duration and timing of the Study, including a timetable for the preparation and execution of the Study and the presentation of the Final Report to the Customs administration;
- Sampling size and sampling selection methods (where a sampling method is used);
- TRS questionnaire form for the data to be collected manually;
- Instructions and guidelines for the collection of data manually or electronically;
- Method for calculation of thc results;
- Allocation of responsibilities for collection of data by individual parties and within each unit;
- List of definitions to ensure uniformity and consistency in implementation;
- Procedures to be followed for manual and automated procedures or for a combination of both;
- Person (s) to be contacted where clarification is needed; and

- Software to be used for data analysis.

- 研究目的；
- 研究范围和方法；
- 研究的持续周期和时间安排，包括研究的准备和开展以及向海关高层提交最终报告的时间表；
- 抽样规模和抽样选择方法（如需进行抽样）；
- TRS 调查问卷表（用于人工收集数据）；
- 人工或自动方式收集数据的说明和准则；
- 计算结果的方法；
- 各有关方和各单位内部收集数据的责任分配；
- 用于确保执行过程的统一性和一致性的定义清单；
- 人工、自动或两者兼有的操作方式应遵循的程序；
- 需要进行问题澄清时的联系人；
- 用于数据分析的软件。

9. The instructions and guidelines should be provided to the following persons or groups:

9. 应向下列个人或组织提供开展 TRS 的说明和指南：

- Customs officials and other stakeholders in the office where the Study is to be conducted;
- Customs staff and other stakeholders who will be directly involved in recording and collecting the data for the Study;
- Customs staff and other stakeholders who are not involved in the Study but who are involved in the operations where the Study is to take place, to ensure the smooth implementation of the Study; and
- Any others necessary.

- 开展研究所在地的海关官员和其他利益相关方；
- 直接参与记录和收集研究数据的海关关员和其他利益相关方的工作人员；
- 未参与研究但参与了研究所在地的操作的海关关员和其他利益相关方的工作人员，以确保研究顺利实施；
- 其他必要人员。

10. To enable the Study to proceed smoothly, the Working Group should identify the following:

10. 为确保研究顺利进行，工作组应确定以下事项：

- Only relevant processes and events in the clearance chain;
- All the documents required for the clearance process;
- The data to be collected and its source, as well as by whom and how;
- How the evaluation of the data is to be done;
- The release times to be captured and evaluated in terms of the type of traffic and goods;
- Whether the data to be captured identifies the reasons for any delays; and
- Whether the evaluation will be based on capturing the total time and/or capturing each intervening process.

- 仅与清关过程相关的流程和事项；
- 清关过程中所需的所有单证；
- 要收集的数据及其来源，以及相关数据的收集人和收集方法；
- 如何评估数据；
- 对哪些运输方式和货物类型的放行时间进行采集和评估；
- 如果有延迟，能否通过所收集的数据来确定延迟的原因；
- 评估是基于对整体时间的收集还是对每个干预过程数据的收集。

11. The Working Group should be particularly sensitive to the anxieties and fears that employees might have concerning this Study. It is suggested that the Group prepare an information paper detailing the importance and advantages of the Study to the organization, with a special focus on those elements that will help to dispel any misgivings which staff might have as to the Study's outcome or as to their interests. This paper may include information on the expected improvements in processes and procedures, and the benefits that staff would gain, as a result of the Study.

11. 工作组应特别注意，相关工作人员可能对该研究产生疑虑和担忧。建议工作组编写一份资料文件，详细介绍该研究对组织的重要性和益处，着重介绍那些有助于消除工作人员对研究成果或其利益可能产生疑虑的因素。这份资料可以包括流程和程序的预期改进，以及研究结果可能会给工作人员带来的好处等内容。

12. The Working Group should meet as often as necessary to discuss the following tasks:

12. 工作组应根据需要召开会议并讨论以下工作：

- Ensure that all the decisions pertaining to the Study are taken in a timely manner;
- Review progress and determine the steps to be followed;
- Use the WCO TRS online software for the input and calculation of data;
- Analyse the results;
- Compare the results with data from previous Studies or pre-set standards, if any;
- Prepare the draft TRS Report, including proposals for improvements; and
- Present the results of the Study to the Customs administration and other agencies involved in the clearance process, and consider releasing the final TRS Report to the general public.

- 确保及时做出与研究有关的全部决定；
- 回顾工作进展情况并确定应遵循的步骤；
- 使用 WCO TRS 在线软件输入和计算数据；
- 分析结果；
- 如与预期结果有偏差，将结果与之前的研究或预设标准进行比较；
- 编写 TRS 报告草案，提出改进建议；
- 向海关部门和其他参与清关过程的机构介绍研究结果，并考虑向公众发布最终 TRS 报告。

B. Establishing the Working Group

B. 组建工作组

13. When developing a TRS coordination mechanism, it is recommended that the national Customs administration act as the agency with overall responsibility for coordinating the TRS process. Customs should ideally have policy or administrative responsibilities that are relevant to the trade process, as well as the capacity to support and drive TRS

implementation.

13. 在建立 TRS 协调机制时，建议各国将海关部门作为全面负责协调 TRS 流程的机构。理想情况下，海关应具有与贸易流程相关的政策或行政责任，并具有支持和推动 TRS 开展的能力。

14. Having decided on the appropriate stakeholders to include, the next step is to establish the TRS Working Group for effective implementation of the TRS, obtaining expertise and timely input from all relevant stakeholders. Once the TRS Working Group is created, it may first approach existing frameworks and obtain information on the objectives, methodology, expected outcomes and utilization of the outcomes which the Customs administration will be in a position to give.

14. 在确定了适当的利益相关方后，下一步是组建 TRS 工作组，以便从所有利益相关方获取专业知识和及时支持，从而有效开展 TRS。TRS 工作组可以采用现有的框架，并从海关部门获得目标、方法、预期成果和成果利用等方面的信息。

15. Next, the Working Group should convene a meeting of the nominated agency representatives. At the meeting, it should outline the roles and responsibilities of the contact points, communication protocols, logistic arrangements, the schedule for subsequent meetings of the Working Group, and any other administrative matters impacting on the implementation of the TRS.

15. 接下来，工作组应召开一次提名机构的代表大会。会上，应概述联络点的作用和职责、通信方式、后勤安排、工作组后续会议的时间安排以及影响 TRS 开展的其他行政事项。

16. The general functions and responsibilities outlined earlier in this Appendix should be adhered to. They can be applied in all circumstances but might progressively become routine as countries conduct Time Release Studies periodically and in a consistent manner. However, it is recommended that staff who have been involved in previous Studies take part in the subsequent TRS as well, to ensure consistency and coherence.

16. 工作组应遵循本附录前面概述的一般职责。“工作组的一般职责”具有广泛的适用性，随着 WCO 各成员以定期、一致的方式开展 TRS，它们会逐渐成为惯例。建议曾经参与过 TRS 的工作人员继续参与随后的研究，以确保该研究的一致性和连贯性。

C. Business processes with respective questionnaire forms

C. 各类业务流程及其对应的调查问卷表

Model of Sea Business Process and its Questionnaire

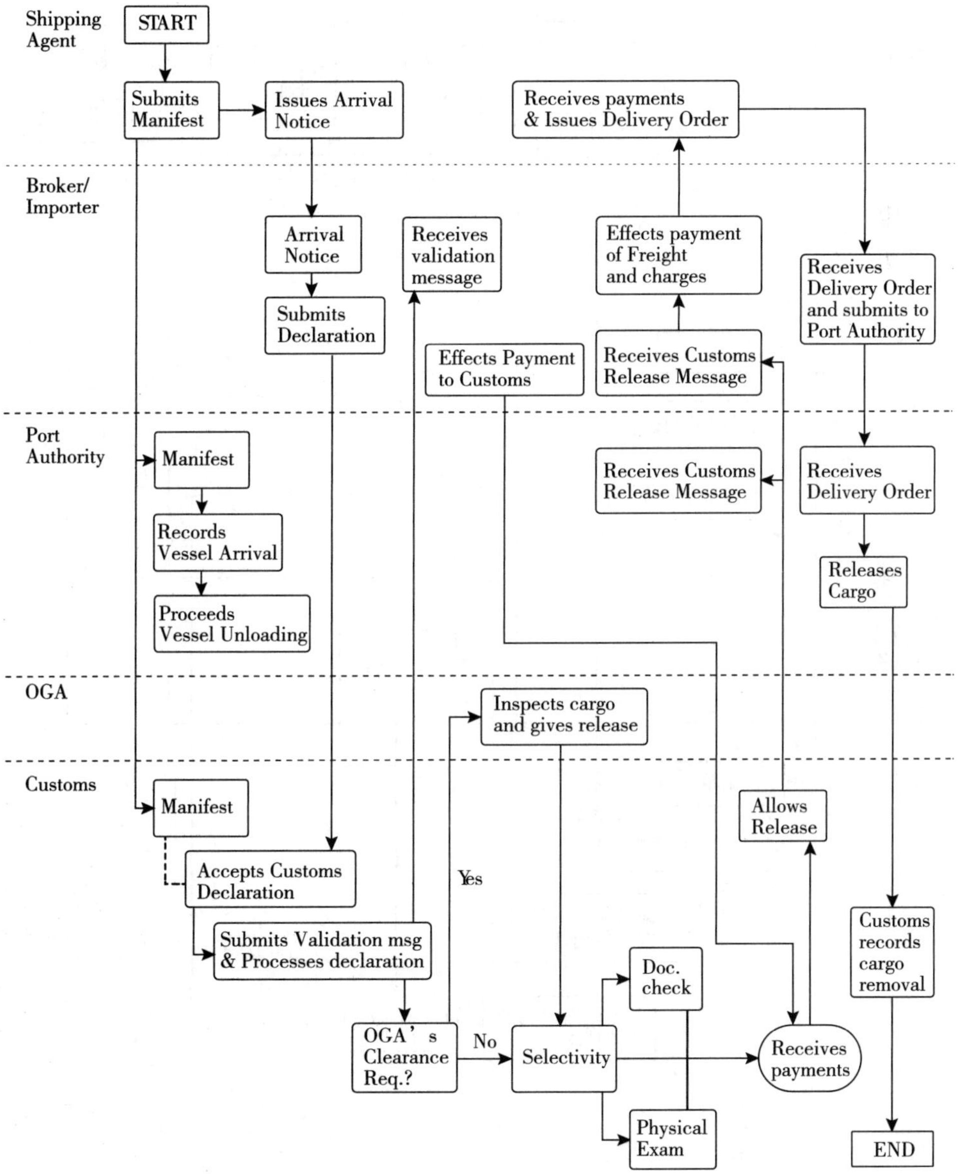

海运业务流程及其问卷调查表模板

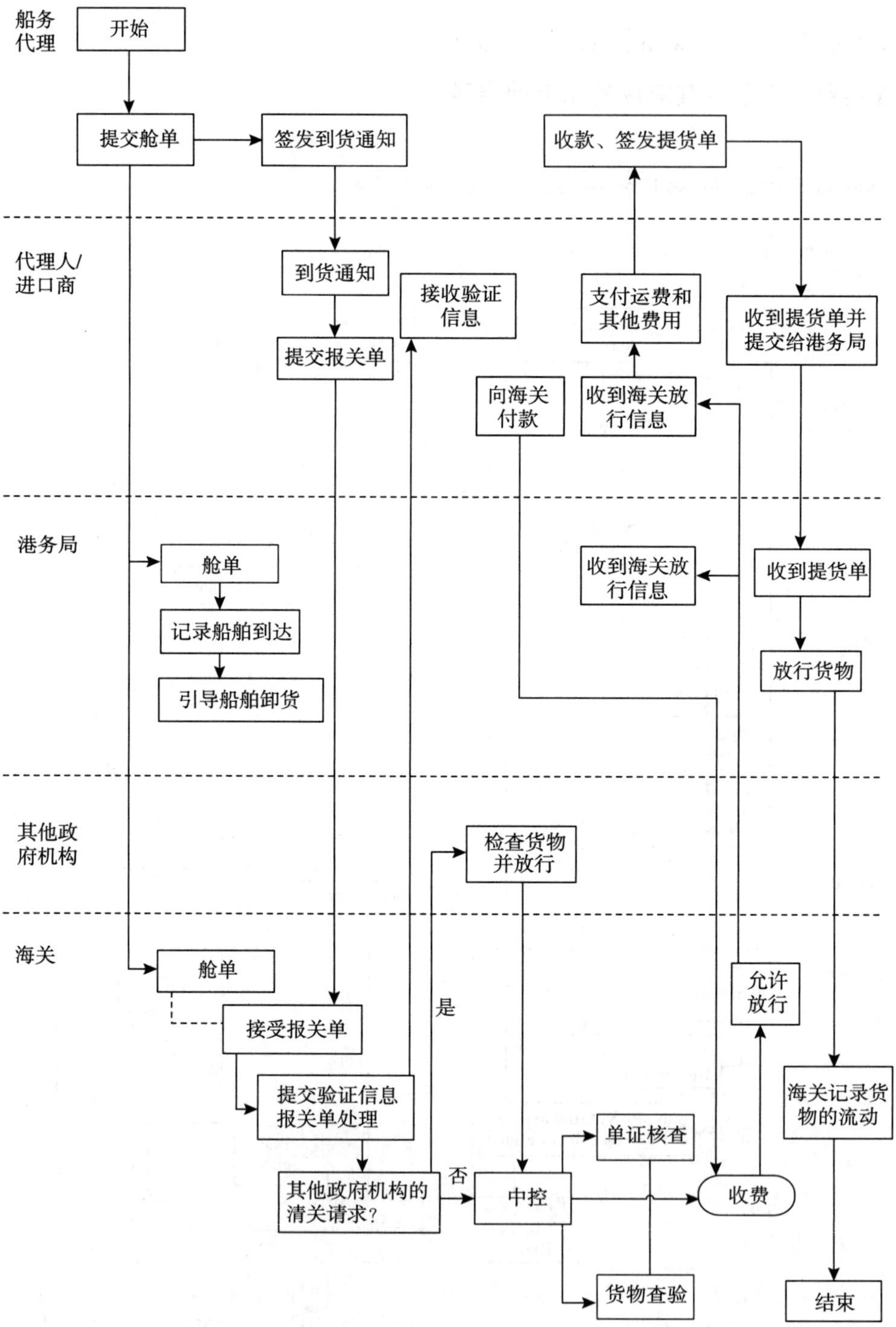

Time Release Study – Sample Questionnaire for Sea Cargo FCL

Identification*	
1. Office*	Office A ☐ Office B ☐ Office C ☐
2. Shipping Agent*	-
3. B/L Number*	-
4. Broker ID*	-
5. Goods Declaration ID*	-
Goods arrival and declaration submission*	
6. Manifest Submission*	☐ day ☐ mth - ☐ hr ☐ min
7. Vessel Arrival*	☐ day ☐ mth - ☐ hr ☐ min
8. Start of Unloading*	☐ day ☐ mth - ☐ hr ☐ min
9. End of Unloading*	☐ day ☐ mth - ☐ hr ☐ min
10. Declaration Submission*	☐ day ☐ mth - ☐ hr ☐ min
OGA Inspection	
11. Agency	Health ☐ Agriculture ☐ Veterinary ☐ Standard Bureau
12. Start of OGA Inspection	☐ day ☐ mth - ☐ hr ☐ min
13. End of OGA Inspection	☐ day ☐ mth - ☐ hr ☐ min
Processing by Customs*	
14. Declaration Channel*	Green ☐ Yellow ☐ Red ☐
15. Start of Documentary Check	☐ day ☐ mth - ☐ hr ☐ min
16. End of Documentary Check	☐ day ☐ mth - ☐ hr ☐ min
17. Start of Physical Inspection	☐ day ☐ mth - ☐ hr ☐ min
18. End of Physical Inspection	☐ day ☐ mth - ☐ hr ☐ min

19. Receive Payment for Duty and Taxes	□ day □ mth - □ hr □ min
20. Customs Release *	□ day □ mth - □ hr □ min
Processing after Customs release *	
21. Payment of Freight and Charges *	□ day □ mth - □ hr □ min
22. Issue of Delivery Order *	□ day □ mth - □ hr □ min
23. Submission of Delivery Order to Port Authority *	□ day □ mth - □ hr □ min
24. Cargo Release by Port Authority *	□ day □ mth - □ hr □ min
25. Physical Release *	□ day □ mth - □ hr □ min

* = Mandatory – if indicated for a section, mandatory questions for the section must be completed; if indicated for a question, the question must be completed if the section is used.

TRS——整柜海运货物调查问卷示例

标识 *	
1. 海关 *	海关 A □　海关 B □　海关 C □
2. 船舶代理 ID *	–
3. 提单编号 *	–
4. 代理人 ID *	–
5. 报关单编号 *	–
到货及报关 *	
6. 提交舱单 *	□月□日 – □时□分
7. 轮船到达 *	□月□日 – □时□分
8. 开始卸货 *	□月□日 – □时□分
9. 结束卸货 *	□月□日 – □时□分
10. 提交报关单 *	□月□日 – □时□分

（续表）

其他政府机构查验	
11. 机构	卫生□ 农业□ 兽医□ 标准机构□
12. 开始查验	□月□日 - □时□分
13. 结束查验	□月□日 - □时□分
海关流程*	
14. 报关通道*	绿色□ 黄色□ 红色□
15. 开始单证审核	□月□日 - □时□分
16. 结束单证审核	□月□日 - □时□分
17. 开始实货查验	□月□日 - □时□分
18. 结束实货查验	□月□日 - □时□分
19. 收到相关税/费	□月□日 - □时□分
20. 海关放行*	□月□日 - □时□分
海关放行后的其他环节*	
21. 支付相关税/费*	□月□日 - □时□分
22. 签发提货单*	□月□日 - □时□分
23. 向港务局提交提货单*	□月□日 - □时□分
24. 港务局放行货物*	□月□日 - □时□分
25. 实货放行*	□月□日 - □时□分

注：带 * 处为必填项。

Model of Air Business Process and its Questionnaire

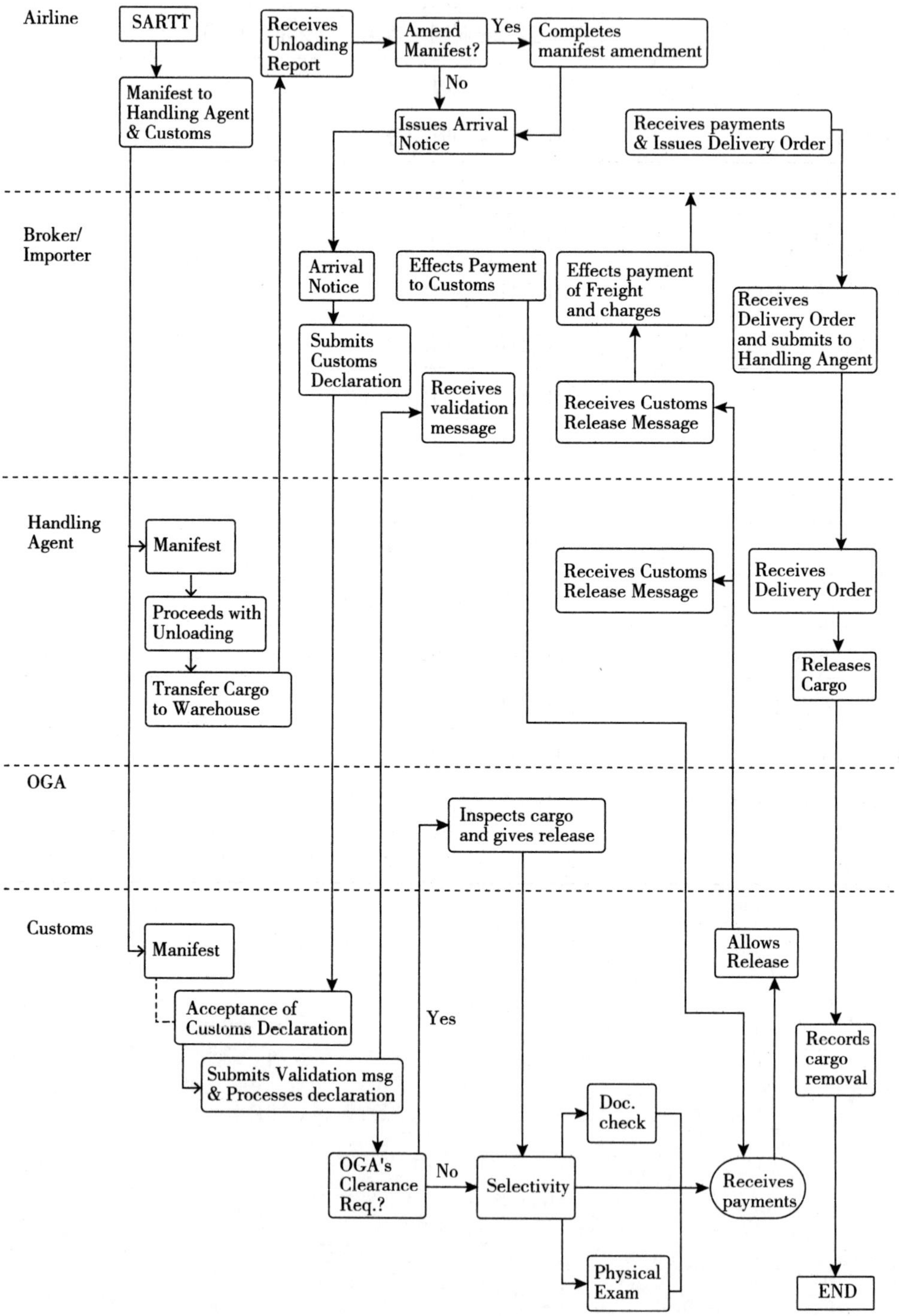

空运业务流程及其问卷调查表模板

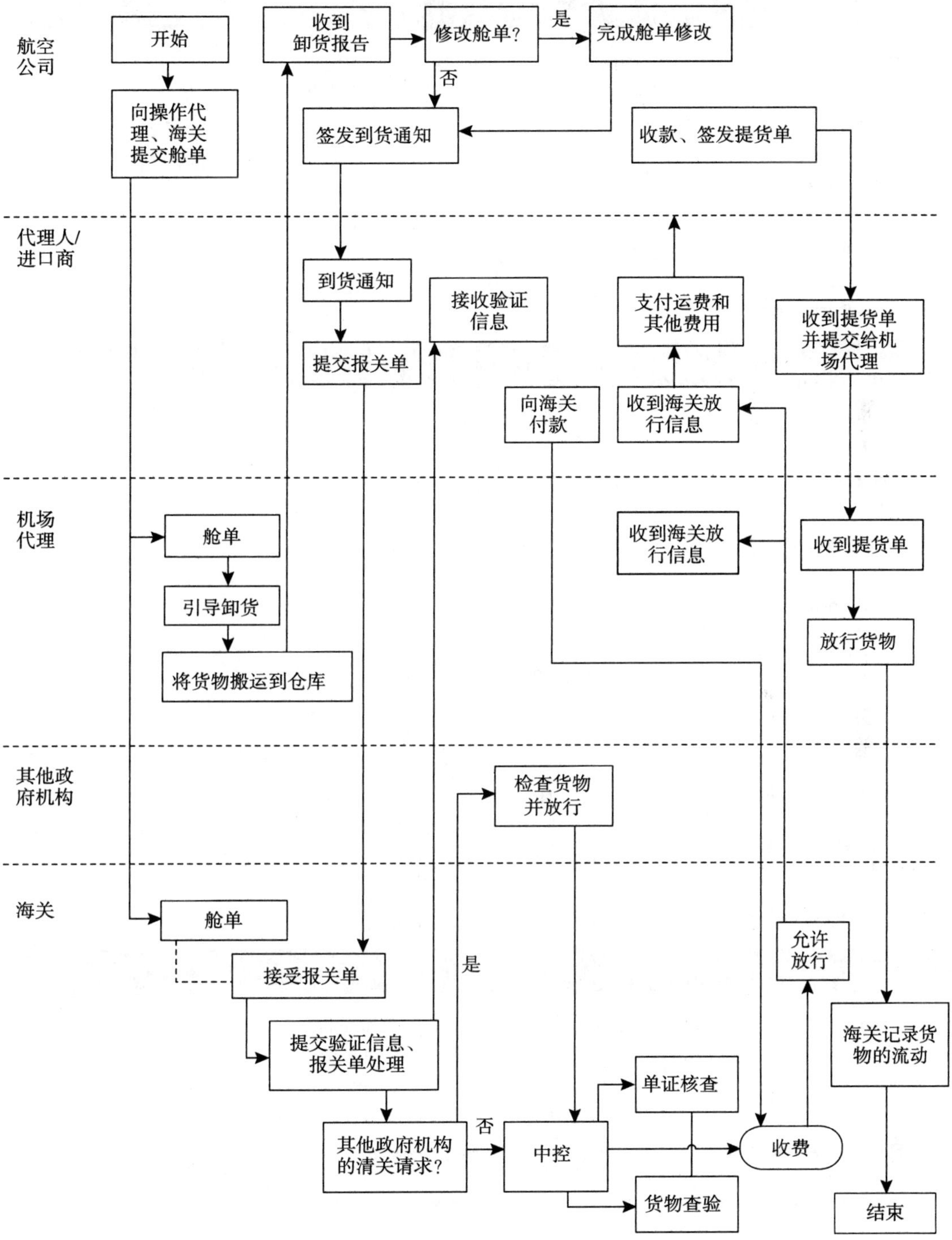

Identification *	
1. Office*	Office A ☐ Office B ☐ Office C ☐
2. Airline *	-
3. AWB Number *	-
4. Broker ID *	-
5. Goods Declaration ID *	-
Goods arrival and declaration submission *	
6. Manifest Submission *	☐ day ☐ mth - ☐ hr ☐ min
7. Aircraft Arrival*	☐ day ☐ mth - ☐ hr ☐ min
8. Start of Unloading *	☐ day ☐ mth - ☐ hr ☐ min
9. End of Unloading *	☐ day ☐ mth - ☐ hr ☐ min
10. Start of Transfer to Warehouse *	☐ day ☐ mth - ☐ hr ☐ min
11. End of Transfer to Warehouse *	☐ day ☐ mth - ☐ hr ☐ min
12. Manifets Amendment	Yes ☐ No ☐
13. Completion of Manifest Amendment	☐ day ☐ mth - ☐ hr ☐ min
14. Declaration Submission *	☐ day ☐ mth - ☐ hr ☐ min
OGA Inspection	
15. Agency	Health ☐ Agriculture ☐ Veterinary ☐
16. Start of OGA Inspection	☐ day ☐ mth - ☐ hr ☐ min
17. End of OGA Inspection	☐ day ☐ mth - ☐ hr ☐ min

* = Mandatory – if indicated for a section, mandatory questions for the section must be completed; if indicated for a question, the question must be completed if the section is used.

Processing by Customs *	
18. Declaration Channel*	Green ☐ Yellow ☐ Red ☐
19. Start of Documentary Check	☐ day ☐ mth - ☐ hr ☐ min
20. End of Documentary Check	☐ day ☐ mth - ☐ hr ☐ min
21. Start of Physical Inspection	☐ day ☐ mth - ☐ hr ☐ min
22. End of Physical Inspection	☐ day ☐ mth - ☐ hr ☐ min
23. Receive Payment for Duty and taxes	☐ day ☐ mth - ☐ hr ☐ min
24. Customs Release *	☐ day ☐ mth - ☐ hr ☐ min
Processing after Customs release *	
25. Payment of Freight and Charges *	☐ day ☐ mth - ☐ hr ☐ min
26. Issue of Delivery Order by Airline*	☐ day ☐ mth - ☐ hr ☐ min
27. Submission of Delivery Order by Warehouse *	☐ day ☐ mth - ☐ hr ☐ min
28. Cargo Release by Warehouse *	☐ day ☐ mth - ☐ hr ☐ min
29. Physical Release *	☐ day ☐ mth - ☐ hr ☐ min

* = Mandatory – if indicated for a section, mandatory questions for the section must be completed; if indicated for a question, the question must be completed if the section is used.

TRS——空运货物调查问卷示例

标识*	
1. 海关*	海关 A ☐ 海关 B ☐ 海关 C ☐
2. 航空公司 ID*	–
3. 空运单号*	–
4. 代理人 ID*	–
5. 报关单编号*	–
到货及报关*	
6. 提交舱单*	☐月☐日 – ☐时☐分

（续表）

到货及报关*	
7. 飞机到达*	□月□日 - □时□分
8. 开始卸货*	□月□日 - □时□分
9. 结束卸货*	□月□日 - □时□分
到货及报关*	
10. 开始向仓库搬运*	□月□日 - □时□分
11. 结束向仓库搬运*	□月□日 - □时□分
12. 修改舱单	□月□日 - □时□分
13. 完成舱单修改	□月□日 - □时□分
14. 提交报关单*	□月□日 - □时□分
其他政府机构查验	
15. 机构	卫生□　农业□　兽医□
16. 开始查验	□月□日 - □时□分
17. 结束查验	□月□日 - □时□分
海关流程*	
18. 报关通道*	绿色□　黄色□　红色□
19. 开始单证审核	□月□日 - □时□分
20. 结束单证审核	□月□日 - □时□分
21. 开始实货查验	□月□日 - □时□分
22. 结束实货查验	□月□日 - □时□分
23. 收到相关税/费	□月□日 - □时□分
24. 海关放行*	□月□日 - □时□分
海关放行后的其他环节*	
25. 支付相关税/费*	□月□日 - □时□分
26. 航空公司签发提货单*	□月□日 - □时□分
27. 向仓库提交提货单*	□月□日 - □时□分
28. 仓库放行货物*	□月□日 - □时□分
29. 实货放行*	□月□日 - □时□分

注：带 * 处为必填项。

Model of Road Business Process and its Questionnaire

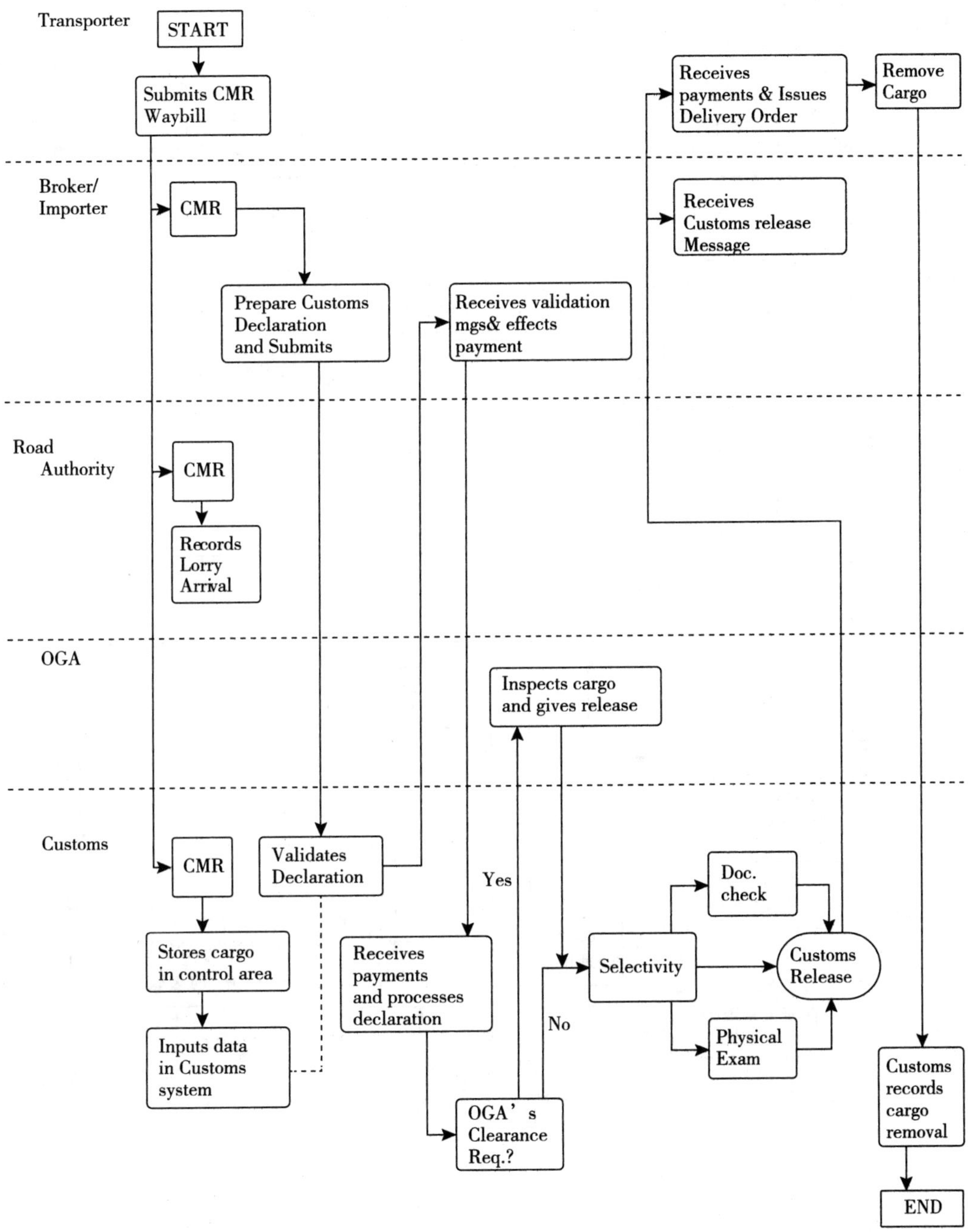

公路运输业务流程及其问卷调查表模板

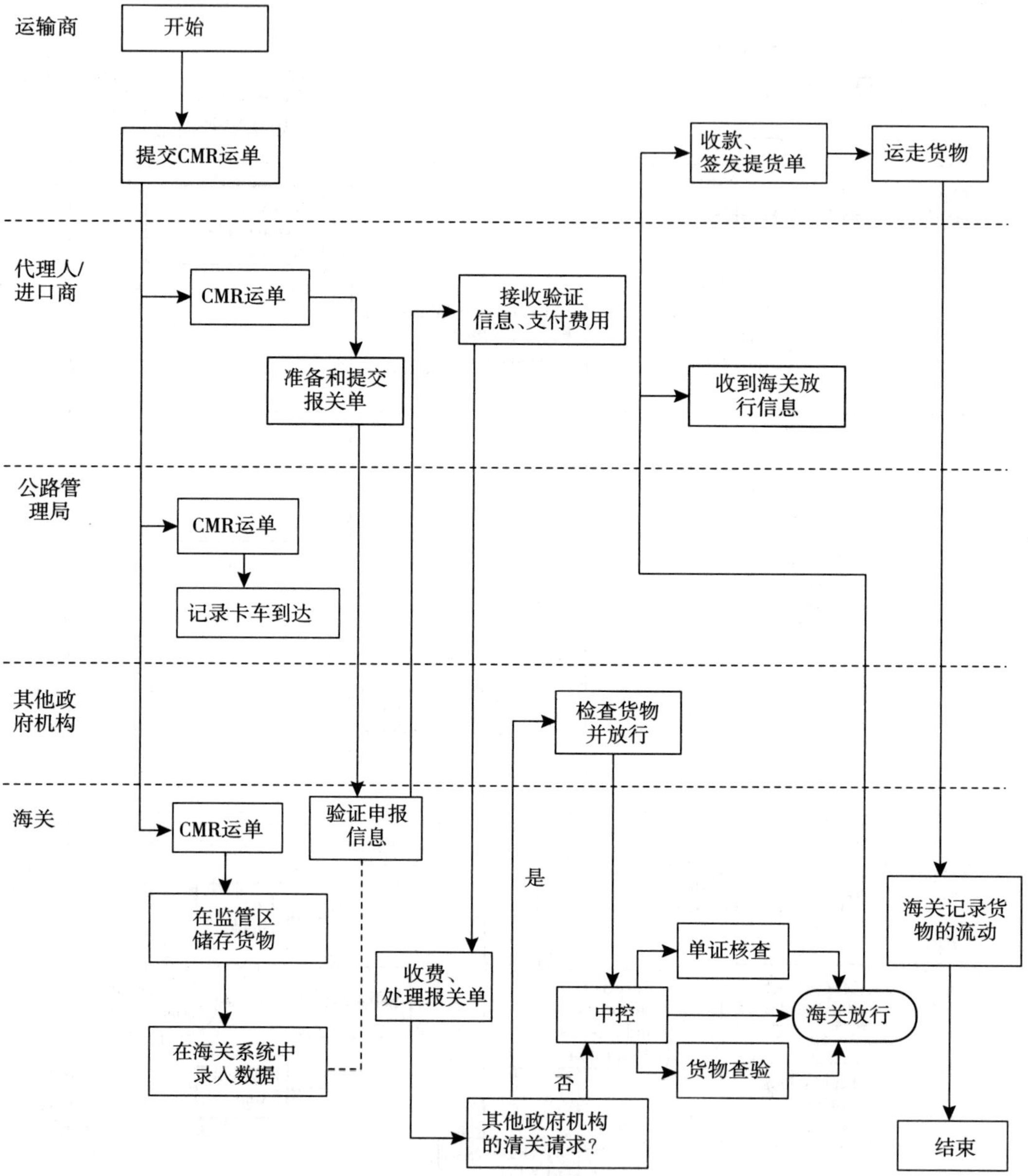

Time Release Study – Sample Questionnaire for Road Cargo

Identification *	
1. Border Post *	Border Post A ☐ Border Post B ☐ Border Post C ☐
2. CMR Waybill Number *	-
3. Broker ID *	-
4. Goods Declaration ID *	-
Goods arrival and declaration submission *	
5. CMR Submission *	☐ day ☐ mth - ☐ hr ☐ min
6. Lorry Arrival *	☐ day ☐ mth - ☐ hr ☐ min
7. Storage in Customs Control Area *	☐ day ☐ mth - ☐ hr ☐ min
8. Declaration Submission *	☐ day ☐ mth - ☐ hr ☐ min
9. Payment of Duty and Taxes *	☐ day ☐ mth - ☐ hr ☐ min
OGA Inspection	
10. Agency	Health ☐ Agricluture ☐ Veterinary ☐
11. Start of OGA Inspection	☐ day ☐ mth - ☐ hr ☐ min
12. End of OGA Inspection	☐ day ☐ mth - ☐ hr ☐ min
Processing by Customs *	
13. Declaration Channel *	Green ☐ Yellow ☐ Red ☐
14. Start of Documentary Check	☐ day ☐ mth - ☐ hr ☐ min
15. End of Documentary Check	☐ day ☐ mth - ☐ hr ☐ min
16. Start of Physical Inspection	☐ day ☐ mth - ☐ hr ☐ min
17. End of Physical Inspection	☐ day ☐ mth - ☐ hr ☐ min
18. Customs Release *	☐ day ☐ mth - ☐ hr ☐ min
Processing after Customs release *	
19. Release of Customs Release by Tranporter *	☐ day ☐ mth - ☐ hr ☐ min
20. Physical Release *	☐ day ☐ mth - ☐ hr ☐ min

* = Mandatory – if indicated for a section, mandatory questions for the section must be completed; if indicated for a question, the question must be completed if the section is used.

TRS——公路运输货物调查问卷示例

标识 *	
1. 边境检查站*	边境检查站 A □　边境检查站 B □　边境检查站 C □
2. CMR 运单编号*	–
3. 代理人 ID*	–
4. 报关单编号*	–
到货及报关*	
5. 提交 CMR 运单*	□月□日 – □时□分
6. 卡车到达*	□月□日 – □时□分
7. 货物储存于海关监管区域*	□月□日 – □时□分
8. 提交报关单*	□月□日 – □时□分
9. 支付相关税/费*	
其他政府机构查验	
10. 机构	卫生□　农业□　兽医□
11. 开始查验	□月□日 – □时□分
12. 结束查验	□月□日 – □时□分
海关流程*	
13. 报关通道*	绿色□　黄色□　红色□
14. 开始单证审核	□月□日 – □时□分
15. 结束单证审核	□月□日 – □时□分
16. 开始实货查验	□月□日 – □时□分
17. 结束实货查验	□月□日 – □时□分
18. 海关放行*	□月□日 – □时□分
海关放行后的其他环节*	
19. 给运输商签发海关放行单*	□月□日 – □时□分
20. 实货放行*	□月□日 – □时□分

注：带 * 处为必填项。

APPENDIX 3 – THE TRS WITHIN AN INTERNATIONAL/REGIONAL ENVIRONMENT
附录3　国际/区域环境下的 TRS

1. The policy document "Customs in the 21st Century" ("C21") identifies Globally Networked Customs (GNC) as the first of ten building blocks setting out the role and mission of Customs in the 21st century. This critically important concept provides a unifying means of bringing C21 to life, since every other building block depends upon effective communication, coordination and collaboration between Customs administrations globally.

1. WCO 政策指导性文件《21 世纪海关》（C21）中将全球网络海关（GNC）确定为 21 世纪海关的十大任务之首。这一重要理念为 21 世纪海关的实现奠定了基础，其他任务的开展均有赖于全球海关之间的有效沟通、协调与合作。

2. GNC highlights the importance of mutual recognition and coordination protocols between exporting, transit and importing administrations to eliminate unnecessary duplication of controls within international supply chains. In this context, the International Convention on Simplification and Harmonization of Customs Procedures (as amended) (Revised Kyoto Convention), which is a WCO instrument, sets out provisions on juxtaposed Customs offices, cooperation at juxtaposed Customs offices, and new Customs offices at common borders.

2. 全球网络海关强调在出口、过境和进口监管部门之间相互识别和协调协议的重要性，以消除国际供应链中不必要的重复操作。并且，作为世界海关组织的一种手段，《关于简化和协调海关业务制度的国际公约》（修正案）（《经修订的京都公约》）阐明了关于公共边境的同级海关、同级海关间合作和新设立海关的相关规定。

3. In practice, one-stop and joint control arrangements, including the One Stop Border Post (OSBP), have been attempted or applied in some regions to further facilitate legitimate trade.

3. 实践中，为了进一步促进合法贸易，在一些地区已经尝试或实施了一站式联合监管安排（包括海关、边境检查等边境监管机构在内的合署办公），例如一站式边境检查站模式（One Stop Border Post，OSBP）。

A. The Joint TRS at a bilateral level

A. 双边联合开展 TRS

4. This part of the Appendix has been developed for countries which desire to undertake a Bilateral TRS with a neighbouring country, including cases where the TRS is undertaken by a landlocked country alongside another country having the entry seaport, in order to provide standardized instruments for the Joint TRS.

4. 本部分是为那些希望与邻国开展双边 TRS 的国家制定的，包括内陆国与有入境港口的国家一起开展双边 TRS 的情况，其目的是为联合 TRS 提供标准化工具。

5. The initial step for the two countries which desire to conduct a Joint TRS is to agree on creating a bilateral instrument in the form of a MoU or letter of intent, through which the countries concerned will express their determination to conduct the Joint TRS.

5. 开展联合 TRS 的第一步是两个国家同意以谅解备忘录或意向书的形式制定一项双边文件，有关国家通过该文件表达其开展联合 TRS 的决心。

6. The MoU or letter of intent symbolizes the country's national commitment to cooperate and conduct the TRS on a bilateral basis (i. e. within the context of two countries). It also serves as an instrument which can be used to encourage the private sector and other government agencies to cooperate and commit to the successful implementation of the Joint TRS. The MoU or letter of intent can be signed by the Ministry of Foreign Affairs or any competent state department, including the Customs administration of each respective country.

6. 谅解备忘录或意向书象征着有关国家承诺在双边基础上（在两国范围内）合作和开展 TRS。它还可以作为一种用来鼓励私营机构和其他政府机构进行合作、致力于成功开展联合 TRS 的手段。谅解备忘录或意向书可由相关国家的外交部或任何主管部门，包括各国的海关部门签署。

7. Each Customs administration, in consultation with other stakeholders, will nominate a representative from each country who willbe responsible for coordinating the Study in that country and who will have the authority to engage with all relevant actors to be identified by each national Customs administration. The designated representative will report to the head of Customs at national level, who in turn will act as the government representative in relation to the Joint TRS. The representative should also coordinate his/her activity with the regional bloc in the context of the integration process, thereby possibly acting as a catalyst for the Joint TRS.

7. 各国海关当局应与其他利益相关方协商，每个国家提名一位代表，负责协调该国开展的研究工作，并有权与该国海关当局确定的所有相关参与者进行沟通和联系。指定代表应向该国的海关当局负责人汇报工作，而海关当局负责人又将担任该国开展联合 TRS 的政府代表。指定代表还应协调相关机构整合通关流程，积极推进联合 TRS 的开展。

8. Each country, through the Custom administration or the NCTF, will create a national Working Group which will execute national actions for TRS implementation. If the countries have already conducted a TRS within a national or bilateral context, the previous TRS Working Group can be reinstated, and tailored, as necessary, to reflect the scope of the Joint TRS.

8. 每个国家应通过海关当局或国家贸易便利化委员会组建一个国家工作组，负责开展该国的 TRS。如果这些国家已经在该国或双边范围内开展过 TRS，则可以恢复先前的 TRS 工作组，并根据需要进行调整，以适应联合 TRS 的要求。

9. It is important to bear in mind that a Joint TRS can be very technical. The officials involved should not only be in a position to make decisions, but also have good technical knowledge of cross-border transactions.

9. 要牢记，联合 TRS 具有非常强的专业性，有关官员不仅应具有决策权，而且应具有与跨境贸易相关的专业知识。

10. In order to achieve a successful outcome to the Joint TRS, it is critical to engage the key stakeholders that intervene in the flow process of the cargo to be analysed, including the private sector, and to take their views into consideration. For example, in cases where cross-border corridors are operated by a private sector or semi-governmental organization, that organization should be involved in the Joint TRS so that transportation between the two countries can also be taken into account as part of the outcome.

10. 为成功取得联合TRS成果，主要利益相关方（包括私营部门）的参与以及对其意见的考虑是非常必要的。例如，在私营部门或半政府组织管理跨境贸易走廊的情况下，该部门或组织应参与联合TRS，以便研究成果能涵盖两国间的运输环节。

11. Collecting data might be quite challenging in the context of a Joint TRS. However, it can be done by choosing one of the data collection methods indicated in Phase II of this Guide. As conducting a Joint TRS is more complex than conducting a TRS at national level, countries may sometimes temporarily employ Questionnaire Assistants to ensure that questionnaire forms are correctly completed, or to insert the times in the questionnaires themselves.

11. 在联合TRS的情况下，收集数据可能会具有挑战性。但可以根据本指南阶段Ⅱ中指出的一种数据收集方法来完成该工作。由于进行联合TRS比在该国层面开展TRS更加复杂，因此相关国家可考虑临时聘请第三方问卷调查公司，以确保调查问卷表填写正确，或由他们在问卷表中填写各项活动所需的时间。

12. Ideally, once the Joint TRS has been conducted, a single Report, as per the model format of a Final Report (Appendix 5), should be produced.

12. 理想情况下，一旦开展了联合TRS，应按照最终报告（附录5）的模板格式编制一份研究报告。

B. The Joint TRS at a multilateral/regional level

B. 多边/区域内联合TRS

13. This part of the Appendix has been developed for countries which desire to undertake a

Joint TRS with multiple/neighbouring countries or with members of a regional economic community. A Joint TRS at a multilateral level can focus on two or more border posts, or even a transit corridor. Further, a regional economic community may give a mandate to its members to undertake a TRS within the bloc.

13. 这部分是为那些希望与多个邻国或一个区域经济共同体开展联合 TRS 的国家而制定的。多边层面的联合 TRS 可以集中在两个或多个边境口岸、过境走廊。此外，区域经济共同体可以授权其成员在该共同体内开展 TRS。

14. The initial step for the countries which desire to conduct a Joint TRS is to agree on creating a multilateral or regional instrument in the form ofa MoU or letter of intent, through which the countries concerned will express their determination to conduct the Joint TRS.

14. 开展联合 TRS 的第一步是同意以谅解备忘录或意向书的形式制定多边或区域性文件，有关国家通过这些文件表达其开展联合 TRS 的决心。

15. The MoU or letter of intent symbolizes the countries' national commitment to cooperate and conduct the TRS. It also serves as an instrument which can be used to encourage the private sector and other government agencies to cooperate and commit to the successful implementation of the Joint TRS. The MoU or letter of intent can usually be signed by the Ministry of Foreign Affairs or any competent state department, including the Customs administration of each respective country.

15. 谅解备忘录或意向书象征着相关国家合作开展 TRS 的国家承诺。它还可以作为一种用来鼓励私营机构和其他政府机构进行合作、致力于成功开展联合 TRS 的手段。谅解备忘录或意向书可由相关国家的外交部或任何主管部门，包括各国的海关当局签署。

16. However, in the context of a regional economic community, a regional trade instrument can be used to seek each country's cooperation. Regional economic communities are increasingly adopting Joint Time Release Studies as tools for strengthening the regional integration process and promoting intra-regional trade.

16. 然而，在区域经济共同体背景下，可以使用区域贸易手段来寻求各个国家的合作。区域经济共同体越来越多地采用联合 TRS 作为加强区域一体化进程和促进区域内贸易发展的工具。

17. Each Customs administration, in consultation with other stakeholders, will nominate a representative from each country who will be responsible for coordinating the Study in that country and who will have the authority to engage with all relevant actors to be identified by each national Customs administration. The designated representative will report to the head of Customs at national level, who in turn will act as the government representative at the regional forum.

17. 各海关当局应与其他利益相关方协商，每个国家提名一位代表，负责协调该国的研究工作，并有权与该国海关当局确定的所有相关参与者进行沟通和联系。指定代表应向该国的海关当局负责人汇报工作，海关当局负责人将在区域论坛上担任该国的政府代表。

18. Each country, through the Customs administration or NCTF, will create a national Working Group which will execute national actions for the Joint TRS. If the countries have already conducted a TRS, the previous TRS Working Group can be reinstated, and tailored, as necessary, to reflect the scope of the Joint TRS.

18. 每个国家应通过海关当局或国家贸易便利化委员会组建一个国家工作组，负责开展该国的 TRS。如果这些国家已经在该国或双边范围内开展过 TRS，则可以恢复先前的 TRS 工作组，并根据需要进行调整，以适应联合 TRS 的要求。

19. As has already been mentioned above, due to the technical nature of a Joint TRS, the officials involved should have in-depth knowledge of cross-border transactions. Furthermore, in order for the TRS to be successful, it is imperative that all key stakeholders in the cargo flow process be involved.

19. 如上所述，由于联合 TRS 的技术特性，有关官员应对跨境贸易有深入的了解。此外，为了成功开展 TRS，必须让货运流程中的所有关键利益相关方都参与进来。

20. Collecting data might be quite challenging in the context of a Joint TRS at multilateral/regional level. However, it can be done by choosing one of the data collection methods indicated in Phase II of this Guide. As conducting a Joint TRS is more complex than conducting a TRS at national level, countries may sometimes temporarily employ Questionnaire Assistants to ensure that questionnaire forms are correctly completed, or to insert the times in the questionnaires themselves.

20. 在多边/区域层面的联合 TRS 的背景下，收集数据可能具有相当大的挑战性。但是，可以根据本指南阶段II中指出的一种数据收集方法来完成该工作。由于开展联合 TRS 比在国家层面开展 TRS 更加复杂，因此相关国家可考虑临时聘请第三方问卷调查公司，以确保调查问卷填写正确，或由他们在问卷表中填写各项活动所需的时间。

21. Ideally, once the Joint TRS has been conducted within a regional economic community, each country's report will be used to produce a single TRS Report, as per the model format for a Final Report in this Guide. The Report should reflect the actual situation in each country where the Study was conducted, such as the time taken to accomplish the process, findings, bottlenecks and recommendations. Additionally, the single TRS Report should be comprehensive and list the crucial obstacles hindering intra-regional trade, with proposals for improving trade within the countries involved in the Joint TRS.

21. 理想情况下，一旦在区域经济共同体中开展了联合 TRS，则每个国家应根据本指南中最终报告的模板格式编制一份 TRS 报告。报告应反映开展研究的每个国家的实际情况，例如完成清关程序所需的时间、研究发现、瓶颈和建议。此外，单一 TRS 报告内容应全面，除了列出区域内贸易的关键障碍，还应提出改善参与联合 TRS 的国家之间贸易状况的建议。

APPENDIX 4 – A BASIC GUIDE TO THE USE OF THE WCO TRS ONLINE SOFTWARE

附录4　WCO TRS 在线软件使用指南

1. User ID and Password from the WCO

1. WCO 提供的用户名及密码

The WCO TRS online software is available to all WCO Members free of charge. Upon request, the WCO Secretariat provides Members with a User ID and Password for the National Survey Administrator, which is valid for a single survey.

WCO TRS 在线软件可供成员方免费使用。应成员方的要求，WCO 秘书处可为成员方提供一个调查管理员的用户名及密码，该用户名及密码仅对一次调查活动有效。

2. Log in to the TRS software

2. TRS 软件的登录方法

The Survey Administrator goes to http://members.wcoomd.org/trs/index.asp and inputs his/her User ID and Password to log in to the software.

调查管理员可打开网页 http://members.wcoomd.org/trs/index.asp，输入用户名和密码，登录 TRS 软件。

3. User ID and Password for users in your administration

3. 调查管理员用户名及密码的使用

A Survey Administrator can allocate a User ID and Password to the other Survey Administrator (s) and End User (s) in his/her administration, so that they can also access the software for the single survey being worked on.

调查管理员可为其他调查员和终端用户分配用户名和密码，以便他们在调查时使用该软件。同样地，这些用户名及密码仅对一次调查活动有效。

4. Developing a survey form (questionnaire)

4. 设计调查表（问卷调查）

The Survey Administrator develops a survey questionnaire in accordance with the detailed TRS conditions set up by his/her TRS Working Group.

调查管理员可按照 TRS 工作组的具体要求设计调查问卷。

5. Distribution of printed blank questionnaires

5. 纸质空白问卷的分发

The Survey Administrator prints the blank questionnaires and distributes them to the officials responsible for TRS implementation, including those in other border agencies, as well as to businesses, where appropriate.

调查管理员打印空白问卷并分发给开展 TRS 的工作人员。若需要，也可分发给其他边境机构和企业。

6. Inputting data into the TRS software

6. 将数据录入 TRS 软件

Having collected all the necessary data from the responses to the survey questionnaire, the Survey Administrator inputs all the data into the TRS software using the "New Data Input" and "Data Collection" functions. You can also allocate this task to an End User in your administration.

通过回收问卷收集到所需数据后，调查管理员使用 TRS 软件的"新数据录入"和"数据收集"功能，将所有数据录入系统。调查管理员也可以将该任务分配给终端用户完成。

7. Developing a Report

7. 形成报告

Lastly, the Survey Administrator can use the "Quick Report" function to calculate automatically the Average Time, Standard Deviation and Largest Deviation in any patterns he/she designs. The "Full Data Excel" function allows you to obtain all data in MS-Excel format so that you can use it for various purposes.

最后，调查管理员可使用“快速报告”功能并通过自己设计的模式自动计算平均放行时间、标准偏差和最大偏差。“全数据 Excel”功能支持将所有数据导出到 Excel 表格中，以满足各种使用需要。

For details, please see "User Manual: INTERNET SOFTWARE FOR THE TIME RELEASE STUDY", which is available on the WCO Members' Website at: http://www.wcoomd.org/members/files/Members%20PDF%20EN/FacilitationProced_PDF/TRS%20user%20manual-updated.pdf

详细内容见 WCO 成员国网站《TRS 在线软件用户手册》，其网址为：http://www.wcoomd.org/members/files/Members%20PDF%20EN/FacilitationProced_PDF/TRS%20user%20manual-updated.pdf。

APPENDIX 5 – MODEL FORMAT OF A FINAL REPORT

附录 5　最终报告的格式模板

1. This model format is a guide to assist the Working Group in preparing a Report of the Time Release Study. The format proposed includes the main areas to be addressed in the Final Report. These areas are not exhaustive and countries may include any other details which reflect their own requirements and concerns.

1. 该格式模板是为工作组撰写 TRS 报告提供的指南，它包含最终报告中应涵盖的主要内容。这些内容并不详尽，各国可根据自身需求和关注重点予以调整。

2. Although raw data should prove very valuable, the Report should provide average times, supplemented by information on the category of goods, inspection channels, mode of transport, interventions by other government agencies (OGA), and use of pre-arrival processing, etc.

2. 尽管原始数据中包含着丰富的信息，但体现在报告中的往往只是整个流程中各环节所需的平均时间，辅以商品类别、查验通道、运输方式、其他政府机构的干预情况以及“到货前信息审核”措施的实施情况等。

3. Depending on the objectives, the TRS Report requires dynamic, as well as static, data: e. g. how backlog cargoes are processed, congestion, peak-time and non-peak time, hourly or daily patterns of traffic and transportation. Statistical data processing models (mean, median, mode, range, how to define extreme data, etc.) may also be useful for inclusion in the Report. In this regard, a Working Group member specializing in statistics should provide comments about the data analysed.

3. 根据研究目标的不同，报告中既要有动态数据，也要有静态数据，例如，记录积压在港货物处理过程的数据，以及反映拥堵期、高峰期和非高峰期，或每小时（或每天）的交通运输情况的数据等。各种数据统计处理模型（均值、中位数、众数、范围、极限数据定义等）的使用也是有帮助的。在这方面，专门从事统计工作的工作组成员应就数据分析提供意见。

4. In general, the following areas should be covered in the Report:

4. 一般情况下，报告应包含以下几个方面的内容：

- Executive Summary
- Objectives
- Scope
- Methodology
- Analysis and Findings
- Recommendations and Conclusions
  - 摘要；
  - 目标；
  - 范围；
  - 方法；
  - 分析和发现；
  - 建议和结论。

Ⅰ. Executive Summary

Ⅰ. 摘要

5. The Executive Summary should provide an outline of the Study and, most importantly, of the major findings, challenges and recommendations.

5. 摘要是对该研究报告进行概述。最重要的是，它应包括主要发现、挑战和建议。

Ⅱ. Objectives

Ⅱ. 目标

6. The Report should explain what the Study was intended to measure. The Study objectives

should cover the following:

6. 报告应对测算对象进行说明。内容应涵盖以下几个方面：

- To measure the average time taken from arrival of the goods to their release;
- To measure the average time taken for each activity in the release process, for example, the time taken for physical inspections;
- To measure performance following the implementation of new policies/procedures/initiatives relating to cargo clearance;
- To identify weaknesses in the release process (including for each individual activity in the process);
- To identify the constraints affecting release; and
- To suggest corrective/remedial measures to improve the time required for the release of goods.

- 货物从运抵到放行所需平均时间的测算；
- 放行过程中各环节平均所需时间（例如现场实际检查所需的时间）的测算；
- 对与货物清关有关的新政策、新流程、新措施执行效果的评测；
- 对放行过程中薄弱环节的识别，包括放行过程中每个环节的薄弱点；
- 对货物放行制约因素的识别；
- 关于缩短货物放行时间纠正/补救措施的建议。

Ⅲ. Scope

Ⅲ. 范围

7. The scope must outline the extent and limits of the Study. Some points to include are:

7. 该部分应对研究的范围（深度和广度）进行概述，包括以下几个方面：

- Was it a comprehensive Study, capturing all the processes leading to release of the goods, or did the Study capture only the clearance procedures of government agencies?
- Did the Study capture all the elements in the Customs release process, or was it a simplified Study, capturing only the key elements in the Customs release process?

- Did the Study involve measuring the time from the arrival of the goods in the Customs territory to their release (total time), or did it cover only the time from when the goods declaration was lodged to the time of release (Customs time)?
- What modes of traffic were studied (e. g. sea, air, land, rail)?
- Which Customs office (s) was (were) involved in the Study?
- Was the Study based on automated or manual Customs procedures, or a combination of both?
- Which other agencies were involved in the Study and what was their role?
- Was the time taken by pre-shipment inspection companies captured?

- 这是一项涵盖货物放行全过程的综合研究，还是仅涵盖政府机构清关程序的简化研究？
- 这是一项采集海关放行流程中全部要素的研究，还是仅采集海关放行流程中关键要素的简化研究？
- 研究是测算从货物运抵边境到放行的总时间，还是仅测算从递交货物报关单到海关放行货物所需的时间？
- 研究涉及哪些运输方式（例如，海运、空运、公路运输还是铁路运输）？
- 研究涉及哪些海关？
- 研究对象是基于自动化系统的海关监管程序，还是人工操作的海关监管程序，或者是既涉及自动化系统又涉及人工操作的海关监管程序？
- 研究还涉及其他哪些机构？它们在清关过程中有什么作用？
- 研究是否采集装运前检验公司所需时间的信息？

Ⅳ. Methodology

Ⅳ. 方法

8. The methodology used in the Study should be explained, as it will impact on the validity and reliability of the results obtained. The following should be covered under this section:

8. 研究所使用的方法会影响研究结果的有效性和可靠性，因此需对其进行说明，包括以下几个方面：

- Were all transactions covered in the Study, or was a sampling methodology used?
- If sampling was used, how were the samples chosen from the whole population or from the sub-population studied?
- What data was captured and how was it collected?
- What was the duration of the Study?
    - 研究使用所有业务数据还是采取抽样方式？
    - 如果使用抽样方式，如何从总体中选择样本？如何从部分总体中选择样本？
    - 研究采集了什么数据？这些数据是如何收集的？
    - 研究持续了多长时间？

Ⅴ. Analysis and Findings

Ⅴ. 分析和发现

9. This section should contain details of the total number of transactions dealt with over the duration of the Study, the number of questionnaire forms issued, the number returned, and the number used in the analysis.

9. 本部分应详细说明在研究期间的总体业务量以及发出的、得到反馈的和分析时使用的调查表数量。

If sub-populations were analysed, it is also important to indicate:

如果分析了业务分类数据，则应指明以下内容：

- The number of transactions;
- The number of forms issued;
- The number of forms returned; and
- The number analysed for the sub-population.
    - 业务量；
    - 发出的调查表数量；
    - 反馈的调查表数量；
    - 业务分类数量的分析。

It is important to indicate what data has been included in the analysis. The following elements should be covered in this section:

指出分析中包含哪些数据是很重要的。本部分应包括以下内容:

- The average time taken from the arrival of the goods to their release. This could include, for example, the following key elements:
  - 从货物运抵到放行所需的平均时间，包括以下关键要素:

◇ Time from the arrival of the goods to the lodgement of the goods declaration;

◇ Time from the lodgement of the goods declaration to the assessment of duty and taxes;

◇ Time taken for examination of the goods;

◇ Time from the assessment to the payment of duties and taxes;

◇ Time from the duty payment to the release of the goods;

◇ Time taken in interventions by other agencies;

◇ Average time taken for each individual process by other stakeholders.

◇ 从货物运抵到提交报关单的时间;

◇ 从提交报关单到评估税费的时间;

◇ 查验货物所需的时间;

◇ 从关税和税费评估到支付关税和税费所需的时间;

◇ 从支付关税到货物放行所需的时间;

◇ 其他机构干预所需的时间;

◇ 其他利益相关方为每个相关流程所花费的平均时间。

- If different categories of goods or goods regimes were studied separately (dutiable goods, non-dutiable goods, goods intended for inward processing, free zones, express consignments, etc.), the average time taken for each category or regime;
  - 分别对不同税制或种类的货物进行研究时各税制货物（例如应税货物、非应税货物、进料加工货物、免税区货物、快递货物等）所需的平均时间;

- Time taken for goods declared manually and electronically; and

- 通过人工申报的货物以及通过电子申报的货物所需的时间；

- Time taken for release of goods by different Customs offices.
  - 不同海关放行货物所需的时间。

Ⅵ. Recommendations and Conclusions

Ⅵ. 结论和建议

10. The conclusions to be drawn and the recommendations made will depend largely on the results of the analysis of the data. The results could also be compared with established work standards and/or theresults of previous Studies in order to arrive at useful conclusions.

10. 根据数据分析结果提出研究结论和建议。将研究结果与既定的工作标准以及先期的研究结果进行比较，可得出更有助于实际工作的结论。

11. The conclusions should focus on the processes where delays occur and why they occur. They should also focus on the areas where further improvements could be made.

11. 结论部分应重点关注发生延迟的流程、延迟发生的原因以及可改进的环节。

12. Recommendations, on the other hand, should focus on specific proposals for improvements and should be translated into an Action Plan.

12. 建议部分应重点关注具体的改进方案，并应转化为行动计划。

APPENDIX 6 – MODEL NATIONAL ACTION PLAN FOR IMPLEMENTATION OF THE TRS RECOMMENDATIONS

附录6　实施TRS中建议措施的国家行动计划模板

Objective

目标

This model Action Plan is aimed at providing clear direction on implementation of the national TRS recommendations. It is presented in the form of a Table of Activities, with six numbered column headings and various examples. A guide to the Table headings is below.

该行动计划模板旨在为实施国家层面的TRS建议提供明确的指导。它以行动计划表的形式呈现，包括六列内容并提供了示例。对该行动表表头的说明如下。

Guide to the Table headings

表格表头说明

Ⅰ. Activities

Ⅰ. 行动

This relates to specific actions included in the TRS recommendations.

此列为TRS建议中包含的具体行动。

Ⅱ. Reference to substantial measures in the WTO TFA

Ⅱ. WTO TFA的相关措施

This column is specifically intended for countries which are Members of the WTO. To the extentpossible, each activity should be linked to particular WTO TFA measures, thus supporting the activity's implementation in line with the categorization determined by the country. One activity may be linked to one or more WTO TFA measures. When completing this column, it is essential that the TRS Working Group refer to the WTO TFA.

此列是专为 WTO 成员方准备的。每项行动都应尽可能与特定的 WTO TFA 措施相关联，从而根据国家确定的分类支持该行动。一项行动可能与一个或多个 WTO TFA 措施相关。在填写该列内容时，TRS 工作组必须参考 WTO TFA 的相关内容。

Non-WTO Members are exempt from completing this column.

非世贸组织成员方无须填写此列。

Ⅲ. Outputs (national and international instruments)

Ⅲ. 结果（国家和国际工具）

This relates to the quantitative and qualitative outputs arising from implementation of the activities identified. Such outputs should normally be tangible and measurable.

此列为执行已确定的行动所产生的定量及定性的结果。此结果通常是有形并可测量的。

Ⅳ. Parties responsible

Ⅳ. 责任方

This relates to the leading stakeholder (i. e. public or private entity) responsible for implementation of the activity in question.

此列为负责实施相关行动的主要利益相关方（政府或私人机构）。

Ⅴ. Potential time frame for implementation

Ⅴ. 实施时间

This relates to the anticipated time frame for implementation of each activity.

此列为实施每项行动的预期时间。

Ⅵ. Comments

Ⅵ. 注释

This column should be used to record any relevant information that cannot be included in columns 1 to 5. Specific details on implementation or the approach adopted may be summarized here. For example, specific target dates, or border posts where new procedures are to be implemented, could be mentioned in this column.

此列用于记录在前5列中无法包含的其他相关信息。可以记录实施建议措施或所采用方法的详细信息。例如，此列中可以记录实现具体目标的日期或将实施新流程的边境口岸。

No.	(1) Activities	(2) Reference to substancial measure in the WTO TFA	(3) Outputs (national and international instruments)	(4) Parties responsibles	(5) Potencial time frame for implementation			(6) Comments
					Short-term	Medium-term	Long-term	
1	Establish an elewctronic national Single Window system.	Article 10.4- Single Window	Steamline border procedures, reduce costs and time, and reduce paper documents.	Customs administration, Ministry of trade and other parties.			x	Will be implemented phase-wide. The Ministry of Health and the Quarantine Department will join before the end of 2018.
2	Align working days and hours between Members sharing a border.	Article 8.2 - Border Agency Cooperation	Facilitate cross-border trade.	Public and private international trade stakeholders in the Member States, including the Customs administration and other agencies in the respective countries.		x		
3								
4								

行动计划表

序号	行动	WTO TFA 的相关措施	结果（国家和国际工具）	责任方	实施时间			注释
					短期	中期	长期	
1	建立电子化的国家单一窗口	第 10.4 条：单一窗口	简化边境程序，减少时间和成本，并减少纸质资料的使用量	海关、贸易主管部等各有关方			√	将在全阶段实施。卫生和检疫部门将在 2018 年年底前加入
2	调整共享边境的成员方之间的工作时间	第 8.2 条：边境机构合作	促进跨境贸易	成员方政府和私人国际贸易利益相关者，包括各自国家的海关和其他机构		√		
3								
4								

APPENDIX 7 – MODEL PRESS RELEASE
附录 7　新闻发布模板

This model is a possible format for Customs administrations to use in preparing a press release about the Time Release Study. It is recommended that a brief factual description of the scope, methodology and results of the Study be included, in order to explain the efforts of Customs and other stakeholders in support of trade facilitation.

本模板为海关部门 TRS 的新闻发布模板。为说明海关和其他相关方在促进贸易便利化方面做出的努力，建议应客观简要地介绍研究范围、采用方法和研究结果。

[Name and symbol of the Customs administration]

[海关部门名称及标志]

PRESS RELEASE

新闻发布

[date]

[日期]

[Title]

[标题]

Outline

概要

[ ] Customs today released the findings of its [country name/port/seaport/border post namc] first [second, third......] Time Release Study (TRS), which measures and reports the time taken by Customs and [other stakeholders] to release imported cargo.

今天 [ ] 海关公布首次 [第二次，第三次……] TRS 结果，该项研究测算并公布海关进口货物放行所需时间。

The TRS is a method endorsed by the World Customs Organization for measuring the time taken by authorities torelease import/export cargo, and is recognized as a means of identifying bottlenecks and improving performance in import/export processes. Since entry into force of the WTO Trade Facilitation Agreement (TFA) in February 2017, Members have been required to measure and publish average release times of import/export goods (Article 7.6 of the TFA).

TRS 是世界海关组织认可的海关放行进出口货物所需时间的测算方法，且被看作识别海关进出口流程中存在的瓶颈、提高工作效率的手段。于2017年2月生效的《世贸组织贸易便利化协定》（TFA）要求成员国测算并公布进出口货物的平均放行时间（详见TFA第7.6条）。

The DG of Customs, [ ], said it was pleasing to [see the results of the first/second/third Study as an objective indicator for trade facilitation] and to [see improvements in [year], which he attributed largely to the efforts of Customs, trade-related agencies and trade working together to achieve a seamless flow of cross-border trade].

海关发言人［ ］说：非常高兴［向大家展示作为贸易便利化客观指标的首次/第二次/第三次TRS结果］或者［看到（ ）年海关在货物放行时间方面的改进，这很大程度上得益于海关、相关贸易机构和企业三方为使国际贸易环境更加顺畅而共同合作所做出的努力］。

The TRS [year] found that the average time from arrival to release for sea cargo is approximately [ ] hours, [an improvement of [ ] hours from [year]]. For air cargo, the interval was around [ ] hours [an improvement of more than [ ] hours] and for land cargo, it was around [ ] hours [an improvement of [ ] hours].

［ ］年TRS结果显示，海运货物从运抵到放行所需平均时间大约是［ ］小时，比［ ］年减少［ ］小时。空运货物所需时间大约是［ ］小时，平均减少［ ］小时，而陆运货物所需时间大约是［ ］小时，减少［ ］小时。

The time takenby each agency in the cross-border processing and release of import/export goods is set out below. (This paragraph is optional)

各相关机构在进出口货物的跨境处理和放行过程中花费的时间如下（本段是可选的）。

In particular, the average Customs procedure time, from Customs declaration to release, is as follows. [Each element has greatly improved as a consequence of efforts aimed at trade facilitation and the resulting enhancement of Customs operations.]

以下是完成从报关到放行的所有海关手续的平均时间。[作为海关提高贸易便利化水平而改进业务流程的成果，各环节所需时间都大幅缩短]

For sea cargo: [ ] hours [an improvement of [ ] hours]

海运货物：[ ] 小时 [缩短 ( ) 小时]

For air cargo: [ ] hours [an improvement of [ ] hours]

空运货物：[ ] 小时 [缩短 ( ) 小时]

For land cargo: [ ] hours [an improvement of [ ] hours]

陆运货物：[ ] 小时 [缩短 ( ) 小时]

Similarly, the average release time taken by [Agency Name] is as follows. [Each element has greatly improved as a consequence of efforts aimed at trade facilitation and the resulting enhancement of [Agency Name] operations.]

类似地，[机构名称] 的平均发布时间如下。[由于旨在简化贸易手续的努力以及由此加强的（机构名称）业务，每一个要素都有了很大的改进]

For sea cargo: [ ] hours [an improvement of [ ] hours]

海运货物：[ ] 小时 [缩短 ( ) 小时]

For air cargo: [ ] hours [an improvement of [ ] hours]

空运货物：[ ] 小时 [缩短 ( ) 小时]

For land cargo: [ ] hours [an improvement of [ ] hours]

陆运货物：[ ] 小时 [缩短 ( ) 小时]

The DG of Customs, [ ], acknowledged trade's contribution to the Time Release Study, in particular [ ], [ ], [ ], who provided advice and assistance.

海关发言人 [ ]：感谢企业为 TRS 所作出的贡献，尤其是 [ ] [ ]，他们为该研究提供了建议和帮助。

Key findings and actions to be taken for further trade facilitation are [ ] . It is also intended that regular Time Release Studies continue to be conducted.

主要研究成果以及下一步将采取的贸易便利化措施包括 [　　]。今后将把 TRS 作为一项常态化工作来开展。

[The Time Release StudyReport can be downloaded from the [Name of Customs administration] website: [web address]

TRS 可从 [海关名称] 网站 [网址] 下载。

Media enquiries:

媒体查询:

For further details contact [ ] Customs [tel. and e-mail]

更多信息请联系 [　　] 海关 [电话和邮箱]。

APPENDIX 8 – MEMBERS' EXPERIENCE

附录8　各成员方的经验

AUSTRALIA

澳大利亚

Australia's 2016 TRS

澳大利亚2016年的TRS情况

1. The Australian Border Force (ABF) was integrated into the Department of Home Affairs (Home Affairs) on 20 December 2017. It operates within Australia's international trading environment and must balance its border protection responsibilities with the need to facilitate legitimate trade. Cargo reports, which include a description of the cargo, must be input electronically into the ABF's Integrated Cargo System not less than 48 hours before arrival for sea cargo, and not less than two hours for air cargo. This allows the ABF to start risk assessing the cargo before it actually arrives.

1. 澳大利亚边境管理局（ABF）于2017年12月20日并入内政部。ABF负责协调澳大利亚边境贸易便利化相关工作，其职责是保护边境和促进合法贸易。在澳大利亚，海运货物必须在到达前48小时、空运货物必须在到达前2小时将其货物申报（包括货物描述）以电子方式传输到ABF的货物综合管理系统中。这使得ABF可以在货物实际到达之前就进行风险评估。

2. The ABF describes its approach to managing the flow of sea and air cargo as "intelligence-led and risk-based". Its regulatory philosophy recognizes that the majority of individuals and entities involved in the importation of cargo intend to comply with the regulatory requirements and should be permitted to operate in a self-assessed environment with minimal or no intervention.

2. ABF用"以情报为导向、以风险为基础"的方法管理海运和空运货物。ABF

的监管理念是“参与货物进口活动的大多数个人和实体都倾向于遵守监管要求，因而允许其在自我评估的基础上开展业务，不干预或少干预其贸易过程”。

Australia's international interests and expectations in the field of TRS

Globalization has brought a dramatic increase in cross-border trading. Accordingly, there continues to be heightened dialogue between the WCO and other organizations to discuss and promote the TRS. There is a growing number of joint Studies conducted by WCO Member States actively seeking to work together in order to deliver common solutions to critically important trade facilitation objectives.

In 2010, Australia and New Zealand worked in collaboration to conduct a trans-Tasman TRS. The same TRS methodology used for the Australian experience was applied to the 2010 trans-Tasman experience. The trans-Tasman TRS was conducted to gauge the performance of the import and export clearance processes in Australia and New Zealand. An evidence-based approach was employed, using data gathered during the usual course of border-management business. Overall, it was found that clearance performance for imports and exports was high on both sides of the Tasman. The TRS also indicated that arrangements made under the Australia-New Zealand Closer Economic Relations Trade Agreement (ANZCERTA) contributed to faster processing times at the border.

Critically, the 2010 trans-Tasman TRS embodied the collaborative effort of both Australia and New Zealand in overcoming differences in their approach to border clearance events, definitions, policy and processes to produce a joint consolidated analysis and Study. Key findings from this Study identified factors which affected performance on both sides. An analysis of these findings suggested that there was potential to further augment the clearance performance in trans-Tasman trade.

Opportunities for streamlining included:

- Advance reporting;
- Information for SME traders;
- Regulatory harmonization;
- Data harmonization;
- Risk management; and
- Performance management.

澳大利亚开展TRS的国际利益与期望

全球化带来了跨境贸易的急剧增长。因此，WCO与其他组织之间将继续加强对话，以商讨和促进TRS的开展。WCO成员开展了越来越多的联合TRS，他们积极寻求合作，从而为实现贸易便利化这一极其重要的目标寻求共同的解决方案。

在2010年，澳大利亚和新西兰合作开展了双边TRS。澳大利亚根据之前的TRS经验开展了2010年的双边TRS。该双边TRS旨在评估澳大利亚和新西兰进出口清关流程的效率。该研究采用了基于证据的方法，采集了边境管理业务常用程序中的数据。总体而言，研究发现，双方的进出口清关效率都很高。TRS还指出，《澳大利亚与新西兰更紧密经济关系贸易协定》（ANZCERTA）所做出的安排有助于缩短边境放行时间。

至关重要的是，2010年的双边TRS体现了澳大利亚和新西兰在克服清关要求、释义、政策/流程上的差异以及在进行联合分析和研究方面的合作及努力。这项研究的结果有助于确定影响双方贸易绩效的因素。对这些结果的分析有助于进一步提高双边的清关效率。

以下方面仍需改进：

- 提前报告；
- 中小企业贸易商的信息；
- 监管协调；
- 统一数据；
- 风险管理；
- 绩效管理。

3. Since 2007, the ABF has conducted various Time Release Studies to:

3. 自2007年以来，ABF为实现下列目标开展了各种TRS：

- Provide a holistic view of the cargo-operating environment;
- Enable the measurement of improvements in clearance times;
- Enable the identification of other improvement opportunities to further streamline border clearance processes and facilitate trade; and
- Provide industry with a measure of border agency performance in delivering timely

cargo clearance.

- 提供货运操作环境的整体视图；
- 执行对于清关时间的改进措施；
- 确认其他改进机会，以进一步简化边境清关程序并促进贸易；
- 为行业提供一个衡量边境机构在及时处理货物清关方面的绩效标准。

4. The table below outlines Australia's performance and shows that this has remained stable in the sea cargo environment, but has improved in the air cargo environment. This is a remarkable achievement that supports the significant changes to border security over the past four years.

4. 下表为澳大利亚的通关概况。它表明海运货物的通关情况保持稳定，空运货物的通关情况有所改善。这是一项了不起的进步，表明该国过去四年在边境安全方面有重大变化。

Results * of key measurements – 2016 TRS

	Sea Cargo 2015	Sea Cargo 2016		Air Cargo 2015	Air Cargo 2016
Arrival to release (days)	-0.5	-0.6	Arrival to release (hours)	6.2	2.8
Arrival to clearance (days)	0.5	0.1	Arrival to clearance (hours)	6.4	3.0
Arrival to availability (days)	1.2	1.2	Arrival to availability (hours)	47.4	35.5
* The negative figures indicate that goods were Customs-cleared half a day before they arrived in Australia.					

2016 年的 TRS——主要评测结果*

	2015 年海运货物	2016 年海运货物		2015 年空运货物	2016 年空运货物
货物运抵到放行（天）	-0.5	-0.6	货物运抵到放行（天）	6.2	2.8
货物运抵到清关（天）	0.5	0.1	货物运抵到清关（天）	6.4	3.0
货物运抵到流通（天）	1.2	1.2	货物运抵到流通（天）	47.4	35.5
* 负数表示货物在抵达澳大利亚前半天已完成海关放行。					

5. Key findings from the 2016 TRS are listed below.

5. 2016 年 TRS 的主要发现如下：

- The ABF remains efficient in clearing cargo at the border and is not an impediment to trade.
- Sea cargo and air cargo volumes continue to increase. However, this does not create a corresponding percentage deterioration in the speed at which cargo is processed at the border.
- In sea cargo, the country of origin plays a significant role in determining the timeliness of document reporting for ABF clearance.

- ABF 在边境清关方面保持了有效性，未构成贸易障碍。
- 海运和空运货物交易量继续增长，但是边境通关速度没有下降。
- 在海运货物中，原产国在确定 ABF 清关单证报告的及时性方面起着重要作用。

6. The 2015 and 2016 Time Release Studies measure clearance performance for import processes only, as this approach is more mature for data collection purposes.

6. 为方便数据收集，2015 年和 2016 年的 TRS 仅测算进口流程的清关绩效。

7. The objective of the 2016 TRS was to:

7. 2016 年 TRS 的目标是：

- Replicate the 2015 TRS and produce comparable measurements;
- Compare the year-on-year results to show any performance changes; and
- Identify opportunities to improve performance.

- 与 2015 年的 TRS 进行对比测算；
- 与同期结果进行比较，以评测绩效的变化；
- 确认提高绩效的机会。

8. The 2016 TRS validated the findings of the 2015 TRS and continued the focus on multi-year and year-on-year trends for the air cargo pathway, sea cargo pathway and top ten

loading countries（sea and air）.

8. 2016 年的 TRS 验证了 2015 年的 TRS 结果，并继续关注空运货物、海运货物以及十大贸易国（海运和空运）近年的变化趋势。

Australia's next TRS：Ongoing preparation in 2018

澳大利亚的下一轮 TRS：2018 年正在进行的准备

9. In 2017，decisions were made to conduct the next TRS，with the work on the 2017 TRS scheduled to commence in mid-2018. The Study will cover all transactions from the calendar year，as opposed to a one-week sample. In addition，it will also include a comparison of average clearance times（from arrival to release）between Authorized Economic Operator（AEO）cargoes and non-AEO cargoes. Importantly，the Study will reflect feedback received from the WCO，as well as continued engagement with other border agencies and industry members.

9. 在 2017 年已决定开展下一轮 TRS，该研究计划于 2018 年中期开始且其样本为本年度的所有贸易数据，而不是一个星期内的贸易数据。此外，将对比“经认证经营者”（AEO）货物和“非经认证经营者”货物的平均清关时间（从运抵到放行）。重要的是，该研究还将对从 WCO 收到的反馈信息做出反应，以及与其他边境机构和行业成员持续合作。

10. The methodology applied to Australia's next TRS and to future Studies will be based on the WCO TRS Guide，and modified in line with local conditions and objectives. It is important to point out that the Australian international trade supply chain involves，and relies on，a highly advanced level of technology，with all of Home Affairs rapidly moving towards a“digital-by-default”approach，and embracing instant development related to automation and digital technologies. It is therefore likely that TRS data or time-stamps will be collected electronically.

10. 澳大利亚开展下一轮和未来 TRS 的方法将基于 WCO TRS 指南，并根据当地条件和目标进行修改。需要指出的是，澳大利亚的国际贸易供应链涉及并依赖先进的技术，所有的政务活动都迅速向“数字化”的方向发展，包括最新的自动化和数字技术。因此，届时 TRS 所需数据或时间戳可能以电子方式收集。

Future developments to add value to the Australian experience

澳大利亚的经验将在未来的发展中产生价值

11. TRS has consistently demonstrated the integral link between early reporting of goods by industry, andearlier clearance times. Indeed, the relationship between early reporting and early clearance has been a significant theme through the TRS series. Opportunities to further improve early reporting are currently being explored through greater dialogue with the WCO, and the development of trade assistance programmes, such as the Australian Trusted Trader and the Single Window.

11. TRS 不断证明了按行业提前申报货物信息和缩短清关时间之间具有不可分割的联系。实际上，在一系列的 TRS 报告中，提前申报与早期审批之间的关系一直是一个重要的主题。澳大利亚目前正在与 WCO 进行更多的对话，并制订贸易援助方案，如澳大利亚可信赖贸易商和单一窗口等，来探讨进一步改进提前申报的可能性。

CAMEROON

喀麦隆

Our story: “We have conducted a TRS and will do another one”

我们的故事：“我们已经开展了一次 TRS，并将再次开展 TRS。”

1. Cameroon conducted a Time Release Study (TRS) from 1 to 15 August 2017. The Study was carried out in accordance with World Customs Organization (WCO) rules, under the supervision of a technical committee (group) made up of leading supply chain stakeholders. This team had previously undergone WCO training on TRS tools (methodology, use of software, etc.).

1. 喀麦隆根据 WCO 的规则，在由主要供应链利益相关方组成的技术委员会（小组）的监督下，于 2017 年 8 月 1 日至 15 日开展了 TRS。该小组先前接受过

WCO 关于 TRS 工具（研究方法、软件使用方法等）的培训。

2. The Memorandum from the Director General of Customs establishing the technical committee also defined its remit, which was to identify bottlenecks in the Customs clearance procedure in the port of Douala and to find solutions to overcome them by means of a collaborative approach.

2. 喀麦隆海关总署署长设立了技术委员会并以备忘录的形式界定了其职责，即查明杜阿拉港海关清关程序中的瓶颈，并通过合作的方式找到解决办法。

3. The group took advantage of the experience of WCO and Ivorian Customs experts. Several activities were performed to ensure smooth implementation of the TRS in Cameroon, and some of the activities were executed with the WCO's technical assistance.

3. 工作组采用了 WCO 和科特迪瓦海关专家的经验。喀麦隆开展了若干活动，以确保 TRS 的顺利开展，其中一些活动是在 WCO 的技术援助下进行的。

Ⅰ. Preparation for the Study, including determination of the scope

Ⅰ. 研究准备，包括范围的确定

4. The first activity was to bring the members of the team together to define the Terms of Reference of the Study, on the basis of its mandate. Procedures in the port of Douala were then explained to all those involved so that each participant had the same level of information on the sequencing of Customs clearance and goods release operations. The committee established a seven-point action plan on the basis of which a budget was drawn up and submitted to the authorities, to ensure the proposed Study would be funded. The plan was based on the following activities:

4. 第一项活动是将小组的成员召集在一起，根据研究任务确定研究的职责范围。然后向所有相关人员说明杜阿拉港的通关程序，以便每个参与者都能熟悉相同级别的海关清关和货物放行作业流程的相关信息。该委员会制订了一项 7 点行动计划，在此基础上制定了预算并提交给当局，以确保该研究能获得财政资助。该计划基于以下活动：

- Mapping of procedures, based on specific information collected during the field visit;
- Identification of sequences of the procedure in relation to the TRS;
- Collection of physical and digital data, based on specially designed forms;
- Determination of intermediate time periods and the overall time period;
- Identification of bottlenecks likely to hinder the smooth movement of goods; and
- Formulation of recommendations for reducing Customs clearance times.
  - 根据实地访问期间收集的具体信息绘制流程图；
  - 确定与 TRS 相关的程序的顺序；
  - 根据专门设计的表格，通过人工和自动化方式收集数据；
  - 确定中间时段和总时段；
  - 确定可能阻碍货物顺利流动的瓶颈；
  - 提出缩短海关清关时间的建议。

5. This approach made it possible to identify not only relevant chronological sequences, but also the various factors or stakeholders that were likely to have an impact on the respective time periods.

5. 该方法不仅可以确定相关的时间顺序，而且可以确定可能对各个时间段产生影响的各种因素或利益相关方。

6. One of the working group's first decisions was to define the target population and units of observation as a whole. Given that this was Cameroon's first experience of a TRS, it was decided to carry out the Study on containers imported for direct consumption, offloaded in the port of Douala from 1 to 15 August 2017, and released by 30 September 2017 at the latest. The team did not wish to take the risk of focusing on all traffic going through the port of Douala (transit, suspensive procedures, etc.). The second issue to be resolved was the choice of month for the Study, bearing in mind the time limits imposed upon the committee. The month of August was selected, and the analysis of available data showed that this period did not normally experience significant increases or decreases in traffic.

6. 工作组最初的决定之一是确定目标总体和整体观察单位。鉴于这是喀麦隆首次开展 TRS，工作组决定对进口用于直接消费的、于 2017 年 8 月 1 日至 15 日在杜阿拉港卸货的、最迟于 2017 年 9 月 30 日放行的集装箱货物进行研究。工作组不愿冒险去研究所有通过杜阿拉港的货流（过境、暂停手续等）。考虑到对委员会规定的时间限制，要解决的第二个问题是选择研究的月份。最终该研究选择了 8 月，通过对现有数据的分析发现，这一时期的货流量通常不会出现明显的增加或减少。

Ⅱ. Collection and recording of data by Cameroon

Ⅱ. 数据收集和记录

7. Two data sources were identified: the various IT systems of port chain stakeholders, and manual data collected from the form previously designed by the technical team responsible for the TRS. This data collection form was designed on the basis that certain information should come from the IT systems of the other parties involved.

7. 数据有两个来源：港口链利益相关方的各种信息系统中的电子数据和从负责 TRS 的技术团队先前设计的表格中收集的手工数据。该数据收集表在设计时已考虑到部分信息需要从其他相关方的信息系统中收集。

8. Physical data collection was preceded by a pilot survey period that was initially scheduled to last two weeks, but which in fact took over one and a half months. This enabled the data collection mechanism to be run in, and difficulties to be identified and corrected before going on to the live stage. This lasted as long as planned, the main problems being lack of involvement of certain supply chain stakeholders and a low level of returns of the form. The group responsible for carrying out the Study therefore decided to increase awareness-raising by means of several field visits.

8. 试点调查前的手工数据收集，最初计划持续两周，但实际上花了一个半月的时间。这使得数据收集机制能够正常运行，并且在进入运行阶段之前能够识别和纠正各种问题。这种情况持续了很长时间，主要问题是缺乏某些供应链利益相关者的参与，表格反馈率较低。因此，负责该研究的工作组决定通过多次实地访问来提高其认识。

9. During the collection period (1 August to 30 September 2017), a memorandum was

issued to make the data collection form a mandatory document to be attached to the detailed declaration. Authorized Customs Brokers（“CDA”） were accordingly required to fill in the physical forms that had been duly prepared for data collection purposes and submit them when the container was taken to a point indicated for that purpose. The data was then captured in the WCO software and a previously identified key was used to combine the manual information with the digitized data to produce a single database.

9. 在数据收集期间（2017 年 8 月 1 日至 9 月 30 日）签发了一份备忘录，使该数据收集表成为附在具体申报表之后的强制性文件。因此，经授权的报关行（“CDA”）必须填写为收集数据而准备的纸质表格，并在集装箱运至指定地点时提交该表格。这些数据随后被 WCO 软件捕获，并使用先前确定的密钥将手工信息与数字化数据相结合，以生成一个单一的数据库。

10. During the survey period，7，046 containers were offloaded，4，143 of which involved goods imported for direct consumption. Containers offloaded during this period which left before 30 September 2017（end date of physical data collection）totalled 3，747（i. e. 90% of containers offloaded which met the Study criteria）. The return of questionnaires，however，was not complete：only 2，471 were actually returned（i. e. a rate of return of forms of 66%）. This rate was regarded as satisfactory for the requirements of the analysis.

10. 在调查期间，共卸载了 7,046 个集装箱，其中 4,143 个为直接消费的进口货物。到 2017 年 9 月 30 日之前（人工收集数据的截止日期），卸载的集装箱总计为 3,747 个（符合该研究标准的 90% 的集装箱已卸载）。然而，调查问卷的反馈并不完整：实际上只返回了 2,471 份（表格的反馈率约为 66%）。该比例被认为满足了分析所需的基本要求。

11. Prior to the analysis，the chronological coherence of data was monitored and the lines of analysis that could best guide decisions favouring a reduction in dwell times in the port of Douala were defined. The second step was to eliminate variables for which there was no，or insufficient，information，and variables for which the information was available but could not be ascribed to a container.

11. 在分析之前，首先监测相关数据的时间顺序，并确定决策的分析路线，以便为缩短杜阿拉港货物的滞留时间。其次剔除没有信息或信息不足的变量，以及那些虽然可用但与集装箱无关的变量。

12. The key variables were then identified, i. e. variables which, irrespective of the procedure (or type of operation), were consistent with some form of chronological sequencing of the procedure. A total of 11 variables were selected, with a rather linear Customs clearance process. These variables were used to define the key sequences. The advantage of the variables was that they enabled the overall dwell time between container offloading and release to be measured by recording the sum of the time periods of the corresponding key sequences.

12. 最后确定关键变量，即与流程（或操作类型）无关但与流程的某种时间顺序一致的变量。总共选择了与海关清关流程相关的 11 个变量。这些变量用于确定关键顺序，其优势在于，它们可以通过记录相应关键顺序的时间总和来测算集装箱从卸载到放行的总滞留时间。

13. Once all the questionnaire forms were collected, they were input into the WCO software and the information from each questionnaire was then compared with the corresponding data available in other electronic systems, including Cameroon's ASYCUDA System.

13. 将所有的调查问卷表都收集完之后，将其输入 WCO 软件中，然后将每个调查问卷中的信息与其他电子系统中相应的可用数据进行比较，包括喀麦隆的 ASYCUDA 系统。

Ⅲ. Data analysis and conclusions: "overall results"

Ⅲ. 数据分析和结论："总体结果"

14. The data analysis showed that the average time taken to release containers for direct consumption in the port of Douala was 22 days. This was consistent with figures produced by the Comité National de la Facilitation des Echanges (CONAFE) [National Trade Facilitation Committee]. This important information showed that a container had to be observed for some 30 days to obtain as much relevant data as possible. In addition, the

container was preferred to the Customs declaration as the principal unit of observation because each container had a single date for exiting the port area. By contrast, since a declaration might cover several containers, the date to be taken as indicating the end of the operation could be problematic (the date of removal of the first container or the date of collection of the last).

14. 数据分析表明，杜阿拉港直接进口用于消费的集装箱的平均放行时间为22天。这与国家贸易便利化委员会（CONAFE）提供的数据一致。这一重要信息表明，为了获得尽可能多的相关数据，必须对集装箱进行大约30天的观测。此外，集装箱比报关单更适合作为主要观测单元，因为每个集装箱都有一个离港的日期。相比之下，由于一份报关单可能涉及多个集装箱，因此若将其视为流程结束的日期可能会有问题（第一个集装箱或最后一个集装箱的提离日期）。

15. Additionally, and according to the fact-based evidence, the average results led to a number of findings, including the following, which have corresponding recommendations to address the problem identified:

15. 此外，以事实为依据，由这些平均结果可获得一些调查发现，包括以下对所发现问题提出的相应建议：

The overall goods release time was rather long: 14 days, 14 hours and 19 minutes. This was largely due to:	Recommendations
• Lack of foresight by shippers, who take an average of over 8 days, 21 hours and 51 minutes to record the declaration after validating the manifest in ASYCUDA. There is a lack of proper communication between shipping agents and importers, meaning that the latter do not have a clear indication of the date and time of arrival of their goods. Moreover, some operators are using the port as a storage area, given that the storage conditions therein are more advantageous. • Late payment of Customs duties (2 days and 6 hours after their calculation). Many importers are facing difficulties in raising the necessary funds to pay their duties and taxes. This is due to the fact that these have to be paid in cash, and credit procedures are yet to be implemented. • Late payment of handling charges (4 days after payment of Customs duties). These charges have to be settled through various manual procedures and this has an impact on delays.	• Promote online services and increase awareness-raising, training and capacity building for shippers and CDAs with respect to foreign trade procedures. • Reactivate the deferred payment procedure and establish the respective conditions for access to this service. • Increase the provision of storage spaces and areas for external goods. • Enhance the dematerialization of foreign trade procedures by introducing a single form (E-Force) in all Customs clearance circuits (pre-Customs clearance/preloading, handling, Customs clearance and collection/embarcwation).

The overall time for the departure of a containerized vehicle is greater than that for a container without a vehicle (5 days, 8 hours and 35 minutes more). This time period is largely due to:	Recommendations
• The time taken for the physical inspection (5 days, 5 hours and 32 minutes), which takes place prior to recording of the declaration. • Late payment of inspection fees: 3 days and 12 hours after approval is granted by the Administration. Inspections of containerized vehicles are carried out prior to submission of the detailed declaration, in order to allow the inspection service provider (SGS) to record all the vehicles' particulars. This procedure is required by SGS so that it can issue its inspection certificate, and can only be carried out with the prior authorization of Customs. Once this authorization has been granted, the importer needs to settle the handling fees and this is precisely where delays have been observed.	• Reduce the number of stakeholders in the procedure for issuing the Customs inspection report on containers transporting vehicles. • Ensure the on-site presence of an inspector scheduled to conduct an inspection in the case of a container transporting vehicles. • Provide DIT (Douala International Terminal) with advance information on containerized vehicles (from shipping lines).

The procedure for electronic payment of port charges takes 2 days, 16 hours and 34 minutes. This time period is largely due to:	Recommendations
• The length of the sequence for submitting the physical file after receiving the pro forma invoice (30% of the time period). • Lengthy port authority procedures, combined with a lack of foresight by Authorized Customs Brokers regarding withdrawal of the pro forma invoice after filing the relevant application.	• Complete the process of digitizing the invoicing and payment of Port Autonome de Douala (PAD) [Autonomous Port of Douala] charges.

整体货物放行时间相当长，为 14 天 14 小时 19 分。主要原因是：	建议
• 托运人缺乏规划，在海关数据自动化系统验证舱单后，平均需要 8 天 21 小时 51 分来申报。船运代理和进口商之间缺乏必要的沟通，进口商没有清楚地说明货物到达的日期和时间。此外，鉴于港口内部的存储条件更方便，一些操作人员将该港口用作存储区域。 • 迟缴关税（计税后 2 天 6 小时）。许多进口商在筹集支付关税和税款必要资金方面面临困难。因为他们必须以现金支付，而且尚未实施信贷程序。 • 延迟支付手续费（支付关税后 4 天）。这些费用必须通过人工进行支付，也导致了延误	• 推动线上服务，增加对托运人和出口货物代理在外贸手续方面的认识、培训和能力建设。 • 重新启动延期付款程序，并为该服务创造相应的条件。 • 增加货物的外部储存空间和区域。 • 通过在所有清关环节（提前海关清关/预装、装卸、清关和收缴/禁运）采用单一表格，提高外贸程序的电子化

（续表）

装载车辆的集装箱放行的总时间要比没有装载车辆的集装箱要长（长5天8小时35分）。主要原因是：	建议
• 在申报之前进行的实物检查需要5天5小时32分。 • 延迟支付检查费：在主管部门批准后3天12小时。在提交详细申报之前，对集装箱车辆进行检查，以便检查服务提供商（SGS）记录所有车辆的详细信息。该程序是SGS要求的，以便其签发检验证书，并且只有在海关事先授权的情况下才能进行。一旦获得授权，进口商需要结清手续费，而这正是本次研究所观察到的出现延迟的地方	• 减少签发运输车辆集装箱海关检查报告流程中利益相关方的数量。 • 对于运输车辆的集装箱，安排检查员在现场进行检查。 • 预先向杜阿拉国际码头提供运输车辆集装箱（来自航运公司）的信息
用电子方式支付港口费用需要2天16小时34分。主要原因是：	**建议**
• 收到形式发票后提交纸质资料的环节所需时间长（占总时间的30%）。 • 漫长的港口当局程序，加上授权的报关行缺乏远见，因此在提交相关申请后无法及时收到形式发票	• 完成杜阿拉自动化港口收费发票和付款的数字化过程

CHILE

智利

1. In 2016, the Chilean Customs Service decided to conduct a Time Release Study (TRS). One of its first activities was to organize a national TRS Workshop in June of the same year, where two World Customs Organization (WCO) experts were invited to share information with Chilean international trade stakeholders on how to carry out a TRS in Chile, taking into account the country's local specificities. The event was attended by officials from the different Customs services throughout Chile, and by representatives from other government agencies, as well as the private sector.

1. 2016年，智利海关当局决定开展TRS。它的首批活动之一是同年6月组织一次国家 TRS 研讨会，邀请了两名 WCO 专家与智利国际贸易利益相关方分享有关如何在智利开展 TRS 的信息，并介绍了该国的特点。智利各地海关部门的官员以及其他政府机构和私营部门的代表参加了此次研讨会。

2. It is important to note that this is the first time that a TRS based on the WCO methodology was carried out in Chile, and the focus was onthe export procedure in a particular port in Chile. The Chilean National TRS Action Plan included seven (7) main stages which incorporated the three phases described in the WCO TRS Guide methodology. The seven stages are described below.

2. 需要指出的是，这是智利首次根据 WCO 的方法开展 TRS，研究重点是智利特定港口的出口程序。智利国家 TRS 行动计划包括七个主要阶段，其中包括 WCO TRS 指南方法中所述的三个阶段。这七个阶段的详情如下：

Stage 1: Creation of a Working Group

阶段 1：组建工作组

3. Overall coordination of the Study was carried out by the Statistical Analysis and Research Unit of the Studies Department, which followed the WCO TRS methodology with some adjustments to ensure that it fitted more closely with the reality of the Chilean international trade environment. The Working Group comprised both permanent members, and members whose participation was on an ad hoc basis.

3. 统计分析和调查部门对此次研究进行了总体协调，该研究对 WCO TRS 的方法进行了一些调整，以确保其符合智利的国情。工作组包括常任理事成员和临时成员。

Stage 2: Determination of the scope of the Study

阶段 2：确定研究范围

4. To determine the scope of the Study, data associated with foreign trade and recordedin National Customs Service databases was previewed and taken into consideration. The criteria

used to define the scope also included a statistical approach, taking into account the importance of consignments to the national economy, and other relevant factors, such as the level of systematization of processes and automatic data recording.

4. 为了确定研究范围，对国家海关数据库中的记录和与外贸有关的数据进行了预览和探究。界定研究范围的标准还包括一种统计方法，其中包括货物对国民经济的重要性及其他相关因素，如系统化水平和自动数据记录。

5. The scope of the Study was based on normal export operations for the aquaculture/fisheries and forestry sectors, at a particular port in Chile where these goods are regularly exported by sea.

5. 该研究的范围是基于水产养殖/渔业和林业部门在智利特定港口的正常出口业务，这些货物定期通过海运出口。

Stage 3: Designing the business process and creating the survey structure

阶段3：设计业务流程并确定调查结构

6. After determining the scope of the Study and conducting some activities, the Working Group designed the business process for the export commodities to be measured. In order to validate the process, in December 2016 the Group made a field visit to confirm the actual procedure followed in the port. The business process described the key points measured relating to the export process.

6. 在确定了研究范围并开展了一些活动之后，工作组设计了待评测出口货物的业务流程。为了验证该流程，专家组于 2016 年 12 月进行了实地访问，以确认港口实际执行的流程。该业务流程涵盖了与出口流程有关的要点。

Stage 4: Determination of the intervals to be measured

阶段4：确定评测的间隔

7. The intervals measured considered the time elapsed between the following stages of the export procedure:

7. 评测的间隔考虑了出口程序以下各阶段之间的时间：

- Authorization for entry into port：In this stage，the physical entry of the goods into the port is authorized，and the National Customs Service confirms if the goods will be inspected or not.
- Authorization for entry into port – Stacking for loading：This stage covers the period after the National Customs Service confirms inspection of the goods，until the goods are placed in the stacking zone，waiting to be loaded aboard the ship.
- Stacking for loading – Loading of goods：This stage covers the time period from the placement of goods in the stacking zone until they are loaded aboard the ship.
- Loading of goods – Departure of ship：Period covering the time between loading the goods aboard the ship，until the ship departs from the port of exportation.

- 批准入港：在这一阶段，获批准的货物实际进入港口，海关部门确认是否对货物进行检查。
- 批准入港—堆放货物：此阶段涵盖从海关部门对货物进行检查之后，直至货物被放置在堆放区，等待被装载到船上的时间段。
- 堆放货物—装载货物：此阶段涵盖从将货物放置在堆放区到将货物装载到船上的时间段。
- 装载货物—船舶离港：涵盖从货物装船到船舶离开港口的时间段。

Stage 5：Data collection

阶段 5：数据收集

8. Once the process had been defined by measuring intervals，and after an in-depth analysis of Customs systems to ascertain what data these systems record，it was felt that the most efficient approach for Chile was to carry out the Study using only the data contained in Customs information systems. Since such data is recorded automatically，a decision was made to collect the data solely via electronic means which keep a record of times，namely the Customs information system.

8. 一旦通过评测间隔确定了流程，而且在对海关系统进行深入分析之后确定了这些系统所记录的数据，发现开展该项研究最有效的方法是使用海关信息系统中的相关数据。由于这些数据是自动记录的，因此仅通过电子方式收集海关信息系统中带时间记录的数据即可。

9. It was further decided that the period for collecting the data would be the second and third quarters of 2016, i. e. between 1 April and 30 September.

9. 收集数据的时间段是 2016 年的第二、三季度，即 4 月 1 日至 9 月 30 日。

Stage 6: Analysis and interpretation of the data

阶段 6：数据分析和说明

10. The final total amount of data for which this desktop measurement was carried out corresponded to 7, 495 export documents.

10. 最终对 7,495 份出口单证进行了测算。

11. These 7, 495 export documents represented 27. 7% of normal exports carried out by the Talcahuano CustomsService and 22. 6% of normal exports carried out at a national level. In both cases, an assessment was made of the aquaculture/fisheries sector and forestry sector, by maritime transport, from 1 April to 30 September 2016.

11. 这 7,495 份出口单证占塔尔卡瓦诺海关正常出口量的 27. 7%，占智利海关正常出口量的 22. 6%。在这种情况下，对水产养殖/渔业部门和林业部门在 2016 年 4 月 1 日至 9 月 30 日间通过海运出境的货物进行了评估。

Stage 7: Findings and recommendations arising from the TRS

阶段 7：TRS 发现和建议

12. The release time was found to be 6. 24 days, a measurement that considers the time from the goods' entry into port, until the ship departs from the port of exportation.

12. 放行时间为 6. 24 天，该时间测算考虑了从货物进入港口到船舶离开港口的时间。

13. The methodology applied by Chile was based on the WCO guidelines. However, some adjustments were made to reflect local conditions and objectives.

13. 智利采用的TRS方法基于WCO发布的指南。但是，为了反映当地的实际情况和目标，对该指南进行了一些调整。

14. Whilst it is recommended that data be considered from all the actors in the export process, one of the difficulties which arose was the definition of a single piece of data that would allow the connection of information from the different actors taking part in the export operation.

14. 虽然建议考虑出口过程中所有参与方的数据，但其困难之一是相关数据定义不统一，还无法将参与出口业务不同参与方的信息关联起来。

15. Although there is an exchange of information between Customs and the port, it is necessary to strengthen that exchange in order to have traceability and thus allow the goods to be controlled in an integrated manner. Some activities at the port are not currently communicated to all the actors in the process. These activities include:

15. 虽然海关和港口之间有信息交换，但有必要加强这种交换，以便信息具有可追溯性，从而使货物得到全面管控。目前，港口的一些活动没有传达给流程中的所有参与者。这些活动包括以下几方面：

a. Automated transfer of the information contained in the consignment note for stored goods; and

b. Transfer of the goods from one ship to another once Customs has authorized the goods' entry into port. These changes can be caused by business and operational issues affecting the shipping company. In turn, this affects Customs, in that goods already declared in a specific export document have to be loaded via a new export document, which is then processed at a later time.

a. 储存货物托运单所载信息的自动传递；

b. 海关批准的货物入港后，将货物从一艘船转移到另一艘船。这可能是由影响航运公司的业务和运营问题引起的。反之，这也会影响海关，因为该货物的出口报关单证需要先更改为新的出口报关单证，然后做处理。

16. The experience gained from this Study will allow Chilean Customs to apply this methodology to other ports or means of transport, as well as to improve procedures, generate indicators and have greater predictability in the context of the release of goods. In addition, knowing the different times involved in the procedure will bring greater transparency to the service delivered by Customs.

16. 从该研究中获得的经验将使智利海关能够将这一方法应用于其他港口或运输工具，并能改进程序、制定指标，在货物放行方面具有更好的可预测性。此外，了解每个程序所涉及的不同时间将使海关提供的服务具有更高的透明度。

17. The automated Customs procedures match the expected outcomes, while the stages that do not have available information show that there are areas for improvement.

17. 自动化的海关监管程序符合预期的结果，而没有可用信息的阶段表明其仍有需改进的地方。

18. A percentage of the information exchanged between Customs and the port was not consistent. A data quality analysis was therefore performed, and it was necessary to exclude 26.7% of the export documents that were initially considered. This occurred because there are operational situations that are not considered in the normal control process. The exceptional procedures used to address them do not reflect reality, resulting in a loss of traceability. This needs to be resolved by modelling and automating all unusual cases that generatc other control and information cycles.

18. 海关与港口之间交换信息的百分比不一致。因此，进行了数据质量分析，有必要排除最初考虑的26.7%的出口单证。这是因为正常控制过程中存在未考虑到的操作情况。用于解决这些问题的特殊程序不能反映实际情况，将导致信息失去可追溯性。这就需要通过建模和自动化所有的可生成其他控制和信息循环的异常案例的方式来解决。

19. The Study showed the need for greater standardization of the information exchanged between the actors in the export process, in order to correctly reflect the traceability of the process measured.

19. 该研究表明，有必要在更大程度上统一出口过程中各参与方之间所交换的信息，以便正确反映所测算过程的可追溯性。

GEORGIA

格鲁吉亚

1. The Georgia Revenue Service (GRS) has been conducting the Time Release Study (TRS) on a periodic basis since 2013, while institutionalizing the TRS as an important tool for trade facilitation in Georgia. GRS carried out its last Time Release Study on Customs Procedures from 16 to 21 February 2016. The TRS was conducted by the GRS Working Group alongside others, and was monitored by representatives of the private sector, acting as observers. It should be noted that a similar Study was conducted from 4 to 11 November 2013. In preparing for the Study, GRS was supported by USAID, the EPI project and business representatives.

1. 自 2013 年以来，格鲁吉亚税收海关服务局（GRS）定期开展 TRS，同时将 TRS 制度化，作为格鲁吉亚贸易便利化的重要工具。GRS 于 2016 年 2 月 16 日至 21 日对海关流程开展了最新的研究。TRS 由 GRS 工作组与其他成员一起开展，并由私营部门的代表作为观察员进行监督。应该指出的是，GRS 于 2013 年 11 月 4 日至 11 日实施了类似的研究。在准备这项研究的过程中，GRS 获得了美国国际开发署、EPI 项目和商业代表的支持。

2. The WCO TRS Guide was adapted to the specificities of Georgia's Customs system, within the scope of the flexibility allowed, taking into account technological arrangements related to the flow process of cargo. The Time Release Study was conducted in three phases: (1) preparation and planning, (2) data collection, and (3) data analysis and conclusions. It is important to point out that all government functions related to the entire clearance process are delegated to GRS.

2. 根据格鲁吉亚海关系统的具体情况并考虑了与货物流通过程有关的技术安排，对 WCO TRS 指南在允许的范围内进行了灵活的调整。TRS 分三个阶段开展：（1）准备和计划；（2）数据收集；（3）数据分析和结论。必须指出的是，与整个清关流程相关的所有政府职能都委托给了 GRS。

Highlights of the 2016 TRS

2016 年 TRS 的亮点

3. The creation of the national TRS Working Group, decisions made, and various other details, are given below.

3. 国家 TRS 工作组的组建、做出的决定和其他细节包括以下方面：

- The Working Group consisted of representatives from GRS, the Business Ombudsman of Georgia, the Business Association of Georgia, the Association of Maritime Agents and Brokers, Panalpina Georgia Ltd (the contractor of BP Exploration (Caspian Sea) Ltd), IDS Borjomi Georgia, the International Freight Forwarders Association and the USAID programme "Governing for Growth (G4G)".

- 工作组由 GRS、格鲁吉亚商业监察员、格鲁吉亚商业协会、海事代理人和经纪人协会、泛亚皮纳格鲁吉亚有限公司［BP 勘探（里海）有限公司的承包商］、IDS Borjomi 格鲁吉亚公司、国际货运代理协会以及美国国际开发署“促进增长（G4G）”计划的代表组成。

- One of the first decisions of the Working Group was to determine the geographical scope of the Study. As this was the second TRS, it was decided to conduct it at the busiest and most important Customs offices only (Customs crossing points and inland Customs offices), a practice accepted and advocated by the TRS Guide.

- 工作组的第一项决定是确定研究的地理范围。由于这是第二次开展 TRS，因此决定在最繁忙和最重要的现场海关（海关过境点和内陆现场海关）开展，这是 TRS 指南提倡的做法。

- The Working Group agreed that the TRS had to be implemented in parallel stages in all of the selected Customs offices. The data collection process took place on six consecutive days, from 16 to 21 February 2016. Georgia's Customs offices operate 24/7.

- 工作组认为，TRS 必须在所有选定的海关办事处同时实施。数据收集工作从 2016 年 2 月 16 日至 21 日连续进行六天。格鲁吉亚的海关办事处全天候运作。

- The selected Customs offices are the largest in the country and serve almost all categories of goods. High-intensity traffic and diversity of goods were some of the main determinants in selecting these Customs offices.

- 选定的海关办事处是全国范围内规模最大的，几乎能为所有类别的货物提供服务。高强度的运输和货物的多样性是选择这些海关办事处的主要因素。

- In line with the Working Group's decision, the TRS was performed for all categories (types) of goods, regardless of country of origin, HS code, means of transport, volume of commodity shipment, or other factors.

- 根据工作组的决定，对所有类别（类型）的货物都开展了 TRS，而不考虑原产国、海关编码、运输工具、商品数量或其他因素。

- As to data collection, it is important to underscore the use of specially designed questionnaires (for Customs crossing points, as well as for inland Customs offices) to collect the necessary information during the TRS process. The questionnaires were agreed with all the parties in the Working Group, and covered all the procedures falling within the scope of the Study, the aim being to gain information that was as precise as possible on specific procedures. The questionnaires also made it possible to determine the overall time spent on Customs formalities for various types of commodity shipments.

- 该研究使用了专门设计的调查问卷（针对海关过境点以及内陆海关办事处）收集必要的信息。调查问卷得到了工作组所有相关方的认可，涵盖了研究范围内的所有程序，目的是获得关于特定流程的尽可能精确的信息。调查问卷还可以确定各类商品运输办理海关手续的总时间。

• Relevant instructions were provided to Customs officers on how to enter data into the questionnaires. The researchers entered information on printed forms, and then transferred the data collected into electronic format, following completion of the questionnaires. Each questionnaire was numbered, and authenticated by the officer's signature, the date and time.

• 向海关关员提供了调查问卷填写说明。研究员在纸质表格上填写相应信息，然后将收集到的数据转换成电子格式。每一份问卷都有编号，并由关员签名、注明填表日期和时间。

• The questionnaires on automated Customs procedures implemented at inland Customs offices were filled out on the basis of the information recorded in the databases, immediately following the completion of the procedures. The sources of information used were e-CUSTOMS (the upgraded version of ASYCUDA World), Oracle, automatic Customs data processing systems, and QMATIC.

• 对于实施了自动化海关监管程序的内陆海关办事处的调查问卷，是在完成相关程序后立即根据数据库中记录的信息填写的。使用的信息来源是电子海关（ASYCUDA World 的升级版）、Oracle、海关自动数据处理系统和 QMATIC。

• It should be noted that the volume of cargo turnover at the Customs offices selected for the Time Release Study is so high that it was impossible to collect information about all commodity shipments. Sampling of shipments was therefore necessary, and the following sampling strategy was followed: at Customs crossing points (CCPs), the information was collected for every 10th commodity shipment in three different shifts over a 24-hour period; in the inland Customs offices, all data on the import of goods was collected.

• 应当指出，为 TRS 选定的海关办事处的货物流量太大，不可能收集到所有货物运输的信息。因此，有必要根据以下抽样策略进行抽样：在过境点海关，在 24 小时的时间分为三个班次、每个班次收集 10 批货物的信息；在内陆海关，收集所有货物的进口数据。

4. An impact analysis of results, focusing on the 2013 and 2016 Time Release Studies, is below.

4. 以下是研究结果的影响分析，重点是2013年和2016年的TRS结果：

• Prior to starting data analysis, the precision and accuracy of the data was verified. Documentary information collected was summarized in electronic format. The results were summarized using statistical processing programs. Final results were then analysed to draw conclusions.

• 在开始数据分析之前，对数据的精度和准确性进行了验证。首先将所收集的单证信息以电子格式汇总，其次使用统计处理程序对数据进行总结，最后对最终结果进行分析以得出结论。

• The institutionalization of this particular project streamlined the critical items specified in the questionnaires, as the Customs administration was able to compare the latest TRS results against the previous ones, and to objectively evaluate positive achievements and remaining shortcomings. The 2016 TRS covered the following main Customs offices: Customs Crossing Point Sarpi (on the border with Turkey), Customs Clearance Zones Tbilisi, Batumi and Poti, and also the Customs Crossing Point "Poti and Kulevi sea ports and Poti Free Industrial Zone".

• 这一特定项目的制度化简化了调查表中的关键项目，同时海关能够将最新的TRS结果与以前的结果进行比较，并客观地评估目前已取得的成就和仍然存在的不足。2016年的TRS涵盖了以下主要海关办事处：海关过境点Sarpi（位于土耳其边境）、通关区第比利斯、巴统和波蒂，以及海关过境点"波蒂和库列维海港和波蒂自由工业区"。

• A comparative analysis of the 2013 and 2016 Studies generally illustrates improvements in terms of the average time taken to accomplish a number of activities. For example, Graph 1.1 shows that, between 2013 and 2016, the average times taken for transit and import procedures decreased in respect of cargo which was not subject to sanitary and phytosanitary (SPS) intervention and which involved the least possible intervention in terms of other controls.

• 对 2013 年和 2016 年研究的比较分析总体上表明，完成多项活动所需的平均时间有所减少。如图所示，对于不受卫生和植物检疫（SPS）干预且受其他管制措施干预最少的货物，在 2016 年完成过境和进口手续所需的平均时间比 2013 年减少了。

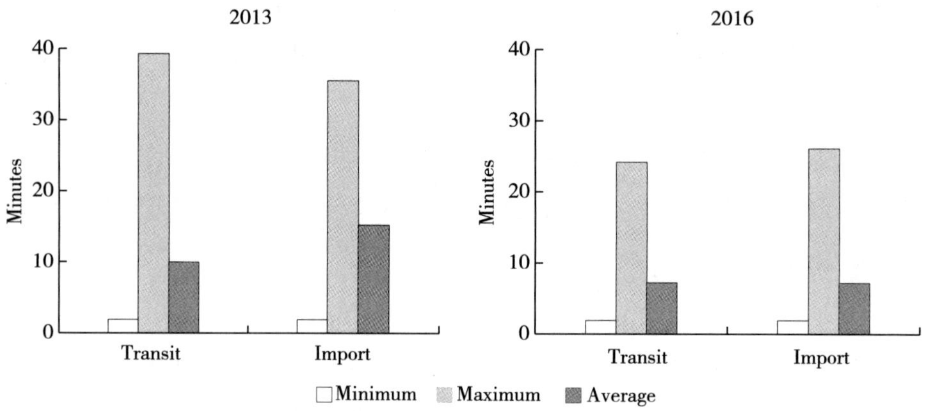

Import and transit times at CCP Sarpi

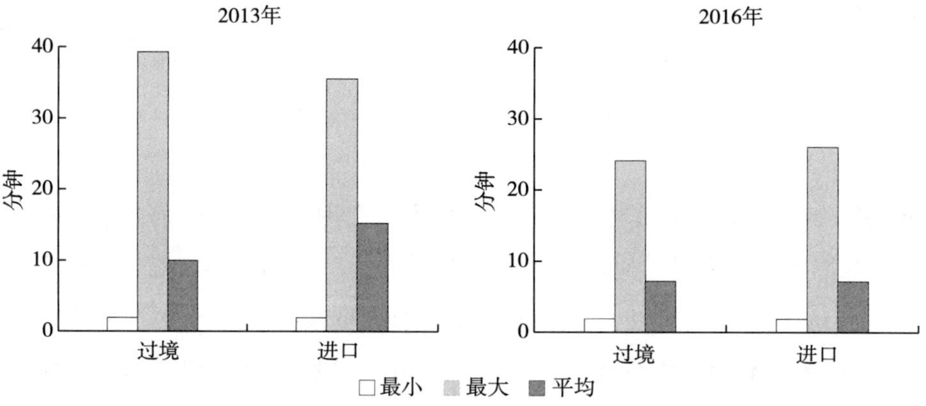

海关过境点 Sarpi 的进口和过境所需时间

• A further example, in relation to importation, can be seen in Graph 1. 2 below. This shows that the average time required in 2016 for cargo to undergo weighing procedures in Georgia was less than in 2013, indicating a clear improvement from one TRS cycle to the next.

• 关于进口的另一个例子，请参见下图。2016 年格鲁吉亚对货物进行称重所需的平均时间比 2013 年有所减少，这表明从一个 TRS 周期到下一个 TRS 周期，情况存在明显改善。

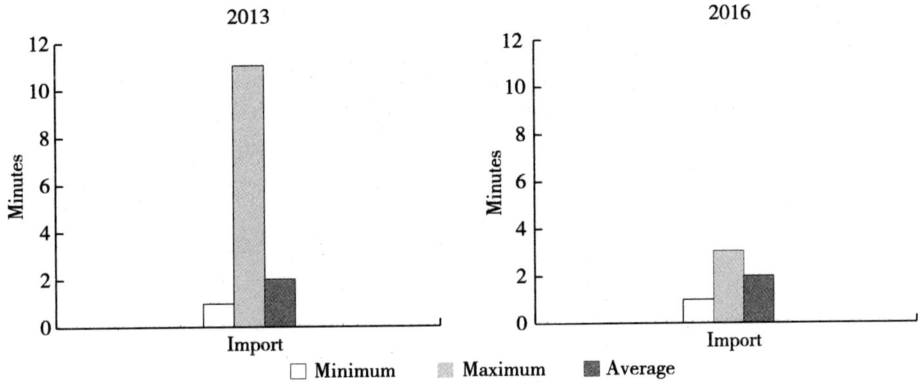

Import clearance times at CCP Sarpi for weight goods

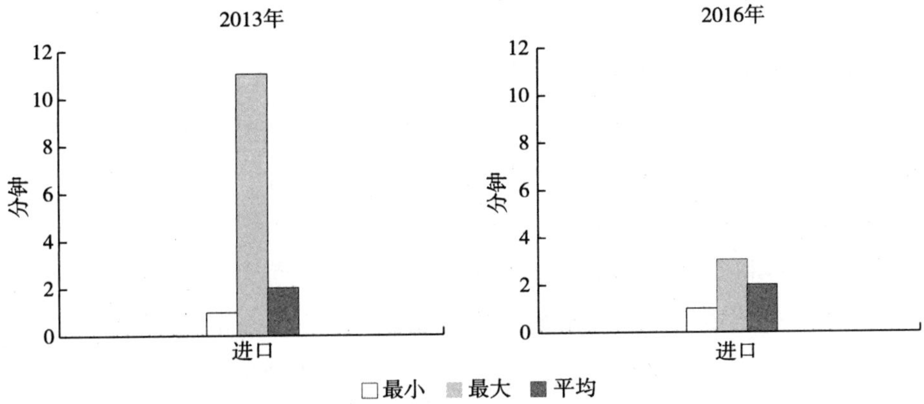

海关过境点 Sarpi 在进口清关流程中货物称重所需时间

• Graph 1.3 below indicates, again with regard to importation, that the process of scanning goods also improved between 2013 and 2016, involving an average reduction of one minute. (This process relates only to the x-raying of cargo).

• 下图也表明，在进口方面，对货物进行扫描这一过程，2016 年比 2013 年有所改善，平均减少了 1 分钟（此过程仅与对货物进行 X 射线扫描有关）。

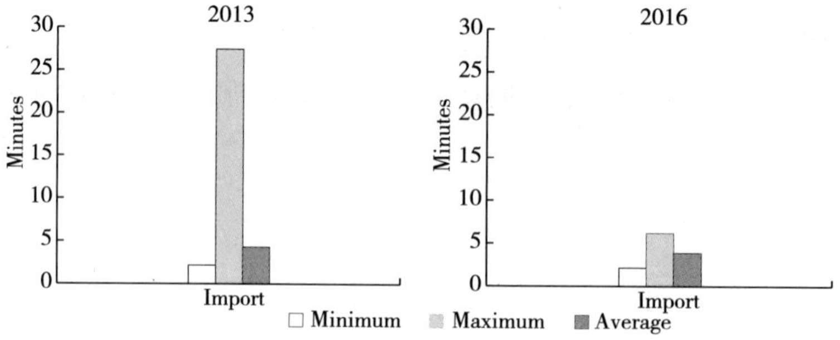

Import clearance times at CCP Sarpi for scanned goods

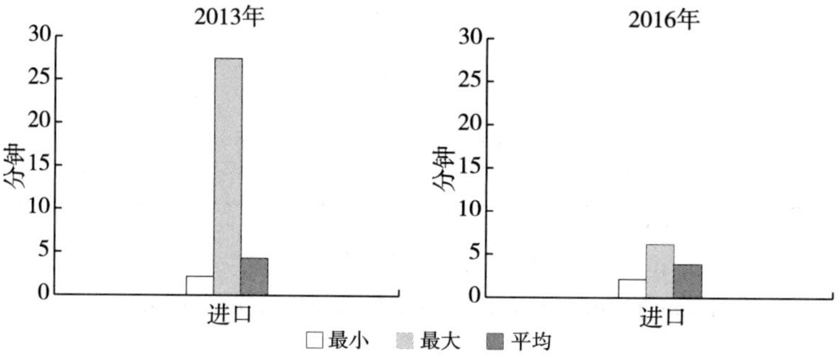

海关过境点 Sarpi 在进口清关流程中货物扫描时间

- In terms of the import procedure for cargo subject to SPS intervention for 2013 and 2016, Graph 1.4 below clearly shows a reduction in average times for sanitary and phytosanitary control. It is important to recognize that SPS intervention in the clearance process was still one of the largest challenges facing the Georgia Revenue Service in 2016.

- 就 2013 年和 2016 年货物受 SPS 干预的进口程序而言，下图清楚地显示了受卫生和植物卫生管制措施所需的平均时间减少了。需要注意的是，SPS 在清关过程中的干预仍然是格鲁吉亚税收海关服务局在 2016 年面临的最大挑战之一。

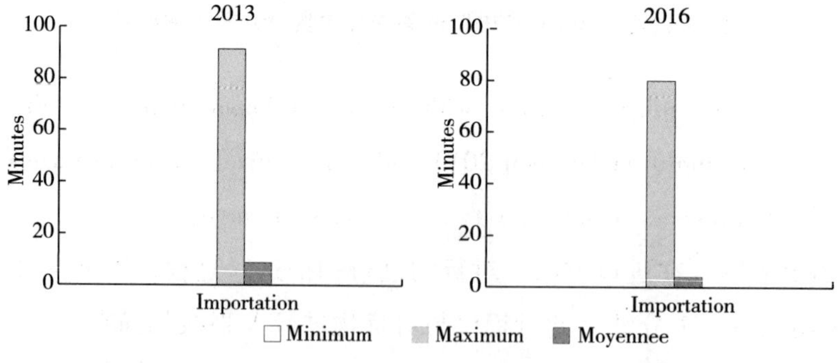

Import clearance times at CCP Sarpi for goods subject to SPS intervention

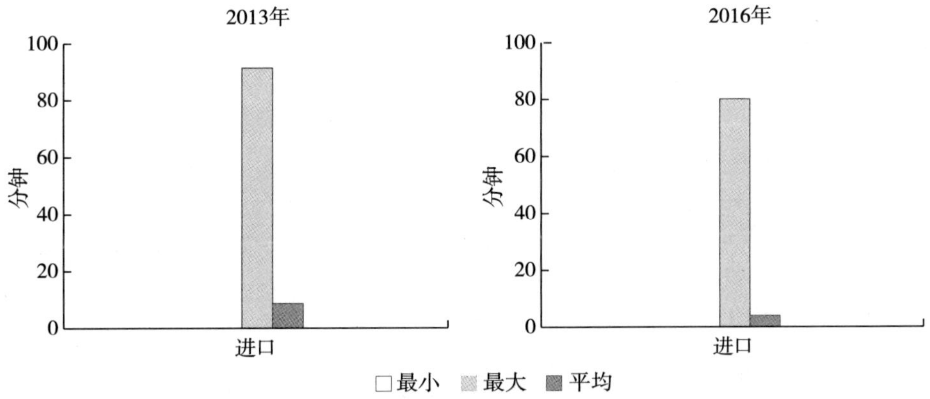

海关过境点 Sarpi 在进口清关流程中货物受 SPS 干预所需时间

5. General findings and recommendations from the 2016 TRS are in the table below.

5. 下表列出了 2016 年 TRS 的发现和建议。

Findings	Recommendations
Georgia's geographic complexity in terms of the natural landscape, and the architectural restrictions on Customs offices, add days in terms of time.	Ensure that alternative means of logistics provision are in place permanently.
Delays to SPS cargo controls due to lack of laboratories.	More laboratories need to be created. Mitigating or addressing this problem will necessitate a greater allocation of financial resources by government.
From 2013 to 2016, the percentage increase in advance cargo declarations was about 30%. However, that increase is not yet sufficient, and it needs to improve further in the short or medium term.	Greater promotion is needed of advance cargo declarations. The GRS therefore needs to introduce a plan to address constraints.
Georgia already has sufficient expertise to increase the scope of TRS so that it extends to other modes of transport or covers other aspects related to the flow of cargo.	Increase or enlarge the scope of TRS so that it includes, for example, other modes of transport relevant to Georgia.
TRS data and results are more reliable for assessing and making judgments on the performance of Georgia's cargo clearance process compared to other international performance indicators or indexes (e.g. the World Bank's Doing Business indicators and Logistics Performance Index, and the OECD's Trade Facilitation Indicators).	International benchmarks evaluating the business climate, including Customs procedures, should consider TRS results in their assessments. Such results are more reliable, since they are based on accurate data and do not allow for perceived performance.

发现	建议
受格鲁吉亚的地理复杂性以及海关的布局限制，在时间上增加了几天	确保替代性的物流方式持续有效
由于缺乏实验室，导致 SPS 管制货物延误	需要建立更多的实验室。政府更多的财政支持才能减轻或解决这一问题
2013 年至 2016 年，提前申报货物的增长率约为 30%。然而，这一增长率还不够，需要在短期或中期内进一步提高	需要加强对货物提前申报的宣传。因此，GRS 需要制订解决此问题的计划
格鲁吉亚已经拥有足够的专业知识来扩大开展 TRS 的范围，使其扩展到其他运输方式或涵盖与货物流通有关的其他方面	增加或扩大 TRS 的范围，例如使之包括与格鲁吉亚有关的其他运输方式
与其他国际绩效指数或指标（如世界银行的营商环境指标和物流绩效指数以及经合组织的贸易便利化指标）相比，TRS 的数据和结果在评估和判断格鲁吉亚货物清关过程的绩效方面更为可靠	评估商业环境的国际基准，包括海关监管程序，应在评估中考虑 TRS 的结果。TRS 的结果更可靠，因为它是基于准确的数据而不是感觉

INDIA

印度

Ⅰ. Background

Ⅰ. 背景

1. The Indian Customs Administration, led by the Central Board of Excise and Customs (CBEC), has been at the forefront of continuously enhancing the facilitation of cross-border trade in line with the Government of India's policy objective of improving the ease of doing business.

1. 由印度消费税和海关中央委员会（CBEC）领导的印度海关当局一直按照印度政府提高便利性的政策目标，不断加强跨境贸易的便利化。

2. Facilitation of legitimate trade is a core objective of Indian Customs' modernization

programme. The National Trade Facilitation Action Plan, developed in response to the WTO TFA, has set a goal of reducing the average release time for import goods to within three days for sea cargo, within two days for air cargo and Inland Container Depots, and to the same day for Land Customs Stations. Similarly, the goal for release of export goods is under two days for sea cargo, and on the same day for air cargo, Inland Container Depots and Land Customs Stations.

2. 促进合法贸易是印度海关现代化计划的核心目标。印度海关根据 WTO《贸易便利化行动计划》制订的《国家贸易便利化行动计划》，设定了一个目标，即将进口海运货物的平均放行时间缩短到三天之内、空运货物和内陆集装箱场站的平均放行时间缩短到两天之内、陆路海关的平均放行时间缩短到当天。同样，出口货物的放行目标是海运货物不超过两天，空运货物、内陆集装箱场站和陆路海关则在当天放行。

3. CBEC and Jawaharlal Nehru Custom House (JNCH) have implemented several recommendations from previous TRS Reports and introduced measures such as electronic Single Window, Direct Port Delivery for imports, and Direct Port Entry for exports to reduce release times. JNCH TRS 2018 was conceived and conducted in the above context. A further aim was to measure the impact of statutory, policy, administrative and ICT improvements undertaken by Indian Customs and JNCH.

3. CBEC 和 Jawaharlal Nehru 海关（JNCH）执行了之前 TRS 报告中的一些建议并采取了一些措施，如电子化的单一窗口、进口方面的港口直接交货和出口方面的直接进入港口，以缩短放行时间。Jawaharlal Nehru 海关就是在上述背景下筹划和开展 2018 年 TRS 的。该研究的另一个目的是评测印度海关和 Jawaharlal Nehru 海关实施的法规、政策、行政、信息和通信技术改进措施等产生的影响。

4. The Jawaharlal Nehru Port Trust (JNPT) is India's largest containerized port, handling about 55% of the containerized cargo across all major ports in India, and is expected to double its capacity to about ten million TEUs by 2022.

4. 加瓦拉尔·尼赫鲁港（JNPT）是印度最大的集装箱港口，处理印度大约 55% 的集装箱货物，预计到 2022 年，其容量将翻一番，达到约 1000 万标准箱。

5. CBEC conducted TRS 2018 at JNCH by engaging various stakeholders as partners, with the scope of the Study covering both imports and exports. It highlighted the role of the partner government agencies, and commodities and processes that may merit greater attention in the national effort to improve the ease of doing business. The rigorous methodology was supported by collecting data from various sources available with different stakeholders. The entire Study was conducted using Customs in-house resources and those of PGAs to obtain the highest level of sensitization and involvement, besides ownership of the results.

5. CBEC 在尼赫鲁港开展了 2018 年的 TRS，邀请了不同的利益相关方作为合作伙伴，研究范围涵盖货物进口和出口。它强调了政府机构伙伴（PGA）的作用，以及在改善营商便利性的过程中值得重点关注的商品和流程。该研究收集了不同利益相关方提供的来自各个方面的数据。整个研究使用的是海关内部资源和政府机构伙伴资源，以获得最高水平的准确性和参与度。

6. Objectives

- Spreading awareness about release times among all stakeholders, and their role in reduction of those times.
- Measuring the distance towards achieving the National Trade Facilitation Action Plan target of a release time of three days for import of sea cargo, and two days for export of sea cargo.
- Identifying categories of bills of entry, commodities and sub-processes that are relatively more time-consuming, with a view to suggesting measures to improve the corresponding release times.
- Improving coordinated border management by seeking to approximate the release times associated with different prominent agencies.
- Assessing the impact of statutory and administrative changes on trade behaviour over time, and identifying reasons for non-compliance through sample surveys among outliers.

6. 目标

- 在所有利益相关方中传播关于放行时间的重要性及其在缩短放行时间中所起作用的意识。

- 评测与实现《国家贸易便利化行动计划》目标的距离，即进口海运货物的放行时间为三天，出口海运货物的放行时间为两天。
- 确定比较耗时的报关单、商品和子流程的类别，以提出缩短相应放行时间的措施。
- 通过设法缩短不同机构的放行时间，协调提高边境管理水平。
- 评估法定和行政的变更对后续贸易行为的影响，并通过对异常值进行抽样调查来确定不合规的原因。

7. In terms of sample size related to import, the Study covered all the 14, 973 bills of entry filed during the sample period of seven days in 2018 (i. e. 1 –7 January 2018), and trackedthem till 7 February, when the data was frozen for analysis.

7. 在与进口相关的样本量方面，该研究涵盖了 2018 年 7 天内（2018 年 1 月 1 日至 7 日）提交的全部 14,973 份报关单，并跟踪这些报关单到 2 月 7 日，在冻结状态下对数据进行分析。

8. It is important to highlight that "release time" in this Study is defined as the time taken from the grant of "entry inwards", to grant of "out of charge" by Customs in respect of both normal bills of entry (where the bill of entry is filed after grant of entry inwards), and advance bills of entry (where the bill of entry is filed before grant of entry inwards).

8. 需要强调的是，该研究中的"放行时间"是指报关单从海关批准"准予进境"到海关发出"放行指令"所用的时间，该报关单包括一般进口报关单（此类进口报关单在批准入境后提交）和预申报进口报关单（此类报关单在批准入境前提交）这两类。

Ⅱ. Results

Ⅱ. 结果

9. Imports

- The all-in-one average release time for imports has improved significantly, from 181. 34 hours in 2017, to 144. 18 hours in 2018. This release time is at variance with the findings of the World Bank's Ease of Doing Business Report. The World Bank perception of the release time for auto components imported from South Korea, at 267 hours, is significantly higher than the comparable release time of 126. 54 hours found under TRS 2018.

9. 进口

- 进口产品的一体化平均放行时间明显缩短，从 2017 年的 181. 34 小时下降到 2018 年的 144. 18 小时。该放行时间与世界银行《营商环境报告》的调查结果不符。世界银行认为，从韩国进口的汽车零部件的放行时间为 267 小时，明显多于 2018 年 TRS 中提出的 126. 54 小时。

- The graph below shows the distance towards achieving the National Trade Facilitation Action Plan target of 72 hrs.

- 下图显示了与实现 72 小时放行的国家贸易便利化行动计划目标的距离。

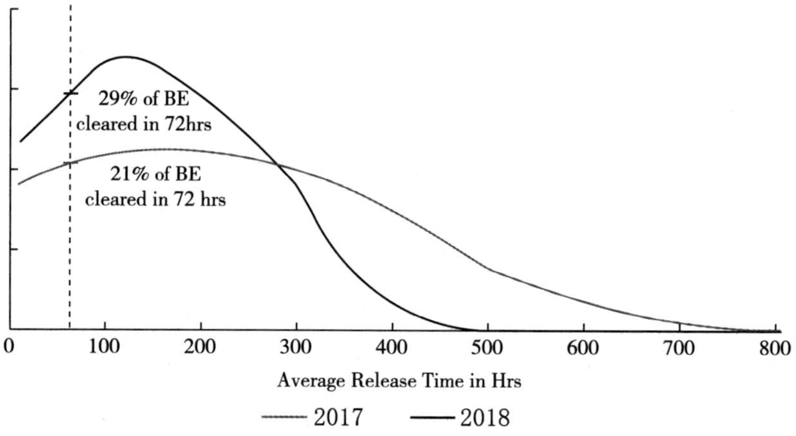

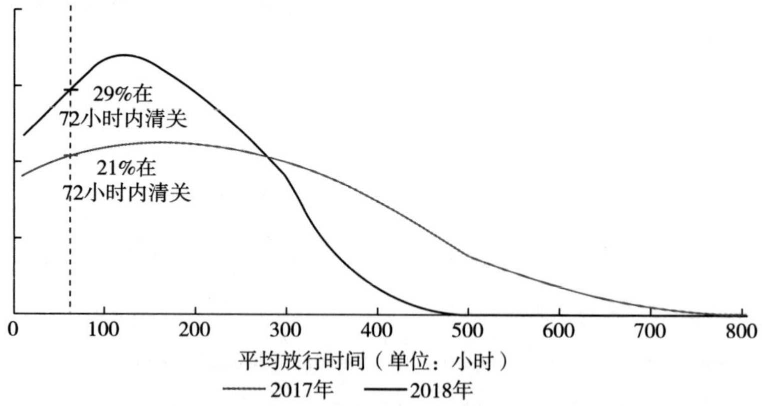

• The normal distribution in the graph shows that: (a) 29% of bills of entry (as against 21% in 2017) were cleared within 72 hours; (b) about two thirds of the bills of entry were cleared in less than the average release time of 144 hours, with the remaining one third of consignments adversely impacting the release time; and (c) a significantly lower number of bills of entry entailed inordinate delays.

• 图中的正态分布表明:

(a) 29%的报关单(2017年为21%)在72小时内清关;

(b) 约三分之二的货物在144小时的平均放行时间内清关，其余三分之一的货物对放行时间产生了不利影响;

(c) 过度延误的报关单的数量大大减少了。

• The Study has identified four elements that must be at the core of the drive towards reaching the TFA target of 72 hours, namely: (a) a higher share of advance bills of entry; (b) greater full facilitation, with no assessment or examination; (c) more AEO enrolment; and (d) higher DPD clearances.

• 该研究确定了实现72小时放行目标的四个核心要素，即:

(a) 提高预申报报关单的占比;

(b) 进行更大程度的全面便利化，无须评估或检查;

(c) 增加AEO的数量;

(d) 提高DPD清关。

• The release time for advance bills of entry was 113.54 hours, compared to 187.30 hours for normal bills of entry.

• 预申报报关单的放行时间为113.54小时，而一般报关单的放行时间为187.30小时。

• AEO bills of entry enjoyed higher full facilitation, at 84.6%, compared to 60.2% overall, and had an average release time of 103.06 hours. The advance facilitated bills of entry filed by AEOs had an impressive release time of 69.18 hours.

• AEO进口报关单的完全便利化程度更高，为84.6%，而总体便利化程度为

60.2%，平均放行时间为 103.06 小时。AEO 提交的便利化的预申报入境报关单的放行时间明显缩短，为 69.18 小时。

- The number of DPD bills of entry has increased by 83.7% since 2017. With a full facilitation level of 75.1%, the average release time for DPD advance facilitated bills of entry was 65.36 hours.

- 自 2017 年以来，DPD 入境报关单的数量增加了 83.7%。在 75.1% 的全面便利化水平下，DPD 提交的预申报入境报关单的平均放行时间为 65.36 小时。

- The Study identified six categories of commodities, based on specific requirements associated with them, to highlight their impact on release times, which is sometimes hidden in the arithmetic averages. The average release times are presented below.

- 根据特定要求，该研究确定了六类商品，以明确其放行时间。平均放行时间如下表所示。

S. NO.	COMMODITY	RELEASE TIME (IN HOURS)
1	Food items (chapters 7, 8 and 9)	247.18
2	Pharmaceuticals (chapter 30)	138.49
3	Fertilizers (chapter 31)	134.19
4	Plastics (chapter 39)	131.54
5	Textiles (chapters 59 and 60)	173.06
6	Auto components (tariff heading 8708)	91.52

序号	商品	放行时间（单位：小时）
1	食品（第7、8、9章）	247.18
2	药品（第30章）	138.49
3	肥料（第31章）	134.19
4	塑料（第39章）	131.54
5	纺织品（第59章和第60章）	173.06
6	汽车零部件（税目8708）	91.52

10. Single Window – partners in a common pursuit

● The release times for bills of entry that were referred to participating government agencies such as Animal Quarantine, Plant Quarantine, the Food Safety Authority, Textile Committee, Wildlife Control, etc. under Single Window (SWIFT) were quantified separately to obtain a perspective on release times in terms of PGAs.

10. 单一窗口——合作伙伴的共同追求

● 在单一窗口（SWIFT）下，分别量化了提交给其他政府参与机构（如动物检疫机构、植物检疫机构、食品安全局、纺织委员会、野生动物保护机构等）的报关单的放行时间，以清楚地看到其他政府参与机构的报关单放行时间。

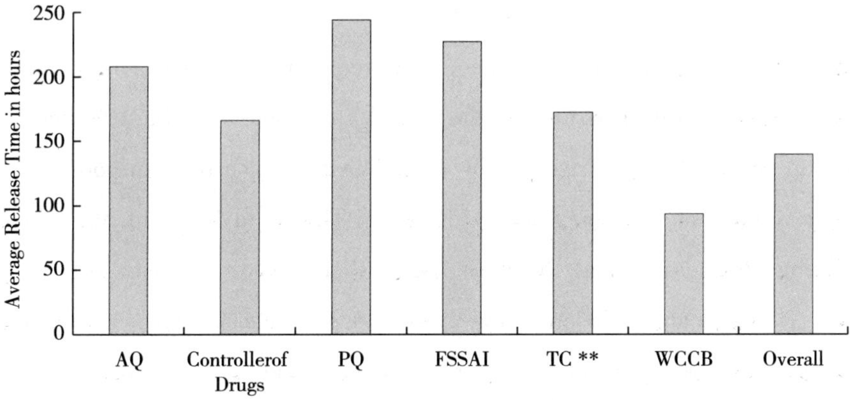

** data pertains to chapter 59 & 60 only

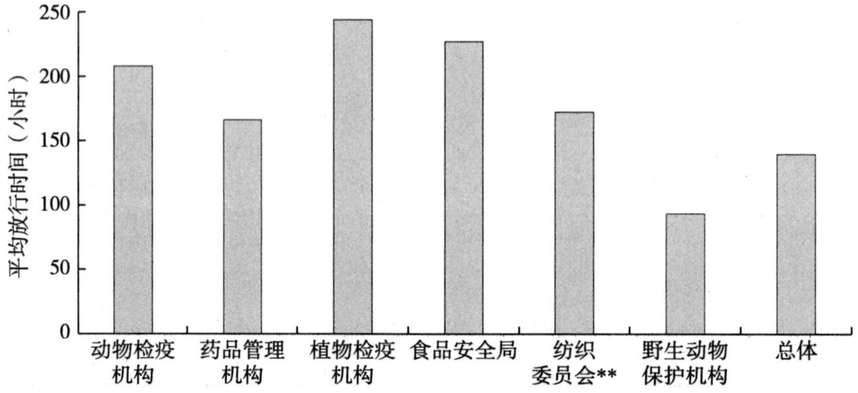

11. Exports

- The methodology adopted for computation of export release involved collecting data concerning the top five exporters of each of six major categories of goods: (i) frozen meat, (ii) frozen fish, (iii) pharmaceuticals, (iv) automobile parts, (v) two-wheelers and three-wheelers (bikes, auto rickshaws), and (vi) electrical machinery (falling under chapter 85).

11. 出口

- 计算出口放行时间所采用的方法涉及六大类商品中排名前五的出口商的数据:(一)冷冻肉;(二)冷冻鱼;(三)药品;(四)汽车零部件;(五)两轮车和三轮车(自行车、汽车人力车);以及(六)电机(属于第85章)。

- The gross average export release time, measured from the time of departure of cargo from factory premises till departure of the vessel, was found to be 108 hours. The net average export release time, arrived at by excluding the domestic transport time from the gross average export release time, was 84.1 hours. This is in line with the World Bank's Ease of Doing Business Report 2018 finding, where export release time is about 85 hours. There is significant variation in the average export release time, with a net average export release time of 53.4 hours for frozen meat, and of 99.7 hours for electrical machinery.

- 总体平均出口放行时间(从货物离开工厂到船舶离开港口的时间)为108小时。将国内运输时间从总平均出口放行时间中剔除后,得出的净平均出口放行时间为84.1小时。这与世界银行《2018年营商环境报告》的调查结果（出口放行时间约为85小时）相符。不同商品平均出口放行时间存在显著差异，冷冻肉净平均出口放行时间为53.4小时、电机净平均出口放行时间为99.7小时。

The average time taken, in terms of stages, in the export process is presented below:

出口过程中各环节所需的平均时间如下图所示。

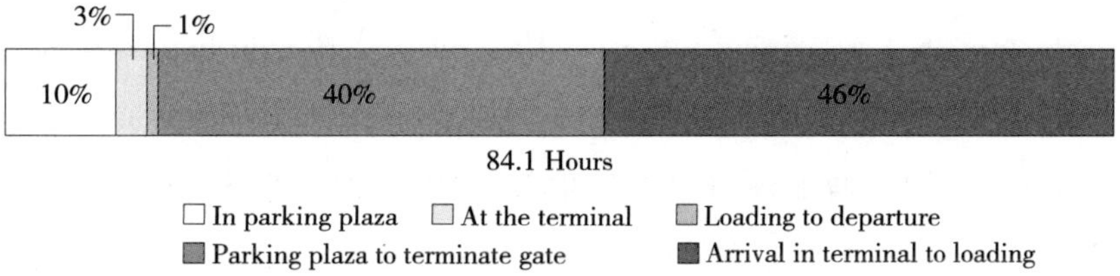

Net Time Share in Export Process

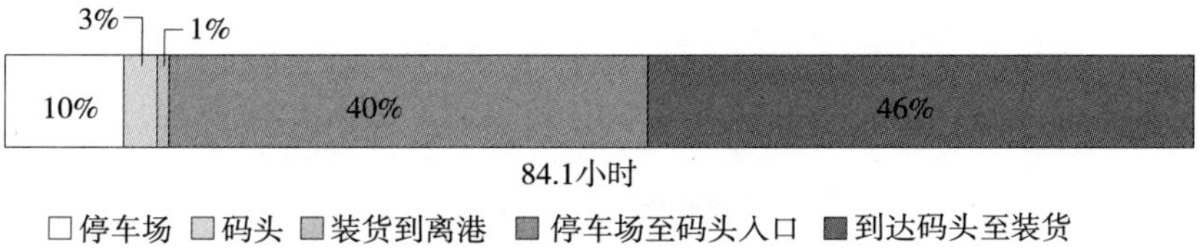

出口过程中各环节所用的时间占总放行时间的比例

Ⅲ. Recommendations

Ⅲ. 建议

12. Based on the detailed analysis, the recommendations below have been made to reduce the release time for import cargo.

12. 根据详细分析，为缩短进口货物放行时间，提出以下建议：

- Constant review of the risk parameters and profile to increase the level of full facilitation (involving neither assessment nor examination).

- 持续审查风险参数和概况，以提高完全便利化水平（既不评估也不涉及检查）；

- The need for physical examination of cargo must be more carefully considered, and scanning capability at the terminal premises should be strengthened.

- 必须更加仔细地审视对货物进行实际检查的需求，并加强码头的 X 光扫描检查能力。

- Enhance the outreach programme to increase the share of advance bills of entry, make use of the e-Sanchit facility (for online uploading of supporting documents with bills of entry in Single Window) to minimize the need to raise queries during assessment, and to encourage prompt filing of normal bills of entry and prompt payment of duty.

- 增强延展计划，增加预申报进口报关单的占比，利用 e-Sanchit 设施（使用在单一窗口在线传送附证明文件的进口报关单），最大程度地减少在评估期间进一步查询的需求，鼓励尽快提交一般入境报关单并及时缴纳关税。

- Effective engagement with regular importers/exporters and logistics operators to increase enrolment under the AEO and DPD schemes.

- 与规范的进口商/出口商和物流运营商进行有效合作，增加 AEO 和 DPD 的数量。

- Partner government agencies, such as FSSAI, ADC, PQ and TC, should review their risk parameters and processes to reduce the share of interdicted bills of entry.

- 与其他政府机构（如 FSSAI、ADC、PQ 和 TC）加强合作，审查其风险参数和流程，以减少禁止入境货物对应报关单的数量。

- Develop a logistics hub in the vicinity of the port to house various offices of PGAs and other stakeholders, and state-of-the-art laboratories.

- 在港口附近建立物流枢纽，以容纳其他政府机构和利益相关方的各个办公室以及先进的实验室。

- Installation of fixed and mobile scanners by port terminals will help reduce the recourse to physical examination of goods and the time involved in such scanning, as well as improve interdiction and consequent effectiveness in risk profiling.

• 通过在港口码头安装固定式和移动式 X 光扫描仪，缩短对货物进行实物检查和 X 光扫描所花费的时间，并改善拦截和由此带来的风险分析效率。

13. The Study recommends the measures below to furtherreduce the export release time.

13. 建议通过采取以下措施来进一步缩短出口放行时间：

• Setting up of a centralized parking plaza, catering for all four terminals, with adequate facilities for scanning and examination of the containers.
• The proposed testing facilities for import cargo may also be equipped with testing facilities for main items of export, including perishable goods.

• 建立一个集中的停车场，为所有四个码头提供服务，并配备足够的对集装箱进行 X 光扫描和检查的设施。

• 同时为主要出口产品（包括易腐货物）配备必要的检测设施。

LAO PEOPLE'S DEMOCRATIC REPUBLIC

老挝人民民主共和国

1. The Lao Customs Department (LCD) has been conducting the Time Release Study (TRS) on a regular basis to measure a key performance indicator of the Customs and Trade Facilitation Project. The Project adopted the "ASYCUDA World" system to support cargo clearance processing, and introduced advanced techniques, such as risk management and advance rulings, to Customs administration in order to enhance trade facilitation. One of the Project's key performance indicators was to reduce the average time required for cargo clearance by 10% each year. This indicator has been measured by conducting the Time Release Study. To date, three Studies have been carried out: in 2009, 2012 and 2016. The first TRS set out the baseline information on the clearance process; the second assessed the impact of the introduction of trade facilitation initiatives, including implementation of an e-Customs system to manage cargo clearance; and the third measured

the achievement of the roll-out of the e-Customs system to major Customs border posts, and the effectiveness of risk management.

1. 老挝海关当局（LCD）定期开展 TRS，以评测海关和贸易便利化项目的关键绩效指标。该项目采用“ASYCUDA World”系统来处理货物清关流程，并在海关管理部门引入了诸如风险管理和预审核等先进技术，以加强贸易便利化。该项目的关键绩效指标之一是每年将清关所需的平均时间缩短 10%。该指标通过 TRS 来衡量。迄今为止，已经开展了三次 TRS，时间分别为：2009 年、2012 年和 2016 年。第一次 TRS 明确了清关程序的基准信息；第二次 TRS 评估了引入贸易便利化举措的影响，包括用电子海关系统管理货物清关流程；第三次 TRS 衡量了将电子海关系统推广到主要海关边境口岸的成就以及风险管理的有效性。

2. A TRS Working Group was established to guide and monitor the Study's progress. It comprised permanent representatives of various trade stakeholders, such as the LCD, the Ministry of Industry and Commerce, the Ministry of Agriculture and Forestry, the Ministry of Health, the Statistics Bureau and the private sector.

2. 组建 TRS 工作组，以指导和监督研究进度。该工作组由各种贸易利益相关方的常任代表组成，例如老挝海关、工业和商业部、农业和林业部、卫生部、统计局和私营机构。

3. Four time intervals were measured as follows:

3. 四个时间间隔的测量如下：

T0: Arrival – Removal was the overall interval between the arrival of a shipment at the checkpoint and its physical removal after receiving permission for release. It represented the average time required for cargo clearance at the border crossing.

T0：到达—提离是指货物到达检查站与收到放行许可后货物实际提离之间的总时间。它代表过境点货物清关所需的平均时间。

T1: Arrival – Unloading was the interval between the arrival of a shipment at the checkpoint and the end of unloading of the cargo at the temporary storage warehouse.

T1：到达—卸货是指货物到达检查站和货物在临时仓库卸货完毕之间的间隔。

T2：Declaration – Permission was the interval between the lodgement of the Customs declaration and permission to release the cargo granted by Customs.

T2：报关—放行许可是指提交报关单与海关放行之间的间隔。

T3：Permission – Removal was the interval between the granting of permission for release and the physical removal of the goods from the temporary storage area.

T3：放行许可—提离是指海关许可放行与从临时存储区实际提离货物之间的间隔。

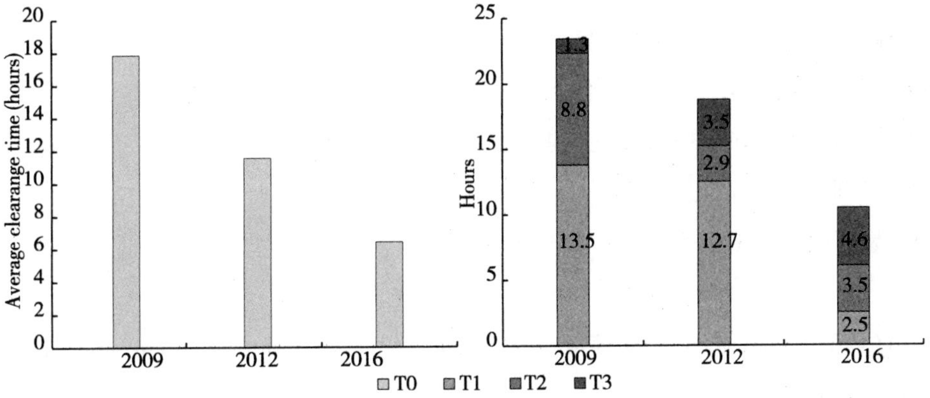

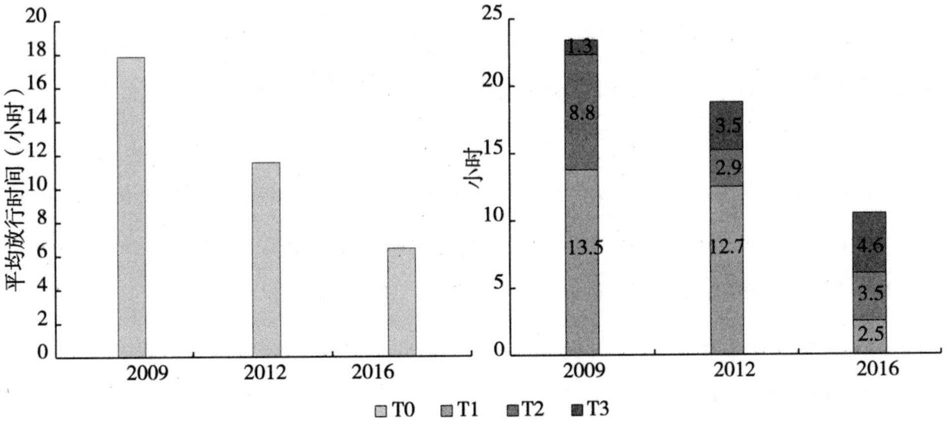

4. The design of the 2016 Lao TRS was as follows:

- Traffic modes: road and air
- Duration: 21 March-24 May 2016
- Types of goods: all shipment types
- Survey sites: ten Customs border posts and one Customs office at the international airport
- Numbers of samples: 832 declarations for road shipments
- And 45 for air shipments
- The data was collected manually.

4. 2016 年老挝开展 TRS 的设计如下：

- 运输方式：公路运输和空运；
- 时间：2016 年 3 月 21 日至 5 月 24 日；
- 商品类型：所有货物类型；
- 调查地点：国际机场的十个海关边境检查站和一个海关办公室；
- 样本数量：832 份公路运输报关单；
- 45 项航空运输报关单；
- 数据收集方式：人工。

5. The WCO TRS software was used to develop questionnaires and for data collection. However, different software was used to analyse the data, as the Lao Customs Department wanted to analyse other parameters, such as medians and percentiles.

5. 使用了 WCO TRS 软件来开发调查问卷和收集数据。但是由于老挝海关当局想分析其他数据，例如中位数和百分位数，因此使用了不同的分析软件。

6. The results of the 2016 TRS allowed LCD, among other things, to observe the impact of the successful implementation of various policies and actions in the national clearance process. The figures above clearly indicate that one of the major outcomes of LCD carrying out periodic TRS is that average clearance times have been significantly and steadily reduced between 2009 and 2016.

6. 2016 年开展的 TRS 结果使老挝海关当局可以观察到成功实施各种政策和行动后对全国通关流程的影响。上面的数据清楚地表明，老挝海关当局定期开展 TRS 的主要结果之一是平均清关时间明显缩短（2009—2016 年）。

7. As per the WCO TRS methodology, one of the main purposes of the TRS wasto identify bottlenecks in the clearance process, and to formulate recommendations to address these bottlenecks. The 2016 TRS found some areas for improvement. These are detailed below, together with the respective recommendations.

7. 根据 WCO 发布的 TRS 方法，TRS 的主要目的之一是找出清关流程中的瓶颈，并提出解决这些瓶颈的建议。2016 年开展的 TRS 发现了一些待改进之处。以下是各研究发现的详情及其建议。

Findings

研究发现

Risk analysis results were dominated by the high risk category, with 42% of cases flagged as requiring physical examination. Selectivity was introduced in 2012, but risk profiles have not been updated in a consistent manner.

风险分析结果以高风险类别为主，其中 42% 的事件标记为需要实物检查。虽然 2012 年引入了抽查机制，但是风险状况并未得到持续更新。

Recommendation

建议

Higher-risk shipments require mandatory inspection, and therefore incur substantially longer clearance times. Improving the accuracy of risk categorization is therefore an obvious area for improving overall clearance times. The risk profiles should be reviewed and updated more regularly by incorporating changing factors, such as trade patterns, levels of compliance, records of seizures, and intelligence.

高风险货物需要进行强制性检查，从而需要更长的通关时间。因此，提高风险分类的准确性是缩短总体清关时间的一个明显措施。应根据不断变化的各个因素，如贸易模式、守法程度、缉获记录和情报等，定期审查和更新风险概况。

Findings

研究发现

Operational hours were too short. The trade volumes transacted through each Customs border post varied widely. Service hours in all offices were the same (08.00 - 16.00) on the working days of Monday to Friday.

工作时间太短。各个海关边境检查站的业务量差异很大。周一至周五的工作日，所有海关办公室的服务时间均相同（08：00—16：00）。

Recommendation

建议

The Study revealed that 62 shipments, or 9% of the total, took over 48 hours to process from arrival to removal. Analysis of these shipments showed that the main reason for the delays was that declarations were lodged at the end of the week (Thursday or Friday), and thus the completion of the permission stage was delayed until the following Monday. Extending the hours of operation at each checkpoint from five to six days a week, and/or extending working hours beyond 16.00, would address these delays and should lead to a decrease in the T0 and T2 intervals observed.

这项研究显示，有62批货物（占总数的9%），从运抵到提离这一过程所需时间超过48小时。对这些货物的分析表明，通关延误的主要原因是在每周最后2个工作日（星期四或星期五）提出申报，因此完成许可放行被推迟到下星期一。将每个边境检查站的工作时间从每周5天延长到6天，和/或将工作日的工作时间延长到16点以后，将解决这些延误问题，并可缩短T0和T2阶段的时间间隔。

Findings

研究发现

Telecommunications connections in several Customs offices located in remote areas were not stable, interrupting the cargo clearance process as a result.

位于偏远地区的几个海关检查站的网络连接不稳定，致使货物清关过程出现中断现象。

Recommendation

建议

- The ASYCUDA system also needs to establish a connection to the central database, so disruptions to the network either at the local checkpoint or at the central database do not stop the system from being able to process shipments.
- The Lao Customs Department should focus on improving the reliability of the ASYCUDA system network. Additionally, an emergency plan should be established. For example, a paper-based process could be used during network outages, which would slow down the Customs process but enable the checkpoint to continue operating. The data could then be entered into the system when it came back online.

- 海关数据自动化系统还需要与中央数据库建立连接，因此，无论是在本地检查站还是在中央数据库，网络中断都不会妨碍系统的运行。
- 老挝海关当局应注重提高海关数据自动化系统网络的可靠性。此外，还应制订应急计划。例如，在网络中断期间可以使用纸质流程，这将使货物清关所需时间延长，但可使检查站能够继续正常运行。当网络恢复时，就可以将这些数据输入系统中。

Findings

研究发现

The implementation of the ASYCUDA system helped standardize the Customs process in many checkpoints in the country. Nonetheless, there are still variations in Customs procedures at different checkpoints. A number of these are due to the layout of the checkpoint, as some have warehouses and storage spaces that are far away from the actual border checkpoint.

海关数据自动化系统的实施能够使该国许多检查站的海关监管程序实现标准化。尽管如此，不同检查站的海关监管程序仍有一些差异。其中一些是由于检查站的分布状况造成的，因为有些仓库和储存场地距离实际的边境检查站较远。

Recommendation

建议

Lao Customs should standardize its cargo clearance procedures to ensure a seamless clearance process. Staff relocation and facility improvement may be needed at some border crossing checkpoints.

老挝海关应使其货物清关程序标准化，以确保清关流程的无缝对接。一些过境检查站可能需要工作人员重新配置和改善现有设施。

JAPAN

日本

The TRS as a Tool for Measuring the Performance of Trade Facilitation Measures

TRS 是衡量贸易便利化措施绩效的工具

1. Japan is a WCO Member which is regarded as one of the pioneer countries in terms of carrying out Time Release Studies, having undertaken them on a periodic basis since the 1990s. Japan Customs has used the TRS results as a Customs performance indicator, and to evaluate the efficiency of new trade facilitation measures, including Customs schemes and procedures. The normal scope of the TRS in Japan is illustrated below, covering the key intervals.

1. 日本是 WCO 的成员，从 20 世纪 90 年代开始定期开展 TRS，因此被视为开展 TRS 的先驱国家之一。日本海关已将 TRS 结果当作考核海关绩效的指标，并评估了包括海关计划和程序在内的新贸易便利化措施的效率。日本开展 TRS 的通常范围如下图所示，涵盖了关键时间间隔。

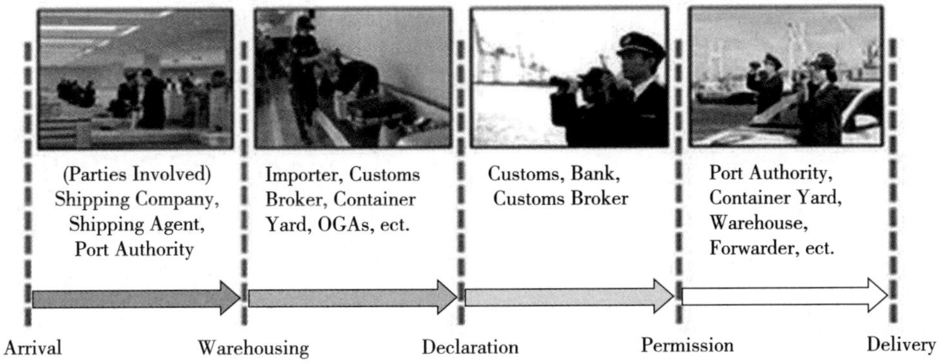

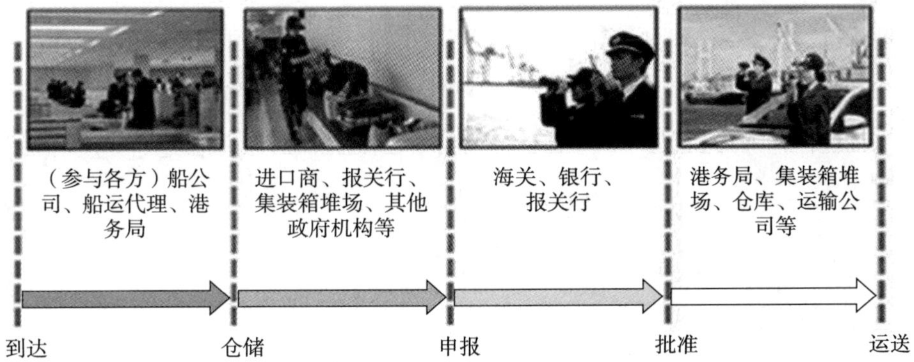

2. Each TRS cycle allows Japan Customs to evaluate the impacts of a number of measures it has undertaken on the import clearance of goods. The "Changes in the mean time required for clearance" in the results of the 2015 TRS clearly show that the introduction of various measures, such as pre-arrival lodgement of the goods declaration, and the Single Window and AEO programmes, have made a positive contribution to reducing the time required for release over the years.

2. 每个 TRS 周期都可以让日本海关评估其采取的一系列措施对进口货物清关流程的影响。2015 年 TRS 结果中的“平均清关所需时间的变化”清楚地表明，多年以来，多种措施的实施，例如在货物到达前进行预申报、单一窗口和 AEO 计划，为缩短放行所需时间都作出了积极贡献。

3. Taking the results for general sea cargo (not including AEOs) as an example, the mean time has decreased by 108.7 hours over the last two decades. This is shown in the graph below, which also includes the results of the 2015 TRS in Japan. The graph clearly illustrates the steady reduction in times required over the years in which Japan has carried out TRS.

3. 以一般海运货物（不包括 AEO 的）的结果为例，在过去 20 年中，平均放行时间缩短了 108.7 小时。如下图所示，其中还包括 2015 年日本 TRS 的结果。这张图表清楚地说明了在日本开展 TRS 的这些年间放行所需时间在稳步缩短。

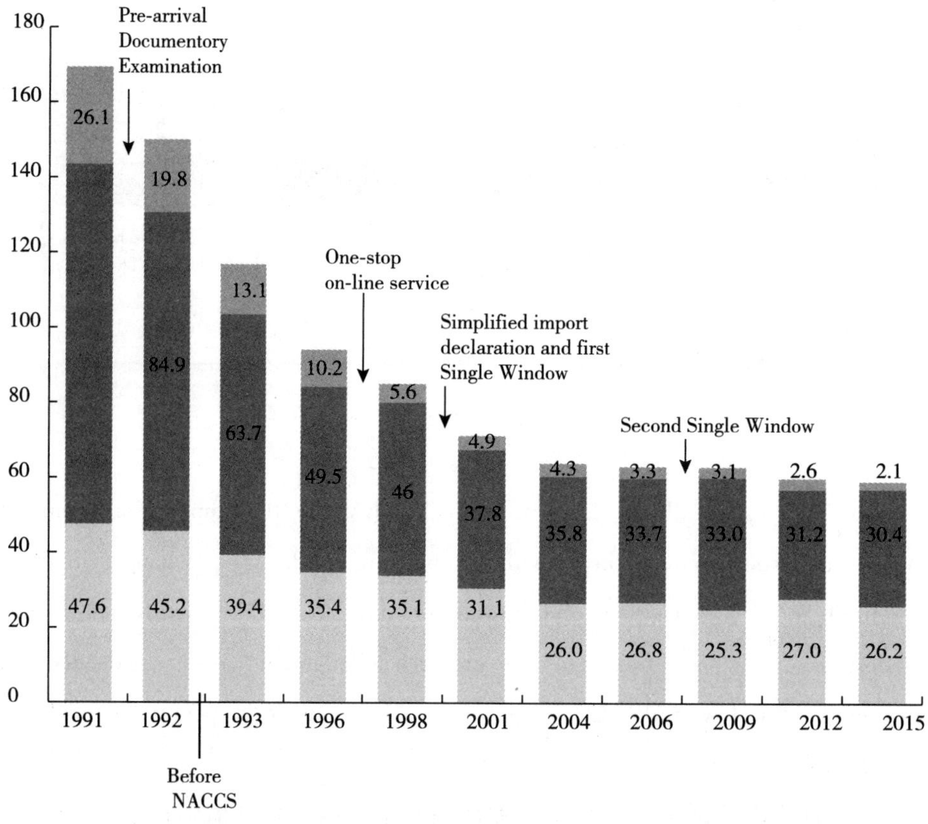

Changes in the mean time for a time period from arrival to release (Sea Cargo)

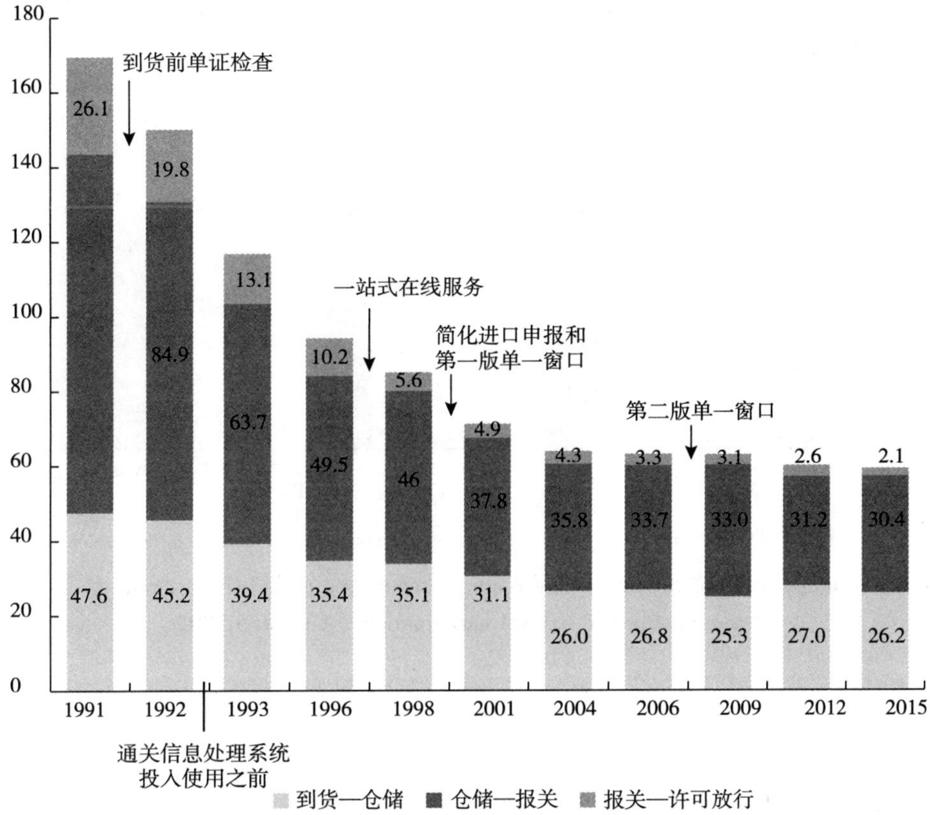

从运抵到放行的平均时间变化（海运货物）

4. In addition to the general trends relating to the mean time required from arrival to release, a number of additional comparisons can be made on the basis of results of the previous Studies. These include analysis by mode of transportation or by specific measure. The graphs below illustrate the analyses made in respect of the 2015 TRS for the Air and Sea modes of transport. The graphs explicitly show the benefits of conducting TRS when different measures are implemented well.

4. 除了能分析出与从运抵到放行所需平均时间有关的变化趋势外，还可以根据以前的研究结果进行其他比较分析，包括按运输方式或按特定措施进行的分析。下图是 2015 年 TRS 中针对空运和海运所做的分析，它们清楚地表明了在实施不同措施后开展 TRS 的益处。

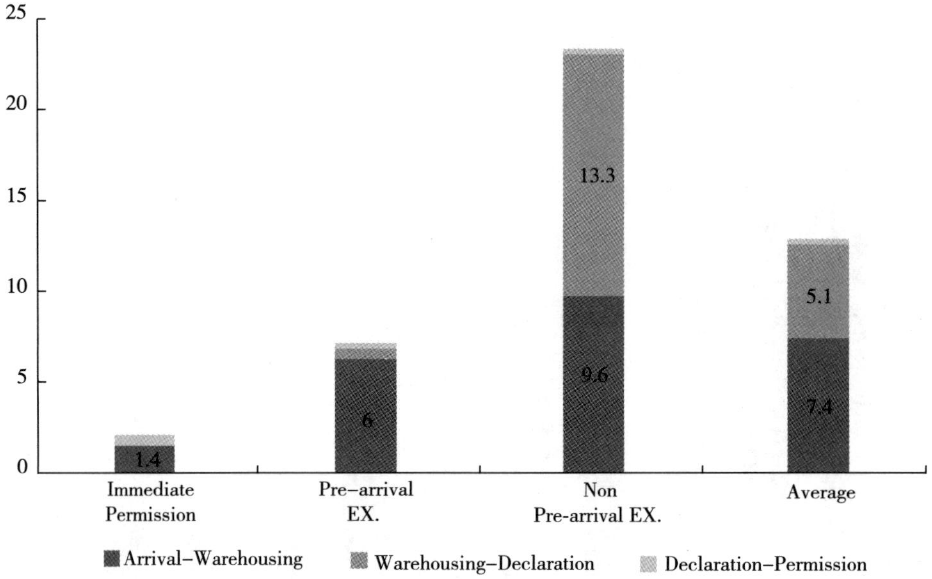

Comparaison of the mean time required for a time period from arrival to release aplying Pre-Arrival Examination (Air Cargo 2015)

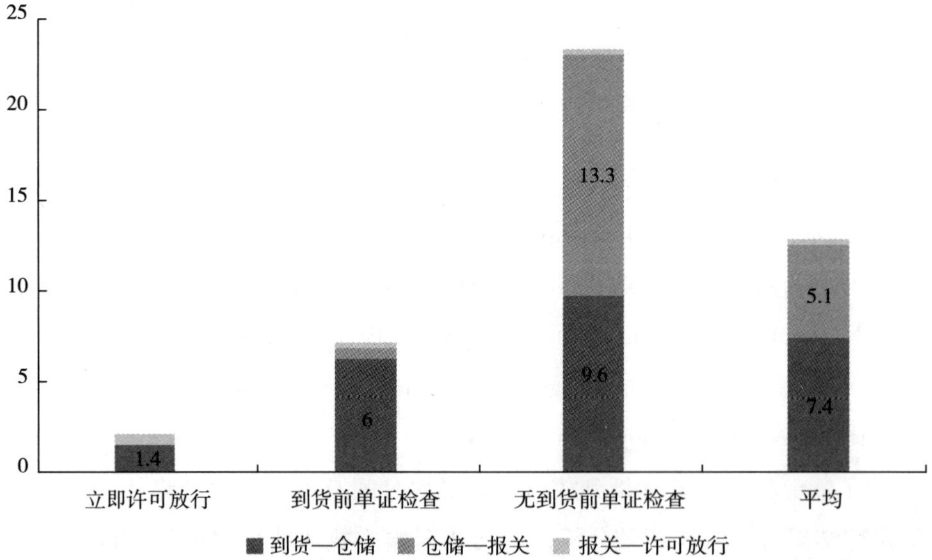

从运抵到放行，应用抵港前检查所需平均时间进行比较（2015 年空运货物）

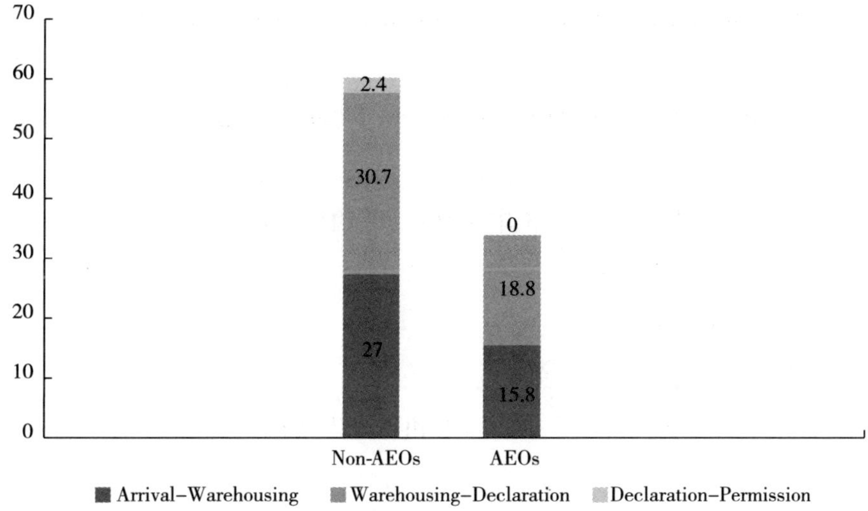

Comparaison of the mean time required for a time period from arrival between AEOs and non-AEOs（Sea Cargo 2015）

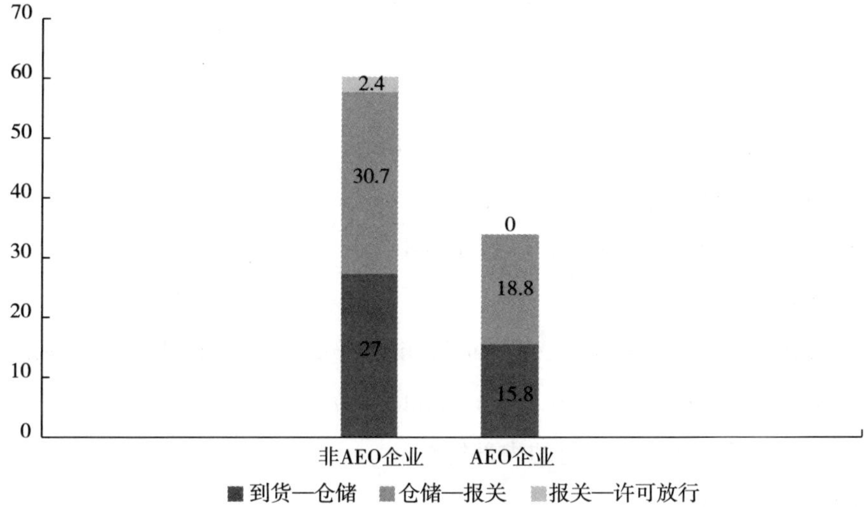

AEO 与非 AEO 从运抵到放行平均时间的比较（2015 年海运货物）

5. In total，24 major seaports/airports out of 188 points of entry were chosen within the scope of Japan's 2015 TRS，which had the following design：

- Duration：seven consecutive days（9 – 15 March 2015）
- Traffic modes：sea and air
- Types of goods：all cargoes
- Geographical scope：all regional Customs

- Choice of Customs offices: 16 major seaports and eight major airports.

5. 在日本2015年TRS的范围内，总共选择了188个入境点中的24个主要海港/机场，其设计如下：

- 持续时间：连续七天（2015年3月9日至15日）；
- 交通方式：海运及空运；
- 货物类型：所有货物；
- 地理范围：所有地区的海关；
- 海关办事处的选择：16个主要海港和8个主要机场。

6. It took approximately six months to complete the 2015 TRS project, from preparation to issue of a press release on the results. The various stages of implementation are described below.

6. 2015年TRS项目从准备到发布有关结果，大约花了6个月的时间。各实施阶段如下所述。

January-February 2015: Pre-survey internal coordination to:

- Set the dates of the survey
- Determine the number of samples to be taken
- Review elements of the survey
- Prepare survey forms (air/sea), including lists of factors taking longer than average
- Coordinate with Customs brokers and relevant Other

2015年1月至2月：调查前的内部协调。

- 设定调查日期；
- 确定要采集的样本数量；
- 审查调查内容；
- 准备调查表（空运/海运），包括比平均时间长的因素列表；
- 与报关行及其他相关部门进行协调。

7. Japan Customs established a cooperative framework for collaborating with other government agencies and business. Nine regional Customs offices played significant roles in

communicating with OGA and Customs brokers, and in collecting/recording data under the guidance of the Customs and Tariff Bureau, and the Ministry of Finance (parent Ministry). OGA and Customs brokers provided regional Customs offices with detailed data on the TRS. The workflow for collecting the data is illustrated below.

7. 日本海关建立了与其他政府机构和企业进行合作的框架。九个地方海关在与其他政府机构和报关行沟通以及在海关和关税局以及财政部（上级财政部）的指导下收集/记录数据方面发挥了重要作用。其他政府机构和报关行向地方海关提供了开展 TRS 所需的详细数据。数据采集的工作流程如下所示。①

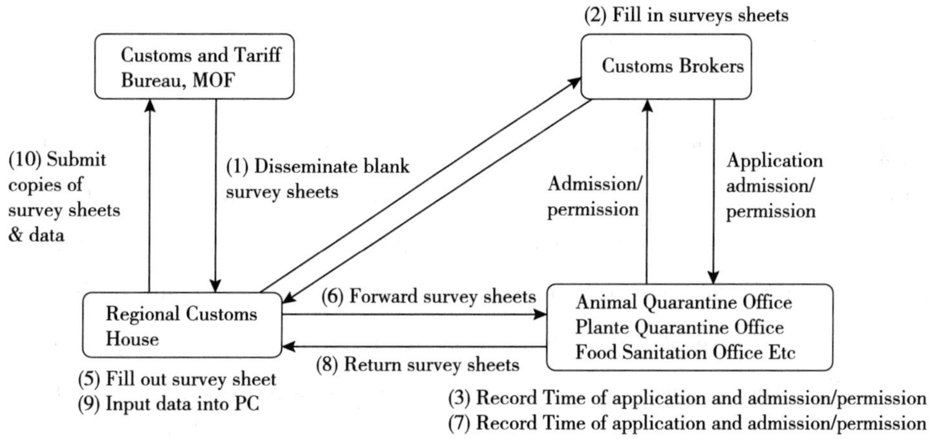

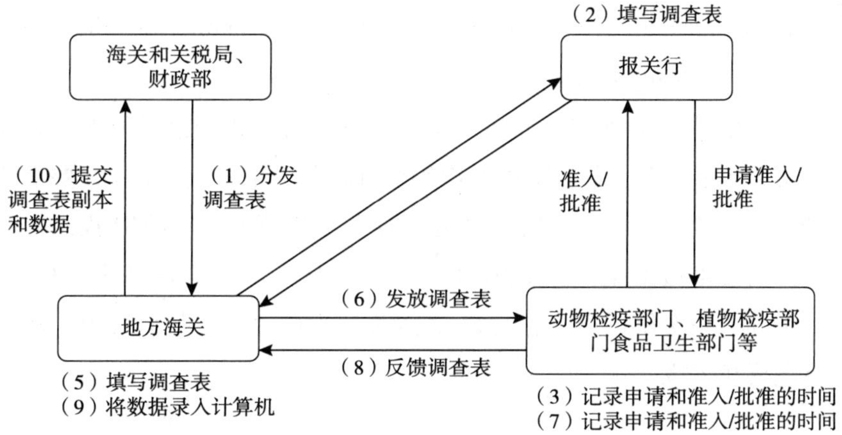

8. Given the importance of continuing these Studies on an ongoing basis for the purposes of performance measurement, Japan Customs has conducted a TRS every two to three years

① WCO 原文件中缺少流程（4），此处尊重原文翻译。

over the last 20 years. Japan conducted its latest TRS in March 2018, and the results will be published in due course.

8. 鉴于持续进行这些研究以进行绩效评估的重要性，日本海关在过去 20 年中每 2 至 3 年开展一次 TRS。日本在 2018 年 3 月开展了最新的 TRS，其结果将在适当时候公布。

MAURITIUS

毛里求斯

Background

1. 背景

In 2015, Mauritius, which was among the first five countries to ratify the WTO Trade Facilitation Agreement (TFA), categorized Article 7.6 ("Establishment and Publication of Average Release Times") as a Category C provision, requiring the acquisition of assistance and support for capacity building. A request was therefore made to the WCO for provision of technical assistance to build the capacity of public and private representatives in order to conduct Time Release Studies, and a workshop was held in April 2016, with financial support from the Customs Cooperation Fund of Japan (CCF/Japan). The workshop was attended by some 50 participants, representing all the major actors intervening in the cargo supply chain.

毛里求斯是最早（2015 年）批准 WTO《贸易便利化协定》（TFA）的五个国家之一，并将第 7.6 条（“建立和发布平均放行时间”）列为 C 类条款，要求获得援助和支持以进行相关能力建设。此后，毛里求斯为开展 TRS，向 WCO 提出提升公共和私人机构能力的技术援助请求。2016 年 4 月，在日本海关合作基金（CCF/日本）的资助下，举办了一次研讨会。有约 50 人参加这次研讨会，他们代表了参与货物供应链的所有主要相关方。

2. Objective of the TRS

2. TRS 的目标

Following the workshop, a decision was made to carry out a TRS in Mauritius from 5

September to 9 October 2016. It was expected that the TRS would positively contribute to trade facilitation and improve the ranking of Mauritius in the World Bank's Ease of Doing Business Report.

研讨会结束后，毛里求斯决定于 2016 年 9 月 5 日至 10 月 9 日开展 TRS。预计 TRS 将对贸易便利化作出积极贡献，并提高毛里求斯在世界银行《营商环境报告》中的排名。

Accordingly, the TRS was aimed at achieving the following objectives:

因此，开展 TRS 旨在实现以下目标：

a. Complying with one of Mauritius's Category C TFA commitments pertaining to the "Establishment and Publication of Average Release Times" under Article 7.6; and

a. 遵守毛里求斯关于在 TFA 第 7.6 条中"建立和发布平均放行时间"的 C 类承诺之一；

b. Assisting national efforts to improve the ease of doing business through the:

b. 通过以下方式协助国家努力提高营商环境的便利性：

- Identification of bottlenecks in the clearance of cargo, and
- Formulation of specific recommendations to address these bottlenecks.
  - 找出货物清关流程中的瓶颈；
  - 提出解决这些瓶颈的具体建议。

Setting up of committees

3. 委员会的设立

Three committees, each with a different mandate, were set up for propercoordination and seamless conduct of the TRS. Due care was taken to ensure the participation of all government agencies, as well as private bodies involved in the clearance of goods, and other organizations contributing to trade facilitation.

设立了三个委员会，每个委员会执行不同的任务，以协调顺利地开展 TRS，确保所有政府机构、参与货物清关流程的私人机构以及其他有助于贸易便利化的组织参与 TRS。

Ⅰ. National Steering Committee

Ⅰ. 国家指导委员会

This Committee was set up to define in broad terms the scope and objective of the TRS. Members were invited to join this Committee at the request of the Director of Customs, as chair of the Committee. Given its international impact, the Committee was also responsible for approving the TRS Report before its publication. The Committee was composed of representatives from:

该委员会的设立是为了从广义上界定 TRS 的范围和目标。应海关当局主任（该委员会主席）的要求，邀请相关成员加入该委员会。鉴于该报告会在国际上产生影响，该委员会还负责批准最终的研究报告。该委员会由下列代表组成：

a. Mauritius Revenue Authority – Customs Department
b. Ministry of Finance and Economic Development
c. Ministry of Foreign Affairs, Regional Integration and International Trade
d. Board of Investment
e. Mauritius Chamber of Commerce and Industry

a. 毛里求斯税务局－海关部；
b. 财政经济发展部；
c. 外交、区域一体化和国际贸易部；
d. 投资委员会；
e. 毛里求斯工商会。

Ⅱ. Inter-Agency Technical Committee

Ⅱ. 机构间技术委员会

This Committee comprised members who are actively involved in the cargo supplychain. Most of the members participated in the TRS workshop facilitated by the WCO in April 2016. Its members played the essential role of apprising the group of the different process flows pertaining to their respective organizations and how best to capture the different time-stamps. This Committee was also set up at the request of the Director of Customs.

该委员会由积极参与货物供应链的成员组成。大多数成员参加了 2016 年 4 月由 WCO 主办的 TRS 研讨会。其成员将在向各小组通报与各自组织有关的流程以及更好地采集各个流程所需的时间方面发挥重要作用。该委员会也是应海关当局主任的要求设立的。

Ⅲ. Customs Working Group

Ⅲ. 海关工作组

The Customs Working Group had overall responsibility for coordinating the TRS processes and was composed of 16 Customs officers who had participated in the TRS workshop facilitated by the WCO. They were selected from different sections of the Customs Department so as to provide proper understanding of the various procedures applicable in all sections involved in clearance processes. This Working Group was responsible for:

海关工作组全面负责协调 TRS 流程，由 16 名海关关员组成，他们也参加了 WCO 举办的 TRS 研讨会。他们是从不同的海关部门中选出来的，熟悉清关流程中的各种程序。该工作组负责以下事项：

a. Determining the methodology, sampling method, the data to be collected and the collection method;

b. Designing the questionnaires, and conducting training and awareness sessions with stakeholders on the questionnaires and data to be collected;

c. Distributing, collecting and verifying the questionnaires;

d. Operating a virtual helpdesk to assist with completion of questionnaires;

e. Recording all manual data using Excel;

f. Determining the analysis to be carried out and performing calculations on data collected;

g. Drafting and submitting the TRS Report, together with recommendations, to the National

Steering Committee and to management for approval;

h. Holding regular meetings with the different Committees in order to provide feedback on the progress of the Study and the results obtained.

a. 确定研究方法、采样方法、需采集的数据及数据采集方法；

b. 设计调查问卷，对利益相关方就调查问卷内容和需要收集的数据进行培训，以便达成统一认识；

c. 发放、收集和核实调查问卷；

d. 协助完成调查问卷；

e. 使用 Excel 表记录所有人工收集的数据；

f. 确定要进行的分析工作，并对已收集的数据进行计算；

g. 起草 TRS 报告（连同建议），提交国家指导委员会和管理层批准；

h. 定期与各委员会举行会议，以便反馈研究的进展和取得的结果。

4. Scope of the Study

4. 研究范围

It was decided that, since the country is relatively small, with a single port and a single airport, the Study would be carried out at both locations, for both imports and exports.

会议决定，由于该国面积相对较小，且只有一个港口和一个机场，因此这项研究将在这两个地点进行，研究对象包括进口和出口货物。

The scope of the Study, as directed by the TRS Steering Committee, therefore encompassed the following:

因此，根据 TRS 指导委员会的指示，研究范围包括：

a. Sea and air consignments into Mauritius during the period from 5 to 11 September 2016;

b. Sea and air consignments for which a declaration had been submitted during the same period;

c. Follow-up of the consignments at (a) and (b) above, from the arrival time of the vessel/aircraft, to the gate-out time of the consignment from the landing place/warehouse, up to 9 October 2016.

a. 2016 年 9 月 5 日至 11 日间通过海运和空运进入毛里求斯的货物；

b. 在同一期间内已提交报关单的海运和空运货物；

c. 对上述（a）和（b）项下的货物进行跟踪，记录从船舶/飞机到达机场/仓库到货物提离的时间，并持续跟踪至 2016 年 10 月 9 日。

5. Data collection and analysis

5. 数据收集和分析

The Study findings were based on data retrieved from the various IT systems operated by the main stakeholders in the logistics supply chain. Data pertaining to non-automated processes was collected manually from economic operators by means of specially designed questionnaires. The completed forms were physically submitted/ collected or sent via email, and the data then compiled in the required format（Excel files）.

研究结果基于从物流供应链中主要利益相关方运营的各种信息化系统中检索到的数据。与非自动化过程有关的数据是通过专门设计的调查表从相关运营商处人工收集的。已填好的调查表以纸质方式提交/收集或通过电子邮件发送，然后将相关数据按照所需的格式（Excel 文件）进行汇总。

All data collected/retrieved was compiled in two master databases, one for imports, and the other for export consignments. The analysis was conducted using these two master databases.

收集/检索到的所有数据都汇总在两个主数据库中，其中一个数据库用于存储进口数据，另一个则用于出口。数据分析将使用两个主数据库中的数据。

The table below provides an overview of the number and percentage of records used for the Study.

下表概述了用于研究分析的记录数量及其占总记录数量的百分比。

Consignement Type	Description	Number of records for study period	Number used for analysis	Percentage used
Sea Imports	No. of Full Container Load (FCL) consignments	1,742	769	44%
	No. of FCL containers	1,629	1,401	86%
	No. of declarations for FCL containers	1,575	775	49%
	No. of Less than Container Load (LCL) consignments	2,060	751	36%
	No. of declarations for LCL consignments	698	644	92%
Air Imports	No. of air consignments	1,600	803	50%
	No. of air declarations	1,431	1,344	94%
Sea Exports	No. of declarations	1,666	1,666	100%
Air Exports	No. of air declarations	910	345	38%

货物类型	说明	研究期间的记录数量	用于分析的数量	使用百分比
海运进口	整箱的货物（FCL）数量	1，742	769	44%
	整箱集装箱数量	1，629	1，401	86%
	集装箱整箱申报数量	1，575	775	49%
	拼箱（LCL）的货物数量	2，060	751	36%
	拼箱托运申报数量	698	644	92%
空运进口	空运货物数量	1，600	803	50%
	空运申报数量	1，431	1，344	94%
海运出口	申报数量	1，666	1，666	100%
空运出口	空运申报数量	910	345	38%

6. Overview of results

6. 结果概述

The median was used to calculate the results as it was considered more representative of the central trend of the data collected than the mean, which was greatly influenced by extreme values/outliers collected. The tables below provide a summary of the median time taken for the various key procedures to be completed for the import and export of goods, respectively.

中位数被用来计算结果，因为通常认为中位数比平均值更能代表所收集数据的变化趋势，而平均值受收集的极值/离群值的影响很大。下表分别汇总了货物进、出口各关键流程所需的中位数时间。

It should be noted that "Submission of the BOE up to Customs release" and "Customs release up to gate-in" take comparatively longer for exports by air. This is due to the fact that, unlike exports by sea, where consignments can be transferred to the place of shipment in containers in a single trip, goods pertaining to a single air consignment sometimes have to be transferred in multiple stages.

由表中数据可以看出，对于空运出口货物，"提交出口报关单至海关放行"和"海关放行至集装箱进堆场"耗费的时间相对于海运较长。这是因为，海运货物可以用集装箱一次运输到装运地，而属于单次空运的货物有时必须分多个阶段进行转运。

Import Processes	Sea	Air	Exports processes	Sea	Air
Vessel/aircraft arrival up to submission of the Bill of Entry (BOE)	25.44 hours	22.3 hours	Submission of the BOE up to Customs release	16 minutes	38 minutes
Submission of the BOE up to Customs release	22.56 hours	2.9 hours	Customs release up to gate-in	2.8 hours	10.9 hours
Customs release up to gate-out	27.12 hours	2.3 hours	Gate-in up to loading on vessel/aircraft	28.8 hours	4.2 hours
Vessel/aircraft arrival up to gate-out	5.15 days	1.9 days	Submission of the BOE up to loading on vessel/aircraft	4.4 hours	4.5 hours

进口流程	海运	空运	出口流程	海运	空运
船只/飞机到达至提交进口报关单	25.44 小时	22.3 小时	提交出口报关单至海关放行	16 分	38 分
提交进口报关单至海关放行	22.56 小时	2.9 小时	海关放行至集装箱进堆场	3.8 小时	10.9 小时
海关放行至集装箱出堆场	27.12 小时	2.3 小时	集装箱进堆场至装船/飞机	28.8 小时	4.2 小时
船只/飞机到达至集装箱出堆场	5.15 天	1.9 天	提交出口报关单至集装箱装船/飞机	4.4 小时	4.5 小时

7. Findings and general recommendations
7. 研究发现和一般性建议

The table below provides an overview of the findings derived from a careful analysis of the results obtained, and the corresponding recommendations.

下表是对相关数据进行仔细分析后得出的研究发现以及相应的建议。

Findings	Recommendation
Only 25% of BOEs relating to sea consignments are submitted prior to arrival of the vessel.	Promote pre-arrival clearance through stakeholder meetings and other awareness sessions.
The working hours of Customs, the Cargo Handling Corporation Ltd. (CHCL), logistics operators and agencies involved in the clearance of goods do not match.	Harmonize working hours for border agencies and operators to provide 24/7 uninterrupted service.
Only 47% of sea consignments are physically removed by importers/hauliers within one day of Customs clearance.	Expedite the removal of goods after Customs clearance by providing incentives for early removal.
Not all agencies or organizations involved in the clearance process are present at the port and airport	House all border clearance agencies under one roof or empower Customs to administer the requirements for permits and authorizations.
Only a few importers have a clear picture of the submission and processing of their declarations.	Improve visibility as regards the submission and processing of declarations, through automatic messaging with importers.
616 tariff lines require clearances from multiple agencies. This means that importers sometimes have to go to various offices to obtain clearances for a single consignment.	Review and re-engineer the process for permits and authorizations and expedite the implementation of a Single Window.

研究发现	建议
与海运货物有关的进口报关单仅有 25% 在船舶到达之前提交	通过与利益相关方召开会议和其他宣传途径促进提前申报、提前清关
海关、货物装卸公司（CHCL）、物流运营商和其他参与货物清关的机构的工作时间不一致	协调边境机构和运营商的工作时间，以提供 24/7 全天候服务
在清关后，进口商/运输商仅将 47% 的海运货物在当天提离	鼓励提前清关，加快海关放行后相关货物的提离
不是所有参与清关程序的机构或组织都在港口和机场	将所有边境清关机构安置在一起工作，或授予海关许可和提供相关授权的权力
只有少数进口商清楚地了解报关单的提交和处理进度	通过与进口商的自动消息传递，提高报关单的提交和处理进度的透明度
616 个关税细目需要多个机构的许可。这意味着进口商有时必须为单批货物去多个机构办理清关手续	审查并重新设计相关许可和授权流程，加快单一窗口的实施

In addition to the above recommendations, other issues were brought to the attention ofthe Customs Working Group during the various meetings and discussions with economic operators in the supply chain. Although these are not a direct result of the TRS, some valuable suggestions have been taken up. These are listed below.

除上述建议外，在与供应链经营者举行的各种会议和讨论中，还有一些需要海关工作组注意的其他问题。虽然这些不是 TRS 的直接结果，但会产生一些有价值的建议。这些建议包括以下内容：

1. Create a new exit gate for scanned containers to improve truck turnaround times.

2. Review Customs procedures for the examination of goods, including the automation of appointments with automatic messages to declarants/importers and CHCL.

3. Adopt a comprehensive approach for declaration processing, whereby examination, valuation and classification of goods by Customs can be carried out simultaneously.

1. 为需进行 X 光扫描的集装箱设置一个新的出口，以缩短卡车的周转时间。

2. 审查海关检查货物的程序，包括自动向报关员/进口商和 CHCL 发送预约信息。

3. 采取综合申报处理办法，海关对货物的审查、估价和分类可以同时进行。

NEW ZEALAND

新西兰

New Zealand's history of Time Release Studies

新西兰的 TRS 历史

1. New Zealand has a modern and well-developed cargo reporting system and Customs clearance processes combined with risk management. Cargo is reported electronically and in advance of arrival. The cargo reporting information is electronically risk-assessed and, if accepted, cleared by Customs, often before arrival of the vessel carrying that cargo. Payment of any duty and taxes is by deferred payment account or cash.

1. 新西兰拥有与风险管理相结合的、现代化和完善的货物报告制度和海关清关程序。货物在到达前以电子方式申报。货物申报信息可在信息化系统中进行风险评估，如果申报信息被接受，还装载在船舶上的货物在运抵前通常已由海关清关。相关关税和税款都可通过付款账户或现金方式延后支付。

2. The Time Release Studies carried out by New Zealand Customs have, in the main, been used to confirm and provide the data and evidence in support of the Customs clearance processes, and to measure Customs performance in facilitating trade. That is, the Studies are used as a measurement and validation tool, rather than as a tool for change. In periods between major changes to border clearance processes, it is expected/ assumed that there will be little variation and reasonable stability in the TRS measures, and certainly no variation statistically significant enough to indicate any major changes (ongoing) in performance. That is, once the major change is implemented and settled in, the times required for clearance should remain relatively stable and consistent until the next change.

2. 新西兰海关开展 TRS 主要是为了确认和提供支持清关程序的数据和证据，并衡量海关在贸易便利化方面的绩效。也就是说，该研究被当作测量和验证工具，而不是作为变更的工具。在边境清关程序发生重大变化期间，可以预期/假设通过 TRS 评测的结果变化很小且具有合理的稳定性，当然统计显示的结果也会表明绩效不会有重大变化。也就是说，一旦实施了变更并解决了相关问题，清关所需的时间应保持相对稳定和一致，直到下一次实施变更为止。

3. New Zealand Customs has carried out three Time Release Studies and assisted in one other: there were two Studies in 2009 – a New Zealand only Study and a trans-Tasman Study with the Australia Border Force; in 2010 there was a further New Zealand only Study; and in 2014, a TRS was carried out with Cook Islands Customs.

3. 新西兰海关当局开展了三次 TRS，并提供了一项协助研究：2009 年开展了两次研究——一次是针对新西兰的研究，另一次是与澳大利亚边境管理局开展的双边联合研究；2010 年，又开展了一次仅针对新西兰的研究；2014 年，与库克群岛海关开展了一次研究。

4. The 2009 trans-Tasman TRS was jointly led by New Zealand and Australia. This Study extended the application of the methodology to include exports, with a methodology and measures developed for exports. It measured the performance of both countries' Customs in clearing cargo from export in one country to import in the other, and vice versa. This TRS found that both Customs were efficient in clearing cargo and did not impede clearance.

4. 2009 年的双边联合研究由新西兰和澳大利亚共同开展。这项研究扩大了研究范围，将出口包括在内，并为出口制定了相关方法和措施。它评测了两国之间的进出口货物通关流程。研究发现，两国海关在货物清关方面都是高效的，清关流程比较顺畅。

5. The trans-Tasman TRS is an example of how two Customs organizations worked co-operatively together andovercame differences in policy, processes, border clearance events, and definitions to produce a joint consolidated analysis and Study. A key lesson drawn from this Study is to get together pre-Study, with the aim of understanding each other's border clearance processes, the stakeholders involved, the key parts of the process that need to be measured, and whether it is possible to measure them. It was also important to ensure that both agencies were clear about, and agreed on, the definitions and measurement of the key clearance events measured in the Study.

5. 双边联合研究是两国海关当局紧密合作并克服政策、流程、清关要求和释义方面的差异以进行联合分析和研究的一个范例。这项研究的一个重要经验是，在研究前相关研究人员应集中在一起，以充分了解彼此的边境清关程序、所涉利益相关方、该程序中需要评测的关键部分以及是否有可能对其进行评测。另外，要确保双方机构都清楚并同意研究中拟评测的关键清关事项的定义和评测方法。

6. The 2010 New Zealand TRS enabled comparative analysis with the 2009 Study and reported on changes in the measurements and performance of Customs in the time it took to clear cargo. The 2010 Study verified and confirmed the findings from the 2009 New Zealand Study.

6. 新西兰将 2010 年与 2009 年的研究结果进行了比较分析，发现了海关货物清关流程所需时间和绩效的变化。2010 年的研究验证和确认了 2009 年的研究结果。

7. The objectives of the 2010 Study were to: replicate the 2009 Study to produce comparable measurements; compare the year-on-year results to show any changes over time; and identify opportunities to improve performance.

7. 2010 年研究的目标是：利用 2009 年的研究方法，以产生与 2009 年研究具有可比性的评测结果；根据同比结果明确相关变化；找出提高绩效的机会。

Results of key measurements (days) from the 2010 NZ TRS

IMPORT	Sea 2010	Sea 2009		Air 2010	Air 2009
Arrival to release	-1.8	-1.8	Arrival to release	0.5	0.3
Arrival to gate-out	2.6	2.8	Arrival to availabilitity	0.1	n/k
% release before arrival	74	75	% release before arrival	40	60
EXPORTS	Sea 2010	Sea 2009		Air 2010	Air 2009
Receipt to lodge	0.8	1.5	Receipt to lodge	-0.9	n/k
Clear to load	-4.5	2.8	Clear to load	-1.2	-1
% cleared > 48 hrs loadiing	87	82	% cleared > 9 hrs loading	70	76

新西兰 2010 年 TRS 的关键评测结果（天）

进口	2010 年海运	2009 年海运		2010 年空运	2009 年空运
运抵至放行	-1. 8	-1. 8	运抵至放行	0. 5	0. 3
运抵至集装箱出堆场	2. 6	2. 8	运抵至流通	0. 1	n/k
运抵前的放行率	74	75	运抵前的放行率	40	60
出口	2010 年海运	2009 年海运		2010 年空运	2009 年空运
收货至申报	0. 8	1. 5	收货至申报	-0. 9	n/k
清关至装船	-4. 5	2. 8	清关至装机	-1. 2	-1
装船 48 小时后的清关率	87	82	装机 9 小时后的清关率	70	76

8. There were changes, butmostly minor, in the 2010 measures compared to the 2009 baseline measures. Generally, Customs performance in clearing cargo (trade facilitation) remained at a comparable and similarly high level to that found in 2009. This was expected, given that there had been no changes to the cargo clearance process or systems.

8. 与 2009 年相比，2010 年的研究结果有一些变化，但大多是轻微变化。总体而言，2010 年海关在货物清关（贸易便利化）方面的表现与 2009 年相当。这是意料之中的，因为货物清关程序或系统没有发生变更。

9. The findings from the 2010 Study support those from the 2009 Study. The key findings are:

9. 2010 年的研究支持了 2009 年的研究结果。此次研究的重要发现是：

- Customs is efficient in clearing cargo at the border and does not impede trade unnecessarily.

- 海关在边境清关方面的效率很高，不会对正常贸易产生影响。

- The level of advance or early reporting for imports by sea remains high, with a high percentage of cargo cleared for release by Customs before arrival. Advance reporting was a key finding from the 2009 Study. There are benefits to Customs and traders from completing Customs clearance requirements early. Customs' early receipt of the required documents for assessing and processing release of cargo provides more time and certainty, benefiting both Customs and travellers.

• 海运进口货物保持了很高的预先或早期申报水平，海关在相关货物运抵前完成清关并放行的情况所占比例很高。提前申报是2009年研究的一个重要发现。尽早完成清关对海关和贸易商都有好处。海关提前收到评估和处理货物放行所需的单证，可以节约更多时间并能提供更高的可确定性，使海关和贸易商都从中受益。

• Export reporting and clearance measures for sea cargo have improved, supporting the 2009 finding. Reporting as soon as the cargo enters Customs' control provides time for Customs to assess and process the information and take any action, so as not to impede the cargo before it is loaded.

• 海运出口货物的申报和清关方式有所改善，支持了2009年的研究结果。一旦货物信息传送到海关系统，海关就有时间评估和处理这些信息，并采取必要的处理措施，以免货物在装货前受阻。

• The analysis of export full container load (FCL) shows benefits to exporters who are Secure Exports Scheme (SES) partners. The SES is New Zealand's equivalent to an AEO programme.

• 对整柜出口货物（FCL）的分析表明，作为安全出口计划（SES）合作伙伴的出口商受益匪浅。新西兰的SES相当于AEO计划。

• Unlike sea cargo, air cargo is reported later — after arrival. In 2010, both the reporting time and percentage of entries lodged before arrival declined (did not improve) compared to 2009. The information required to complete Customs' reporting requirements, and shorter transport and dwell times, are the most likely explanations why air cargo is reported later. In addition, it is thought the increase in overseas online purchases has led to an increase in air cargo volume and in the workload to prepare and lodge the documents for import clearance.

• 与海运货物不同，空运货物在到达后才申报。与2009年相比，2010年的申报时间和抵港前提交入境申报的百分比都下降了（没有改善）。需要完成海关申报要求的信息以及运输和滞留时间较短，是空运货物的申报时间较晚的主要原因。另外，海外网购数量的增加导致空运数量的增长以及准备和提交进口清关文件工作量的增加。

Main contribution of the TRS to the Government's goal

TRS 对政府目标的主要贡献

10. At the Government level, the TRS, to date, supports the over-arching goal of delivering greater prosperity, security and opportunity to all New Zealanders, and to growing the economy. The TRS also contributed to the Customs Annual Plan for 2010 – 2013 and supported one of the priorities agreed with the then Prime Minister and Minister of Customs, which was to "Enhance border agency coordination to reduce duplication and improve the experience for traders and travellers" (as per the "Statement of Intent 2010 – 2013"). This was done by identifying opportunities to improve service delivery and hence the experience of traders.

10. 迄今为止，为实现向所有新西兰人提供更加繁荣的经济、更安全的环境和更多的机会以及促进经济增长这一总体目标，TRS 一直在政府层面提供支持。TRS 还为 2010—2013 年海关年度计划作出了贡献，并支持了与当时的总理和海关部长商定的优先事项之一，即"加强边境机构的合作，以减少重复工作并提高贸易商和旅行者的体验"（根据"2010—2013 年意向书"）。这是通过确定增加服务机会、增强贸易商的经验来实现的。

Most recent TRS in New Zealand: the 2014 "Cook Islands TRS"

新西兰最新开展的 TRS：2014 年"库克群岛 TRS"

11. In 2014, New Zealand Customs assisted Cook Islands Customs in carrying out a TRS. This Study was part of the Cook Islands Customs modernization programme, and aimed at measuring the impact on clearance times of a new computer system for processing cargo (CusMod). The system was installed and implemented in November 2013, and represented a major technological step in the modernization of processing import entries and releasing cargo. In effect, the cargo clearance process changed from a manual process to an

electronic process. An earlier Study carried out in May 2013 by the Oceania Customs Organization（OCO）enabled a“before and after”comparison.

11. 2014 年，新西兰海关协助库克群岛海关开展了 TRS。这项研究是库克群岛海关现代化方案的一部分，旨在评测新的计算机货物处理系统（CusMod）对通关时间的影响。该系统于 2013 年 11 月安装并投入使用，是处理进口报关单和放行货物现代化的重大技术步骤。事实上，货物清关程序已从人工方式转变为自动化方式。大洋洲海关组织（OCO）于 2013 年 5 月进行的一项早期研究使得比较实施该项措施“前后”的效果成为可能。

12. The main reasons for carrying out this TRS in 2014 were:

12. 2014 年开展该 TRS 的主要原因是：

- To measure if the new computer system had an impact on cargo clearance times for imports;
- To compare times with the OCO TRS; and
- To provide a baseline set of times.

  - 评测新计算机系统是否对进口货物的通关时间有影响；
  - 与大洋洲海关组织的 TRS 就放行时间进行比较；
  - 提供一组基准时间。

13. The three-phase approach of the TRS methodology was also followedfor the Cook Islands TRS, and adapted to local conditions, cargo volumes, and flows. It is worthwhile to underscore the following in respect of each of the phases:

13. 库克群岛 TRS 也采用了 TRS 的三阶段方法，并根据当地条件、货运量和清关流程进行了调整。每个阶段需强调以下几点：

- Phase One involved planning and preparation in New Zealand, and contact with Cook Islands Customs, to establish a Working Group. The cargo arrival and clearance process was observed and the design of the Study scope and methodology developed and adapted to the local conditions.

• 第一阶段包括在新西兰进行规划和筹备，并与库克群岛海关共同组建 TRS 工作组。熟悉货物运抵和清关过程，确定研究范围、制定研究方法并根据当地实际情况进行调整。

• Phase Two involved the collection of information and data, the observation of arrival and unloading processes, and the recording of times (for example, for manual entries lodged during the TRS week). Much of the data was collected manually.

• 第二阶段涉及信息和数据收集，运抵和卸载过程的观测以及相关时间的记录（例如在 TRS 期间由人工录入相关信息）。许多数据是人工收集的。

• Phase Three involved the analysis of the data and writing of the Report.

• 第三阶段进行数据分析和报告编写。

14. The TRS targeted all international flights for the week spanning Monday 10 November to Sunday 16 November, and the three cargo vessels that discharged cargo during the month of November. Only imports were studied.

14. TRS 的目标是 11 月 10 日（星期一）至 11 月 16 日（星期日）之间的一周内所有国际航班，以及在 11 月卸货的三艘货船。本次研究仅涉及进口货物。

15. This Study showed improved times for cargo clearance for Cook Islands Customs as a result of the investment in the computer system.

15. 这项研究显示，由于对计算机系统的投资，库克群岛海关的货物清关时间得以缩短。

16. Important to the success of this Study was the pre-Study work thatinvolved developing a working relationship, and working with and alongside Cook Islands Customs. This enabled the unique local conditions to be observed, and ensured all aspects of the local cargo arrival and clearance process were incorporated into the TRS scope and methodology (for example, having to adjust the times to account for vessels, aircraft, and cargo crossing the International Date Line).

16. 该研究得以成功的重要因素是研究前的准备工作，包括建立工作关系、与库克群岛海关的合作。这使我们能够观察到当地独特的条件，并确保与当地货物到达和清关过程有关的所有方面都被纳入了 TRS 的范围（例如必须调整时间以考虑跨越国际日期变更线的船舶、飞机和货物）。

Highlights of the Time Release Study: Cook Island Customs

TRS 的亮点：库克岛海关

Events	2013 Study (by OCO - preCusMod period)	2014 Study (by NZ Customs post-CusMod period)	Remarks
Manual vs electronic processing	100% manuel	74% CusMod 26% Manual	Change is a significant outcome. Lodgement via CusMod might increase but due to loca conditions it would be difficult to have 100% entries lodges electronically
Average release time of entries - see cargo	145 hours after arrival	27 hours after arrival	Significant positive outcome
Average release time of entries - air cargo	27 hours after arrival	13 hours after arrival	Significant positive outcome
Lodgement		Lodged 58 hours earlier when compared to	Traders taking up benefits

事件	2013 年研究（来自大洋洲海关组织的研究——使用计算机货物处理系统前）	2014 年研究（来自新西兰的研究——使用计算机货物处理系统后）	备注
人工或自动程序	100% 人工程序	74% 自动程序 26% 人工程序	改变是最明显的结果。通过自动化系统提交的申报资料大幅增加，但由于当地条件有限，还很难实现 100% 的电子化进口申报
海运进口货物平均放行时间	货物运抵后 145 小时	货物运抵后 27 小时	显著的积极成果
空运进口货物平均放行时间	货物运抵后 27 小时	货物运抵后 13 小时	显著的积极成果
申报		与之前相比，提前 58 小时申报	交易方获益

Mode/entry type	Drop-off to RA	RA to EO/Lodge to release	EO to pick-up	Drop-off to pick up
Manual vs electronic processing	100% manuel	74% CusMod 26% Manual		
Average release time of entries - see cargo	145 hours after arrival	27 hours after arrival	Significant positive outcome	
Average release time of entries - air cargo	27 hours after arrival	13 hours after arrival	Significant positive outcome	
Lodgement		Lodged 58 hours earlier when compared to	Traders taking up benefits	

模式/入境类型	还柜至 RA	RA 至 EO/Lodge 至放行	EO 至提柜	还柜至提柜
人工或自动程序	100% 人工程序	74% 自动程序 26% 人工程序		
海运进口货物平均放行时间	货物运抵后 145 小时	货物运抵后 27 小时	显著的积极成果	
空运进口货物平均放行时间	货物运抵后 27 小时	货物运抵后 13 小时	显著的积极成果	
申报		与之前相比，提前 58 小时申报	交易方获益	

17. In summary, the introduction of the computer system for cargo processing significantly reduced the times for processing and clearing import entries, compared to the manual processing days. The electronic processing is faster, freeing up officers' time (otherwise spent on manually checking the import entry and documents) so that it can be spent on other work activities.

17. 总之，与人工处理相比，计算机系统的引入大大减少了处理和清关进口货物的时间。电子化系统的处理速度更快，节省了关员的时间（否则就要在人工审核进口报关单和其他单据上耗费时间）。

18. The findings from this Study can be used as a baseline set of times to compare against

future Time Release Studies; and to make changes to further improvements in the processing and clearance of cargo.

18. 这项研究的结果可作为一组基准时间，与未来开展的 TRS 数据进行比较；并通过采取改进措施进一步改善货物的处理和清关流程。

New Zealand's next Time Release Study: 2018

新西兰下一次的 TRS：2018 年

19. Another TRS is scheduled for 2018. Since the last Study, there have been changes to the clearance of cargo at the New Zealand border. Another TRS will provide data and evidence to measure the impact (in time) of these changes.

19. 下一次 TRS 计划于 2018 年开展。自上次研究以来，新西兰边境的货物通关流程发生了变化。下一次 TRS 将提供数据和证据来评测这些变化的影响（及时）。

SUDAN

苏丹

Sudan 2015 Time Release Study

苏丹 2015 年的 TRS

1. Having already carried out Time Release Studies, in 2014 the Sudan Customs Administration made the decision (unprompted by COMESA) to conduct another Time Release Study (TRS) with the following objectives: to find any bottlenecks hindering trade; to identify opportunities to introduce trade facilitation measures; and to create an environment in which to strengthen Sudan's competitiveness in the international market.

1. 苏丹海关当局已经开展过 TRS。2014 年，苏丹海关当局决定开展另一次 TRS，其目标如下：找出阻碍贸易的瓶颈；确定引入贸易便利化措施的机会；为增强苏丹在国际市场上的竞争力创造良好环境。

2. After receiving technical assistance from the World Customs Organization in conducting a TRS, Sudan Customs established a national Working Group with the mandate to carry out such a Study. In line with the WCO TRS methodology, other Government agencies, besides the national Customs Administration, were involved in the Study, as were representatives from the private sector. The Customs Administration used the WCO TRS software to calculate the average release time.

2. 在获得 WCO 的技术援助后，苏丹海关组建了一个国家工作组，其任务是主持开展这项研究。按照 WCO TRS 的方法，除海关当局外，其他政府机构、相关私营部门的代表也参与了该研究。苏丹海关当局使用 WCO TRS 软件来计算平均放行时间。

3. Based on the sampling method, TRS data or time-stamps were collected from a number of Customs clearance stations, using a survey sample generated with the aid of the WCO TRS software. The total data collected was sufficiently representative to calculate the average release times in different Customs stations.

3. 根据抽样方法，使用 WCO TRS 软件生成调查样本，从多个海关检查站收集 TRS 数据或时间戳。收集的全部数据要足以计算不同海关检查站的平均放行时间。

4. The figure above indicates the average release time at each of the stations where TRS was conducted, covering different modes of transport. It is clear that the average release time was higher than ten days for the sea mode of transport, in comparison with the two other transport modes, namely road and air, which registered an average release time of less than ten days. The container Customs station registered an average release time of 17 days.

4. 下图显示了开展 TRS 的每个检查站（包括不同的运输方式）货物的平均放行时间。很明显，海运方式的平均放行时间多于 10 天，而其他两种运输方式（公路运输和空运）的平均放行时间少于 10 天。海关登记的集装箱的平均放行时间为 17 天。

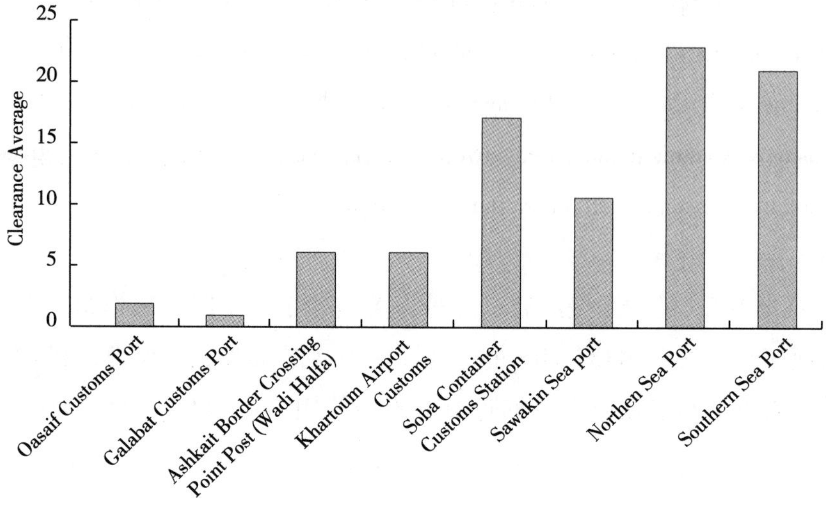

Average clearance times at different Customs stations in Sudan

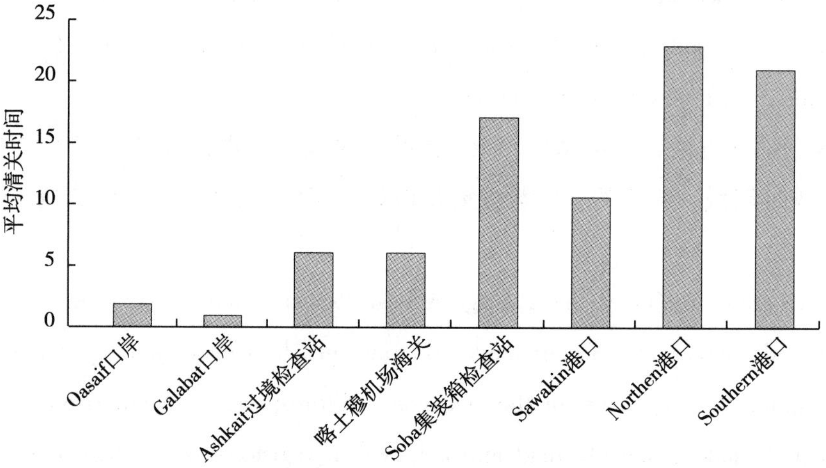

苏丹不同海关检查站的货物平均放行时间

General bottlenecks

瓶颈

5. Although the TRS Working Group identified a number of bottlenecks related to a particular Customs station, broadly speaking the bottlenecks included the following:

5. TRS 工作组确定了一些与特定海关检查站相关的瓶颈，从整体上讲，这些瓶颈包括：

- Operational problems in moving goods to Customs-inspected areas, particularly in the case of goods handled at the Red Sea ports;
  - 将货物运至海关查验场所的操作问题，特别是红海港的货物；

- Delays with regard to verifying manifests submitted by transport companies, mostly related to Khartoum airport;
  - 审核运输公司提交的舱单时产生延误，这主要与喀土穆机场有关；

- Delays in sending original documents related to the consignment to local banks, a requirement stipulated in Sudan's national legislation.
  - 因向当地银行提交国家要求的与托运货物有关的原始单据而引起延误。

General recommendations

建议

6. In order to mitigate or tackle the problems, the following general recommendations were made:

6. 为了减轻或解决这些问题，提出了以下建议：

- Resolve transportation problems in moving cargo;
- Speed up the completion of the Single Window project;
- Amend the circulars of the Central Bank of Sudan concerning the movement of cargo to ensure the smooth flow of goods.
  - 解决货物转移过程中的运输问题；
  - 加快实施“单一窗口”项目；
  - 修改《苏丹中央银行关于货物运输的通知》，确保货物顺利流动。

7. Although the decision to conduct a TRS was made in 2014, the Study was only initiated in 2015, and the Final Report approved in 2015. After national approval of the TRS Report, Sudan decided to share a copy with the WCO.

7. 虽然开展 TRS 的决定是在 2014 年做出的，但在 2015 年才开始进行并批准最终报告。在 TRS 报告获批后，苏丹与 WCO 分享了该报告。

Sudan 2017 Time Release Study

苏丹 2017 年的 TRS

8. More specifically, in the field of trade liberalization and Customs cooperation, COMESA Member States have been engaged in a number of trade facilitation initiatives aimed at eliminating tariffs, and simplifying and harmonizing the Member States' trade documents and procedures. The intention is to reduce the cost of doing business, including transaction costs related to the import and export of goods within the region and beyond.

8. 更具体地说，在贸易自由化和海关合作领域，东南非共同市场成员国参与了一些旨在消除关税、简化和协调成员国贸易单证和程序的贸易便利化举措。其目的是降低经商成本，包括与本区域进出口货物有关的交易成本。

9. Upon a recommendation by COMESA, in 2017 Sudan decided to conduct another TRS as part of a continuous improvement strategy, and to evaluate the impact of earlier trade facilitation measures that had emerged from previous Studies conducted in the country. As per the figure below, Sudan followed the three phases described in the TRS Guide (Version 2). The Study was carried out in accordance with the WCO TRS methodology, using the WCO TRS software.

9. 根据东南非共同市场的建议，作为持续改进战略的一部分并评估该国在先前研究中提出的贸易便利化措施的影响，苏丹决定于 2017 年再开展一次 TRS。如下图所示，苏丹遵循了《TRS 指南（第 2 版）》所述的三个阶段。该研究是根据 WCO TRS 方法并使用 WCO 发布的 TRS 软件开展的。

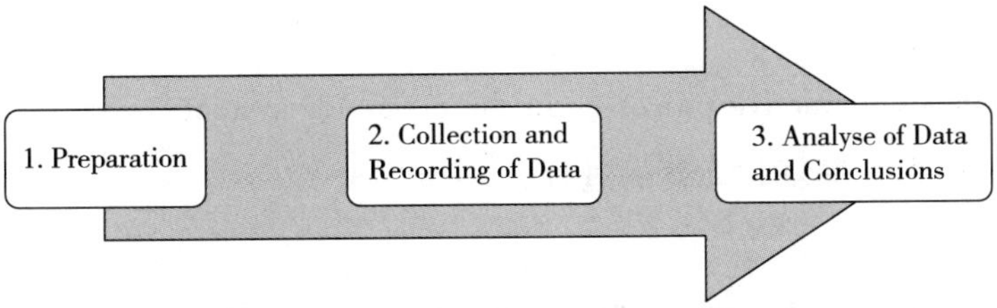

Three-phase TRS methodology followed by Sudan

苏丹采用的三阶段 TRS 方法

10. The TRS was carried out in a number of places, covering three modes of transport and different Customs procedures, such as importand export. As recommended in the WCO TRS Guide, after entering the TRS data collected into the WCO TRS software, a single Report was generated, indicating the average release time at each of the Customs clearance points where the TRS was conducted.

10. 该 TRS 在多个海关检查站开展，涉及三种运输方式和进出口程序。按照 WCO TRS 指南的建议，在将收集到的相关数据输入 WCO 发布的 TRS 软件后，就生成了一份显示参与此次研究的每个海关检查站平均放行时间的报告。

11. As often happens when Sudan carries out a TRS, the average release time was highest in the sea mode of transport, followed by air, and then road. The main reason why the average release time for air was higher than for road is that, for road, Sudan only considered the waiting time for trucks to enter Sudan Customs territory.

11. 正如苏丹之前开展 TRS 所表明的那样，海运方式的平均放行时间最长，其次是空运，最后是公路运输。空运平均放行时间高于公路运输放行时间的主要原因是，在公路运输方面，苏丹只考虑卡车进入苏丹关境的等待时间。

12. The predominant causes of delay in clearance are as follows:

12. 造成放行延误的主要原因如下：

- Repetitive and unproductive processes in the clearance system;
  - 清关流程中有重复和无益的过程；

- Documentary checks based on a transaction approach rather than risk management;
  - 基于交易方式而非风险管理的单证核查；

- Excessive controls on consignments, resulting in checking and rechecking of the same information by several different sections (e. g. valuation, assessment);
  - 对货物过度监管，导致多个不同部门对同一信息进行检查和复核（例如估价、评估）；

- Poor quality of some declarations lodged by clearing agents, resulting in rejection and queries in respect of the declarations at different levels;
  - 清关代理机构提交的部分申报信息质量较差，导致不少申报单被拒绝和被质疑；

- Delays in clearance procedures, due to lack of investment in infrastructure in certain cross-border regulatory agencies;
  - 由于某些跨境监管机构对基础设施的投资不足，导致清关时间延长；

- Delayed payment of duties, taxes and other charges by importers or their clearing agents;
  - 进口商或其清关代理延迟支付关税、税款和其他费用；

- Lack of interconnectivity between Customs and other agencies; and
  - 海关与其他机构之间缺乏沟通；

- Lack of equipment for moving goods to the examination and offloading areas.
  - 缺乏将货物运至查验区和卸货区的设备。

LIST OF ABBREVIATIONS
缩略语列表

AEO	Authorized Economic Operator（经认证的经营者）
CBM	Coordinated Border Management（协调边境管理）
FCL	Full Container Load（整箱货物）
GPS	Global Positioning System（全球定位系统）
ICT	Information and Communication Technology（信息通信技术）
LCL	Less than Container Load（拼箱货物）
NCTF	National Committee on Trade Facilitation（国家贸易便利化委员会）
RFID	Radio-Frequency Identification（射频识别）
RKC	Revised Kyoto Convention（经修订的京都公约）
TFA	Trade Facilitation Agreement（贸易便利化协定）
TRS	Time Release Study（TRS）
WCO	World Customs Organization（世界海关组织）
WTO	World Trade Organization（世界贸易组织）
WTO TFA	World Trade Organization Trade Facilitation Agreement（世界贸易组织贸易便利化协定）

GLOSSARY OF TRS CUSTOMS TERMINOLOGY
TRS 海关术语汇编

Bilateral TRS

双边 TRS

TRS carried out between two countries, either at a single or at multiple border posts or Customs offices, involving the collaboration and participation of officials from both countries.

两个国家之间在一个或多个边境站或海关办事处开展的 TRS，涉及两国官员的合作和参与。

Consecutive TRS

连续 TRS

Within the national, bilateralor multilateral context, TRS conducted at one or more border posts or Customs offices or along different routes, followed by additional Studies conducted at other border posts or Customs offices or along different routes, the results of all Studies being compiled in a single TRS Report.

在本国、双边或多边范围内，在一个或多个边境站或多个海关办事处或沿不同路线开展 TRS，然后在其他多个边境站或多个海关办事处或沿不同路线开展另外的研究，最后将所有研究结果汇集在一份研究报告中。

Multilateral TRS

多边 TRS

TRS carried out between more than two countries in a regional context, either along a single or along multiple routes across all the countries involved, and requiring the collaboration and participation of officials from all the countries concerned.

在区域范围内的两个以上国家之间，或沿一条或多条跨越所有相关国家的路线所开展的 TRS，该研究需要所有有关国家的官员合作与参与。

Physical Release

实货放行

The step of the clearance process when the goods are physically placed at the disposal of the importer or exporter or his/her legal representative for home consumption or export or any other Customs procedure. In the case of export or international transit, it is the stage when the goods are considered to have departed the Customs territory.

货物实际交由进口商或出口商或其法定代理人在国内消费或出口或转由其他海关监管程序处置的清关环节。就出口或国际过境而言，是货物被视为已离开关境的阶段。

Simultaneous TRS

同时 TRS

Within the national, bilateral or multilateral context, TRS conducted at the same time at different border posts or Customs offices or along different routes, the results of all Studies being compiled in a single TRS Report.

在国家、双边或多边范围内，在不同的边境口岸或不同的海关办事处或沿不同路线同时开展的 TRS，最后所有研究的结果都汇集在一份研究报告中。

Test Run

试点研究

A simulation of the data collection exercise to ensure that the Study will be able, as planned, to capture all the required time-stamps necessary to establish average clearance times. The test run will help identify changes required in the plan to allow effective collection of data. Often, countries conduct this exercise for a minimum of two days.

模拟数据收集工作，以确保研究能够按计划采集确定平均放行时间所需的所有时间戳。试运行将有助于完善研究计划，以便有效地收集数据。通常，该试运行至少应进行两天。

TRS Cycle

TRS 周期

List of tasks to be completed in a chronological order when conducting the Time Release Study, namely: Planning, Data Collection, Testing and Validation, Calculation of Results, Analysis, Identification of Findings, Drafting of Recommendations, Reporting, and Monitoring and Evaluation. It is often followed by another cycle after two or three years.

在开展 TRS 时，应按时间顺序完成以下任务清单：计划、数据收集、测试和验证、结果计算、分析、确定研究发现、起草建议、撰写研究报告以及监测和评估。通常在两三年后启动下一个 TRS 周期。

TRS Report

TRS 报告

Report drafted at the end of a Time Release Study to disclose the average physical release times, as well as the average duration of various procedures that have been recorded through the Study. The Report may also contain other details, such as the scope and methodology used for the Study, as well as recommendations to improve release times.

在 TRS 结束后起草的报告，要披露平均实货放行时间，以及通过该研究所记录的不同程序的平均持续时间。报告还可能包含其他信息，如研究范围和方法，以及改进放行时间的建议等。

TRS Statistical Report

TRS 统计报告

The TRS statistical report provides details of the number of transactions used for the Study, as well as details of time-stamps for the completion of the different procedures in the Customs clearanceprocess, and establishes the average release times, either for specific procedures or for the whole process.

TRS 统计报告提供了用于该研究的交易量的详细信息，以及完成海关清关程序中不同流程的时间戳的详细信息，并确定了特定流程或整个流程的平均放行时间。

WORLD CUSTOMS ORGANIZATION
Rue du Marché, 30 B-1210 – Brussels
Belgium
Tel: +32 (0) 2 209. 92. 11 – Fax: +32 (0) 2 209. 92. 92
Web Site: http://www. wcoomd. org
E-mail: information@ wcoomd. org
DATE OF PUBLICATION
January 2019

D/2019/0448/3

世界海关组织
地址：Rue du Marché, 30 B-1210 – Brussels Belgium
电话：+32 (0) 2 209. 92. 11
传真：+32 (0) 2 209. 92. 92
网站：http://www. wcoomd. org
邮箱：information@ wcoomd. org
出版日期：2019 年 1 月

D/2019/0448/3